'An intense adrenalin rush from start to finish, I read *The Laughterhouse* in one sitting. It'll have you up all night. Fantastic!'

S.J. Watson, *New York Times* bestselling author of *Before I Go to Sleep*

'This dark, gripping thriller, the latest in the Tate saga, is as hardboiled as it gets. The surprise ending suspends all disbelief. Like a TV series that ends its season on a cliff hanger, you won't want to wait until next year. This will leave the reader clamoring for the next book in the series.'

Suspense Magazine

'Piano wire-taut plotting, Tate's heart-wrenching losses and forlorn hopes, and Cleave's unusually perceptive gaze into the maw of a killer's madness make this a standout chapter in his detective's rocky road to redemption.'

Publishers Weekly (starred)

'Cleave's horrific narrative takes no prisoners, with the bloody action relentlessly ricocheting around Christchurch at a pace that leaves the detectives near collapse . . . An intense and bloody noir thriller, one often descending into a violent abyss reminiscent of Thomas Harris, creator of Hannibal Lecter.'

Kirkus Reviews

'A wonderful book . . . The final effect is that tingling in the neck hairs that tells us an artist is at work.'

Booklist (starred)

ALSO BY PAUL CLEAVE

PAUL CLEAVE

THE
LAUGHTERHOUSE

MULHOLLAND
BOOKS
HODDER

First published in Great Britain in 2017 by Mulholland Books
An imprint of Hodder & Stoughton
An Hachette UK company

1

Originally published in New Zealand in 2012

A CIP catalogue record for this title is available from the British Library

Paperback ISBN 978 1 473 66470 8
eBook ISBN 978 1 473 66471 5

Typeset in Goudy Oldstyle Std

Printed and bound in Great Britain by Clays Ltd, St Ives plc

Hodder & Stoughton policy is to use papers that are natural,
renewable and recyclable products and made from wood grown in
sustainable forests. The logging and manufacturing processes are expected
to conform to the environmental regulations of the country of origin.

Hodder & Stoughton Ltd
Carmelite House
50 Victoria Embankment
London EC4Y 0DZ

www.hodder.co.uk

To McT, The Mogue, Loony, and Haku

PROLOGUE

It was Christmas in August. A real winter wonderland. Yellow tape decorated the scene like tinsel, wisps of fog snap-frozen across the words *Do Not Cross*, blurring the letters to the point where nobody could tell one from the other. There was a small brown shoe in the snow. It was on its side, and snow had built up around the bottom of it. It had fallen off the girl when she was carried from the car into the building. The air was deathly still and cold, so cold it seemed your breath might solidify in front of your face and fall to the ground, where it would land softly in the snow by your feet and add to the frost biting at your toes. The snow was white in most places, gray where it had been ripped open by footsteps and vehicles. In other areas, mostly closer to the building, it reflected the halogen lamps and the colorful lights coming from the police cars. Those same lights streaked across the nearby dirty windows, the depths of the rooms behind the glass absorbing the light.

It all looked like a Christmas scene; Santa had come to the wrong part of town, met the wrong kind of people, and paid the worst kind of price. The halogens and headlights pointed at the old building, spotlighting the tragedy and turning it into a pageant. The place was abandoned, had been for nearly half a century, empty except for retired equipment and rusted pieces of iron everywhere, old tools and furniture not worth the money or time it'd take to pick them up. And of course the smell. It smelled of the death that had marched through the doors two by two, like animals heading onto the ark, except there wasn't any salvation here for them. The floor had absorbed the blood and shit and urine over the few years the slaughterhouse operated, death and all the messy bits that come with it were entrenched in the cement, buried in the foundations and the walls and even the air, as though the air didn't cycle in here, but was stagnant, too heavy to move outward, too thick to fit anything fresh in.

How much blood had been spilled here, Officer Theodore Tate didn't want to know. He didn't want to think too long or hard about that—he just wanted to do his job, stay alert, and not get in the way. He and his partner, Officer Carl Schroder, were the first on the scene after the call had come through. They had gone inside slowly, carefully, and they had found the young girl with the matching shoe still on her foot, along with the sock, and it was all she was wearing. The rest of her clothes were torn and piled up to her left. Neither of them had seen much in the way of bodies—a few suicides mostly, a couple of car accidents, one where the driver had been cut in half, twenty meters between his legs and chest and they never did find one of the hands—but this was Tate's first homicide, the blood fresh, the eyes cloudy, tragedy by force rather than by bad luck.

They'd secured the area, words at a minimum between them, then waited for the others, spending their time rubbing their hands together and stamping their feet to try and kickstart their circulations. Seeing the young girl made Tate want to give up being a cop, and it also made him want to become a homicide detective. Like his priest had told him, life was full of contradictions and bad people.

The detectives who had arrived since then had nobody to interview. The only witnesses out here were the ghosts of those peddled through the doors of the slaughterhouse on their way to becoming supermarket specials and hamburgers.

It was a little after ten o'clock. A degree or two below thirty. A couple of days away from a full moon. The snow had started the night before. The areas the halogens didn't hit were bathed in pale moonlight. The words *North City Slaughterhouse* were stenciled on the front of the building in big letters. Somebody had blacked out the *S* on the signage, so it now read *laughterhouse*, and others had vandalized the hell out of the place. A day and a half ago the cutting and slicing had started up again, only it hadn't been cows and sheep this time.

They already had the man who did this in custody. They'd had him for twenty-four hours. For twenty-two of those he had given up nothing. The parents had been at the station the entire time, begging to speak to the man who had abducted their girl; they felt like there was a chance they could get their daughter back. The cops knew they'd get her back but not in the condition they'd like.

In the end a detective had marched into the interrogation room and started beating the suspect. He'd just had enough, picked up a phone book, and used it to go to town on the accused. The cop would lose his job, but the suspect had given up the location.

One of the officers came out of the building, spotted Tate, and came over.

"Hell of a scene," Officer Landry said, then patted down his jacket pockets. He stopped when he hit a packet of cigarettes, then pulled them out. "Jesus, my fingers are so damn cold I'm not sure I can even light one."

"It's a sign you should give up," Tate said.

"What, from God? From what we saw in there He's got better things to be doing," Landry answered. "You see that floor?"

Tate nodded. He'd seen it and would never forget it.

Landry carried on. "That's a scary looking floor. Can you imagine that being the last damn thing you ever see?" He drew heavily on the cigarette and the tip of it flared red. He looked up at the lettering on the side of the building. "Laughterhouse," he said. "That supposed to be some kind of sick joke?"

Tate didn't answer. Just kept his hands in his pocket, bouncing slightly on his feet.

"That poor girl," Landry said.

"Jessica," Tate said.

Landry shook his head. "You can't do that. You can't give her a name."

Tate looked at him, then looked down.

"Listen, Theo," he said, taking the cigarette out of his mouth. "I know she has a name, okay? But you can't do that. There will be plenty of future sad stories, and you're going to have to think of these victims as cases, nothing more, otherwise you're not going to last in this job."

Another detective stepped outside of the slaughterhouse, in his hand a bright red schoolbag with a rainbow drawn across the back of it. He was holding it ahead of him with a straight arm, as if carrying a dead mouse his cat had just brought inside.

Landry took another drag on the cigarette. "You heard about the confession, right?"

Tate nodded. He'd heard.

"The son of a bitch is going to get away with it," Landry said, then finished his cigarette. He walked back inside, leaving Tate alone in the snow to stare at the brown leather shoe no bigger than his hand.

CHAPTER ONE

Fifteen Years Later

It's bad funeral weather. The early Monday morning Christ-church sun has given way to rain, a cloudless sky now nothing but gray without a hint of blue, one minute the rain thick and steady, the next nothing more than annoying drizzle that the window wipers on my car struggle to keep up with. It's not much of a car—it's over twenty years old, which puts it around seventy in human years, certainly retirement age. Some mornings it'll start and others it won't, but it was cheap and the truth is cheap is something I can barely afford.

The morning isn't too cold, not yet. March is often kind to us that way, though each morning is certainly cooler than the previous, days marching by on their way toward July and August and a whole lot of cold. My car certainly won't work in those conditions. Perhaps I won't be working either, each paying job a rarity rather than the norm. The only PI work to have come my way recently has been passed on by Detective

Inspector Carl Schroder, small cases not important enough to warrant the attention of the police, mainly because the police these days are too busy trying to stop the good people of Christchurch from ending up in the ground.

Only it's not March anymore. It's been April for the last ten hours, and April is a crueler month. One half of it I've spent asleep, and one half driving from motel to motel with a photograph of Lucy Saunders in my pocket, showing it to clerks behind counters. Lucy Saunders is outgoing and friendly and not yet halfway through her twenties, attractive and warm and with all the attributes perfect for a con woman. It's those attributes that got her into trouble with the police. She skipped on bail and nobody has seen her for two weeks, and the twenty thousand dollars she stole that set her fate in motion still hasn't been recovered. It's not really PI work anymore, it's being a bounty hunter, but it pays the bills. At least I hope that's the case—Lucy Saunders is my first one.

The most sensible thing for Lucy and her boyfriend to have done would be to jump in a car and keep driving, putting as much distance between them and Christchurch as they can, but sensible things don't come easy to people like Lucy and her boyfriend. I step out of my car and use a newspaper to keep the rain off my head and dash to the big glass doors of the Everblue Motel, the kind of motel you wouldn't want to be caught dead in because if you are, it means the pimp wasn't happy with how you treated one of his girls. The guy behind the counter looks like he lives for hamburgers and porn. He's dressed in a shirt stained with food that's unbuttoned to reveal a white mesh undershirt, hair sticking out of it like paintbrush bristles, making me thankful I haven't eaten in twenty hours. The room smells of cigarette smoke and the ceiling is almost blotted out by fly shit.

"Room for two with a double bed is—"

He stops talking when I put the photo down on the counter. "You seen her?" I ask.

"Listen, buddy, we get a lot of cops and fathers and pimps through here, all of them looking for somebody, and I always tell them the same thing—nothing comes for free."

"That's mighty big of you," I say. "A real humanitarian."

"Being a humanitarian doesn't pay the bills," he says.

"Or get you a new shirt. I'm not giving you twenty bucks just to have you tell me she isn't here."

"And I'm not asking for twenty. I'm asking for fifty and you're going to give it to me."

"Yeah?"

"Yeah, because I've seen her," he says, reaching under his shirt and scratching at one of his nipples in a way that would turn the gayest man straight. "Always with the same guy too. That info's for free, like a goodwill gesture, you know? Fifty bucks will get you more."

"If you've seen her that means she's here or just been here," I say. "I could just start kicking down doors and taking a look."

"Good point," he says, and he reaches down and puts his hand on a baseball bat. Somebody has written *Persuader* across it in marker. "But let me counter your point with this. See, if you were a cop you'd have told me already and shown me ID. A cop would have pulled up in a car worth more than the petrol in its tank, and between me and my buddy here," he says, lifting more of the bat into view, "I'm thinking you'd get through one door at the most. So what's it going to be?"

I look out the window into the parking lot. There are a dozen rooms all side by side forming an *L* shape, six rooms from north to south, six rooms east to west. Four of them have cars parked outside.

"I don't have fifty bucks," I tell him. "You've seen my car."

"Then I don't have any idea who the girl is."

"Thanks for your time."

I step outside. The fresh air is a relief after the office. It's almost lunchtime and my stomach is overreacting, trying to convince me I'm going to die if I don't eat soon. If I had a spare fifty bucks I'd spend it on food before handing it over to hairy nipple guy. What I have, though, is a spare five seconds on the way back to my car, and I use them to pull the fire alarm.

Curtains are drawn back from the rooms and faces press at windows, and in the second room from the end of the east-to-west wing is the face of Lucy Saunders. I pull the cell phone out of my pocket and make the call. Nobody in any of the rooms comes running out at the alarm, only the manager, who looks over at me with an angry look. He's holding hands with the *Persuader*. He's weighing up whether or not he wants to try using it on my car, deciding in the end the impact would devalue his bat more than it would my ride. Then he weighs up whether he should try using it on me. I stay in the car and stare out at him, willing him to go back inside, and thankfully he does just that.

Two minutes later a fire engine arrives, the siren loud and wailing and starting up the beginnings of a headache. It pulls into the parking lot and the sirens shut down and nothing much seems to happen then. It's still there a few minutes later, a bunch of firemen standing out in the rain, when Schroder shows up, along with two patrol cars. I watch from behind my windshield, where only the driver's side window wiper works, as Schroder's team approaches the hotel room. He knocks on the door. Within a minute Lucy and her boyfriend are cuffed and on their way to the back of a patrol car, then it's talks with the motel manager, the fire department, and then Schroder slips into the passenger seat of my car, getting water all over the seat. We both stare out at the firemen who are being spoken to by the local hookers.

"Good job," Schroder says. "You managed to only piss off the motel clerk and the entire fire department, which, I have to say, is pretty good for you."

"I appreciate the compliment."

"Hell, I just appreciate you didn't have to kill anybody."

"Life's a learning curve," I tell him.

"You still coming this afternoon?"

"I said I would."

"You don't have to, you know. It's not like you liked him, and he certainly didn't have anything nice to say about you."

"I know," I tell him. "It's a shitty thing," I say, remembering the last time I saw Bill Landry. It was last year. He was accusing me of murdering two people. He was only half right. A week ago Landry followed some bad leads. He drew some wrong conclusions and the price he paid was the ultimate one. Now he's one more cop to have died in the line of duty, one more statistic in a growing world of bad statistics.

"You okay?" he asks.

"What?"

"You're rubbing your head."

I pull my hand away from the side of my head, where there is a small dent beneath the hair and a scar too. I hadn't realized I was rubbing it. Six weeks ago a glass jar containing a severed thumb was smashed into the side of my skull by a man trying to kill me. Ever since then I've been getting some pretty rough headaches. Thankfully this one is already in the tail end of leaving.

"I'm fine," I tell him.

"You should see a doctor."

"How's my application coming along?" I ask.

"It was never going to be an easy process, Tate, too many bad things in your past for that."

"And people are jumping ship every day," I tell him. "In a year's time there aren't going to be any cops left. I don't see why I can't just step in and take over Landry's place."

"Really? You don't see how that wouldn't work?"

"It was just an example," I say, knowing that no cop who dies can be replaced. "But the force is short of good cops, and no matter what, Carl, I was a good cop."

He sighs. "You were, and then you screwed things up and became a bad one. Look, I'm rooting for you, okay? I'm doing what I can. I do think the force would be better off with you on its side than against it. What's more is I think the city will be better off, but the application takes time, and if it's accepted there are still going to be plenty of stipulations. One of which will be a fitness test, and Jesus, Tate, you're not exactly instilling me with any confidence there. Have you even eaten this week?"

"I need the job, Carl."

"There are plenty of jobs."

"No, there's not. I need this job. There isn't anything else I can do."

He nods at me before stepping back into the rain, and it's the same kind of look that we used to give junkies back in the day.

"See a doctor," he tells me, then he shuts the door.

Lucy and her boyfriend are both staring ahead from the back of a patrol car at their futures and the fire engine is pulling away slowly, its lights off, the hookers looking dejected as they watch them go. I twist the key in the ignition and the car doesn't start, not straightaway, not until the fifth attempt. The weather, the dying car, the funeral—it all feels like a bad omen as I drive through the wet streets back home.

CHAPTER TWO

My house has the ghosts of my daughter and my cat but I live with a fully corporeal mortgage that haunts me. I used to be a cop, then a private investigator, then a criminal, and now back to being a private investigator again, one who's hoping to return to the police force. It's the circle of life. But it's not enough. I need something more than following cheating husbands. Being an investigator is all I know. That, and killing people.

I spend an hour eating lunch before putting on my only suit. It's loose on me. At two thirty I head into traffic. The rain hasn't eased up any and the watery surface masks the faded road markings, making them all but impossible to see. I pass ladies in big coats at bus stops and kids in uniforms carrying bags and chatting on cell phones. It takes thirty minutes to reach the cemetery where my daughter is buried and where my priest used to work until he, like Detective Landry, became another statistic. The parking lot is full of cars that show a cross section of society. I have to park two blocks away and walk back. The gutters are jammed with leaves. The red ones are fresh, the brown ones older and turning to sludge. There is a light wind that rips through my clothes. There are more leaves swirling around the parking lot, most coming to rest on the stones, others getting lodged in the bottom edge of the windscreens of the cars. And still the rain keeps coming.

Bad funeral weather.

Police funerals are always big affairs. There are reporter vans parked out front, the journalists being the first to have arrived. They point cameras at me for a few seconds before turning them away. I figure it's a good thing the death of a cop is still important enough to cover. There will be an angle to it though, some kind of spin. It's what separates reporters from monkeys. I climb the steps to the big front door, shake off my umbrella, and hang it up with my jacket. The church is over a hundred years old and made from chunky gray stone with white mortar and has stained-glass windows covered with as much dust as there is color. The inside is about half full, but there's a steady stream of people walking in behind me, other small groups huddling outside getting through a final cigarette before the service. Schroder is talking to an attractive woman who must be in her mid-thirties. He sees me and comes over, the space he leaves filled by another guy who starts his conversation to the woman with a big smile.

"Glad you made it," Schroder says. "Follow me," he adds, and I follow him toward the front of the church where he introduces me to Father Jacob, the priest who replaced Father Julian last year after Julian had his head caved in with a hammer and his tongue cut out.

"Welcome to Christchurch," I tell him.

"I've heard a lot about you," Jacob says, shaking my hand. He's in his early to mid-sixties, with hair more gray than black and a gaunt face resting on top of a body that could hide behind a lamppost. His fingernails are stained with nicotine and there are patches of red skin on his face around his nose as if he is having an allergic reaction to the cold.

"I hope some of it was good," I say.

"Some of it was," he says, and this should be where he gives the warm fatherly smile, but he comes up empty. "And some of it might be worth a visit to the confessional."

We have to talk loudly to be heard over the hammering rain. The church fills up, most of the people in police uniform, the others, like myself, in black. Everybody is talking in soft tones, and the snippets of conversation I can hear don't involve Landry, they involve the weather or other friends or the game last weekend. The front row is reserved for family and for Landry's ex-wives, of which there are three, and they seem to be getting along okay, their struggles of being married to him something in common. I walk with Schroder toward the back of the church and end up sitting next to the woman he was chatting with earlier who is now reading the funeral pamphlet with Landry on the front and some hymns inside. There's a poster-sized picture of Landry next to the coffin, his big smiling face staring out from a memory one or two of these people may have shared with him.

Right on three thirty Father Jacob stands up at the podium and the room goes quiet. The church could do with some heaters. It could also do with some fresh paint. People are rubbing their hands for warmth. It's hard for a man to sum up another man when they've never met, but Jacob gives it a really good try, helped along by a whole bunch of clichés about love, loss, life, and God's greater plan. Then we all have to stand up and sing one of the hymns. When it's done Jacob opens up the podium for others to come and speak, Landry's sister stepping up in front of us and managing only three words before being escorted away, arms around her as she breaks down and cries. Others go up and do better, some do the same, Landry lying there the whole time aware of none of it. The casket is closed because his death wasn't as pretty as a heart attack—he got himself shot several times. Hollywood would have rebuilt him. They'd have added armor and weaponry along with a power source to keep him kicking ass and fighting crime. If Christchurch had rebuilt him, they'd have made him out of recycled plastic, paid him minimum wage, and given him a wet, wound-up towel as a weapon.

Another detective, Detective Watts, steps up to the podium. He smiles out at the crowd, then says nothing for nearly ten seconds, and I know he's fighting the fear of public speaking and he's fighting back the tears, and then he begins to talk. He says he and Landry used to play practical jokes on each other. It's something I never knew about Landry, and it's hard to imagine him ever doing that. Watts tells us about the time they were on a stakeout, about how he had put shoe polish around the binoculars Landry was using, and how for an hour they sat in the car with Landry having black rings around his eyes. He tells us the joke works exactly like it does on TV, then tells us they were called to assist at an armed robbery a few blocks away at a Chinese restaurant, how in front of a restaurant full of patrons, Landry had stood there taking statements for three hours without anybody telling him.

The crowd laughs. Schroder joins in, so does the woman next to me, and so do I. It's not that funny a story, but in that moment it's the funniest story any of us has ever heard.

"He got me back the following night," he says. "We'd been putting in some long nights on this stakeout, and when we got back to the office I fell asleep at my desk. He superglued my face to it."

The funeral lasts ninety minutes. I keep looking at the coffin, wondering how somebody's life can fit into something so small, everything they were no longer existing. We all mingle out in the parking lot as the rain eases off and wait for the coffin to come outside. It's placed in the back of a hearse, then driven deeper into the cemetery. We walk in the drizzle wearing our jackets and carrying umbrellas and we mingle again, this time around the patch of earth where Landry is laid to rest. The priest starts up again and I'm worried he's going to aim for another ninety minutes, but he lasts only five—ashes to ashes, dust to dust.

The rain has eased off and umbrellas are shaken and folded back down, but the sky is starting to darken. A few people leave and the trend catches on. I get back to the car and there's a leaflet hooked beneath the windshield wiper. An ad for a brothel in town, "Bring the voucher and *entry* is half price." Traffic becomes congested as we all try to move out. The funeral procession leads us into town where we all start splitting up looking for parking spots, most of us taking a nearby parking structure. Tires squeal on the ramps, and there are plenty of paint marks on the walls from cars that have taken the turns too narrowly over the years. I park near the top and take the stairs down. At the bottom is a homeless guy who tries selling me Jesus for the price of beer.

Popular Consensus is a nightclub near The Strip, a line of bars operating as cafés and restaurants during the day, then doubling as nightclubs after nine. The club is owned by Landry's brother, and is about five hours away from doing peak business with the thousands of alcoholic teenagers who roam this city at night. But right now the doors are open for those of us who knew Landry and the tables are full of sausage rolls and sandwiches and it's an open bar. Nearly every flat surface has a photograph of Landry on it, and I study one from our days at the academy; him and Schroder and me side by side, hairlines further forward and Landry and Schroder's stomachs not as round as they are now, and I guess those are things Landry doesn't have to worry about anymore. The club has all the lights on and everybody sits around the bar and at the booths sharing stories and tears.

"Here," Schroder says, handing me a drink.

"I'm fine," I tell him.

"It's only orange juice," he says, and I take it from him. I look longingly at his beer as he nurses it, remembering how beer and all of its friends got me into trouble last year. "Seems like a lifetime ago," he says, nodding toward the picture.

"I don't even remember half these people," I tell him.

"Landry's the first."

"Huh?"

He nods toward the picture again. "First one in that photo to have gotten himself killed."

We sip at our drinks and take a few seconds to contemplate what he just said, wondering if he'll be the last, wondering if the others will end up retiring in a few years or quitting now. A stereo is turned on, The Rolling Stones start playing to the bar, Landry's favorite band—one of my favorites too.

"What the hell was he doing working on his own?" I ask.

He shrugs before coming up with something I wasn't expecting. "ME says he had cancer."

"What?"

"He'd have been dead before the year was out. I think he just got sick of the way things play out in this city." He tips up his beer and drains half of it down his throat. "He tried to make a difference by himself and got killed for it."

We move back to the bar. Every detective is trying to drink enough to hibernate through the winter. Landry's brother looks more upset at the tab he's covering than at his brother getting killed. He looks like he's wishing he'd watered down the whiskey more than he already has. Schroder gets another beer and finishes it before I'm even a third of the way through my juice. All the voices are getting louder and there are snippets of stories coming from every direction, less and less of them about Landry the more everybody drinks, more and more of them about Christchurch, about the weather and the crime rate and the boy-racers, the boy-racers who have their teeth in this city and won't let go. They block the streets at night racing their brightly colored cars, cars lowered and modified to look cool and be loud. The conversations get darker as the first hour slips into the second, the words more slurred, theories being thrown about on how to make this city a better place, who we ought to be going around shooting to make that happen. Schroder finishes off his third beer and I start on my second juice. Other cops come over to talk to us, there's lots of "you guys were at the academy with him, right?" and "you should come back to the force, Tate," and "last thing the force needs is you coming back." I sip at my drink, wanting nothing more than to get the hell out of here, wondering how many of these people will resent me if I do make it back onto the team.

"How are things going with the Melissa X case?" I ask Schroder.

He starts on a new beer, sipping at it slowly for a few seconds before lowering it back to the bar. "It's like we're chasing a ghost," he says.

Melissa X is the woman the Christchurch Carver, a notorious serial killer now in jail, partnered up with. She is still on the loose—and still killing. When I was released from jail in February, Schroder was there to meet me in the parking lot, the Melissa X file in his car and needing all the help he could get. We found out her true identity. Her real name is Natalie Flowers—but she started calling herself Melissa when she was attacked and raped three years ago by her college professor. Since then she has tortured and killed at least half a dozen men, the last of which was seven weeks ago.

"Nothing new?"

"We've spoken to all her friends, all her family. Nothing," he says. "We've followed up with surgeons and health clinics, checking to see if she's had any cosmetic surgery, but nothing. It's like she's left this planet, and just when you think that might be true, she'll kill somebody else."

"It does seem that way," I say. I have the file too, and I keep looking at it every day just like Schroder, but for me looking at that file isn't paying the bills.

"We'll get her," he says. "I can promise you that."

The woman I sat next to at the funeral sees us and comes over. Schroder stands up and smiles at her and I do the same.

"Theodore Tate, this is Detective Inspector Kent," he says, introducing us.

"Call me Rebecca," she says, shaking my hand.

Rebecca is a few inches shorter than me, a few pounds lighter, and probably with a few less problems in the world. Athletic and attractive. Both Schroder and myself can't stop smiling at her. She has black hair that hangs to her shoulders that she brushes back behind her shoulder.

"You work with Schroder?" I ask.

"Detective Kent just transferred down here from Auckland," he says. "She's only been with us a week. She was one of their best so we're lucky to have her."

She smiles. "I'm lucky to be back," she says. "I'm Christchurch born and raised."

"Really," I say. "When did you leave?"

"Right after the police academy," she says. "I got posted in Auckland ten years ago and have been trying to get back since."

"That reminds me," Schroder says, turning toward me. "Emma Green has been accepted into the academy."

"I knew she was applying," I say.

"Emma Green. How do I know that name?" Rebecca asks.

"She's the girl who was abducted earlier this year," he says. "Tate found her."

"Oh, of course," she says. "The same girl you . . ." she says, but doesn't finish.

Emma Green is the same girl I ran into with my car last year when I was drunk. It's what landed me in prison.

"I'm sorry," she says. "That was dumb of me. I've had three too many gin and tonics," she says, rattling the ice in the bottom of her empty glass.

"Not your fault. I'm the one who was being dumb last year," I tell her, unsure of how I feel about Emma joining the force.

"Well, it's all in the past now," Schroder says.

He takes another sip of beer, then the conversation changes.

Rebecca gets another gin and tonic and comes back. We start talking about Schroder's family. He pulls out his wallet and shows me photographs of his daughter and his six-month-old son. I've never seen his son before; met his daughter plenty of times but haven't seen her in a few years. Rebecca smiles at the photographs and tells Schroder how cute his children are, before saying she doesn't have children but she does have two cats and laughs that she understands how much work it must be for him.

He just starts telling us about something his son managed to jam into his ear when his cell phone goes off. He has to pat down his pockets looking for it, missing it the first time through. He answers it and I can hear another one ringing. And another. Detectives across the room are patting at their pockets, then there's a chorus of people saying their names, including Detective Kent. The room goes quiet as people start listening. Schroder has one hand on the bar to keep himself steady. He stares at his beer, then slowly pushes it away. Rebecca puts her new drink—still untouched—onto the bar. People start hanging up, then another round of cell phones start ringing, a new set of detectives being called. News is flooding in from somewhere. Other detectives are finishing off their drinks in final gulps and heading toward the door, others to the bathroom. Schroder hangs up. "Call us some taxis," he says to the bartender.

"What's happened?" I ask him, following him to the door.

"You're sober, right?"

"Right."

"And your car's here, right?"

"Right."

"Then give me a lift and I'll explain on the way."

CHAPTER THREE

Caleb Cole is excited. He doubts the old guy is going to remember him, but he'll get there with some explaining. He
wasn't sure what to get him; he did wonder if flowers would
be appropriate before deciding it would just be a little weird.
Showing up empty-handed would be just as strange, so he
settled on a six-pack of beer, which he decided was perfect.
He wasn't sure what Albert drank, but figured at Albert's age
it probably wouldn't matter too much. Beer, wine, he guesses
one type tastes like any other when you're closing in on a hundred. Not that Albert is a hundred, but he's certainly closer to
a hundred than he is to fifty.

He parks outside the retirement home. He doesn't know if
driving in will be enough to wake half of the residents even
though it's only seven thirty, or whether it'd be like waking the
dead, which in a place like this would be a pretty neat trick. He
carries the beer and straightens the fresh shirt he put on only
half an hour ago, after taking a shower. The rain is coming and
going—one moment it's there, the next it's gone.

He's never stepped foot in a retirement community before today. No reason to. His parents both went to one for almost ten years before they died, but he never visited them, and he doesn't have any uncles or aunts that he's kept in touch with. His grandparents—well, half of them were dead before he was born, and the other half not long after. Looking around, the retirement community feels like exactly what it is—a holding pattern for old people between this world and the next. All the homes are made from brick with aluminum windows and are well insulated. They'd stay warm in the winter and cook anything inside in the summer, but they all look the same, and he struggles for a few minutes to figure out exactly which one he's supposed to be heading to. Once he thought it was the kind of place he and Lara would end up living in. The kids would get sick of looking after them and put them into a home. They would grow old together, dreading that day when one of them got sick, picked up pneumonia or a lung infection to complicate the matter, then say goodbye.

He finds the right unit. There are lights on inside. He feels nervous. He tucks the beer under one arm and knocks on the door. He can hear a TV going inside, but nothing else.

He knocks again. "Albert?"

Nothing. He walks around the unit and is able to peek through a gap in the curtain and into the living room. Albert is facing away from him, toward the TV, of which they both have a clear view. Turns out the world is full of reality shows these days. He wonders if his own life would ever make for good reality TV, and decides it probably wouldn't. It would, for lack of a better word, be too *real*. Albert is sitting on a couch with patterns of flowers on it. There is a machine next to him that looks like a dehumidifier, only there's a clear tube leading from it to Albert, providing him oxygen.

Caleb taps on the window.

Albert jumps a little, then turns toward the sound. It's obvious he can't see anything beyond the window, so Caleb taps on the window again, then moves to the door. He knocks and waits, and a few seconds later the front door opens.

"Yes?"

"Albert McFarlane?" Caleb says.

"Yes, that's right," Albert answers. He's bald with ears that are pushed out slightly wider than normal because of the oxygen tube going over them and tucking into his nose, which is red and looks irritated. When he talks, he wheezes, and the effort is making him puff hard. He puts a finger on the bridge of his glasses and pushes them a little closer to his eyeballs, so close the lenses must nearly touch. His eyes narrow as he focuses on the way everything has just been magnified.

"My name is Caleb Cole," Caleb says, "do you remember me?"

"Remember you?" Albert leans forward and takes a closer look. "Are you one of my grandchildren?"

Caleb shakes his head. "No. Do you mind if I come in?"

"Are you trying to sell me something, son?"

He lifts up the beer. "No. I just wanna shoot the breeze," he says, figuring the term will make Albert happy.

"Ah huh, well that's mighty good, son, but I still don't remember you, and I don't drink beer anymore. Doctor's orders. But hell, it's not like I got much more to do, so sure, come on in."

Albert steps aside and Caleb walks in and closes the door behind him. Albert's clothes are hanging from his body with all the shape of laundry hanging on the line, and he's squinting, as if trying to see past the cataracts clouding his vision. He doesn't look well. Caleb has seen people with cancer before, and that's exactly what it looks like Albert has.

"Take a seat," Albert says. "Can I make you a coffee?"

"Sure, thanks," Caleb says, and he sits the beer on the coffee table and makes a mental note to take it with him since Albert doesn't want any. He follows Albert into the kitchen, which isn't far since it's effectively part of the living room. The oxygen tube looks long enough to hang somebody a few times over.

"Kettle just finished boiling a few minutes ago," Albert says, then reaches up into the cupboard for a cup. "How do you like it?"

"Strong," Caleb says. "No sugar. No milk."

"Well, that I can do."

The house is small. From the space between the kitchen and living room he can see down the hallway. It's not a complicated layout. A bedroom, a toilet, a bathroom, not much else. It looks like a lonely life, and he guesses that's just the way it goes when you get to this age. It's not like people are dancing in the streets. Hell, nobody even saw him come in here and no doubt nobody will see him leave either. People in this community can only see about thirty feet ahead and fifty years into the past and not much else.

"What did you say your name was again?" Albert asks.

"Caleb Cole," he says.

"And we know each other," Albert says.

"This is your family?" Cole asks, looking at some of the photographs in the room. There are pictures of a lady in most of them, she ages at the same rate as Albert, then disappears. There are children and grandchildren. The living room is full of the knickknacks of life. There's a cordless phone on a small table to the side of the couch, the phone large and heavy and perhaps one of the first ever built. The TV is on mute, but the oxygen machine is humming like a fridge. He wonders how Albert can sleep at night with it running.

"Yep."

"You see them much?"

"Huh! You've got to be kidding. Here," Albert says, and slides a coffee along the bench toward Caleb. It's hot. He picks it up and both men sit down in the living room, and Caleb rests the coffee on the table next to the beer.

"Caleb Cole," Albert says, then sips at his own coffee, which he was already working at when Caleb arrived.

"That's right," Caleb says, picking his coffee back up and blowing at it, trying to cool it down. People on the TV are chanting at something, yelling at somebody to "jump, jump, jump." Maybe reality TV is all about people standing on rooftops. The room is hot. There is a fan suspended just below the ceiling, slowly circulating the sticky air. If the future he'd meant to have had come true, he's not so sure he'd have liked living in a place like this.

"Can't say it rings a bell."

"Think back," Caleb says. "Seventeen years."

The edges of Albert's face turn downward, and his face seems to shrink in on itself. "Seventeen years? Jesus, son, I'm lucky if I can remember back seventeen hours."

"There was a legal case you were involved with."

"A case? You got the wrong man, son. I'm not a lawyer. I used to be a teacher. A damn good one too. Why, some of my students still write me. I have letters, a whole bunch of them, maybe two dozen from kids who have grown up and made something of themselves. Ah, hell, that's where I know you from, right? You used to be a student. Which year, son? How old are you?"

"Fifty," Cole says. "I turned fifty last year."

"Fifty! Well now, no way you can be one of my grandkids, and I don't see how I would have taught you," he says. "You've got the wrong teacher. What did you say you were? A lawyer? What kind of lawyer?"

"No. I used to be a teacher too."

"You're a teacher? You teach law?"

"I taught high school. At least I used to, I gave it up fifteen years ago."

"Ah, that's what I did. Did that for over forty years. You'd have been ten at the time when I started, unless my math is wrong, which means—ah, hell, you could have been one of my students. Is that where I know you from?"

Caleb shakes his head. "No." He keeps blowing at his coffee, cooling it down. "You were on a case," he says, "seventeen years ago. You were involved in a trial. You were a character witness."

"A witness? Oh, that takes me back. I haven't thought about that in years. When was that? Twenty years ago."

"It was seventeen."

"Seventeen? Well, if you say so. It was an awful case," he says. "Was my first and only time in court. I'd never want to do that again. But what could I do? I had to go. And that poor little girl," he says, "kidnapped and . . . and . . . the things he did to her. She was lucky to have survived. That boy, he was something. Scary as shit. But it wasn't his fault, you know? That's what I said. He used to be one of my students."

"I know."

Albert leans forward and adjusts the flow on his oxygen machine, turning one of the dials up from a three to a three and a half. "I mean, it was pretty obvious he was messed up in the head. His mother, she'd done a hell of a job on him. Ruined him for life. Made him completely mental. Poor bastard never had a chance. The same year he was in my class, she put him into a coma. Beat the shit out of him. He tried coming back later that year, but it just didn't work."

Caleb is nodding. The coffee is finally cool enough to sip at. He's going to either need to clean the cup when he's done or take it with him. "So you got up in the witness box and told the jury and the judge that what he did wasn't his fault."

The old man fixes him an annoyed look. "It wasn't like that. Sure, I got up there and I had to tell everybody what he'd been like as a kid at school. I had to explain how much he changed after the beating, and yeah, of course I said things weren't his fault. He was a victim too. I didn't get up there and say it was okay what he did. If I remember right, he still got locked away. Went to a hospital, didn't he? Jury found him not guilty because he wasn't competent. Not sure how long he got. Ten years. Twenty, maybe."

"Two."

"Two? Are you sure, son?"

"Very."

Caleb keeps drinking, staring over the top of the cup as he does so. When a quarter of it is gone, he looks down at it. "This is good coffee, Al. Do you mind if I call you Al?" And before Al can answer, he puts the coffee back onto the table and stands up. "Let me ask you a question, Al. If I were to kill you right now do you think a jury like the one you spoke to would make the same decision? Do you think they would find I wasn't competent and put me away for two years?"

"How did you say we know each other exactly?" Al asks, his tired old face forming concern.

"Well, I didn't say exactly," Caleb says, "and the truth of the matter is we've never really met until tonight," he says, and he reaches around to his back where he has the handle of the knife tucked into his belt, the blade safely flat against his spine. He pulls it out. "But we're meeting now, so how about I explain why I'm here, see if I can get you to remember why it was only two years and not ten," he says, and then the explaining begins.

CHAPTER FOUR

There are already minivan cabs pulling up outside Popular
Consensus. They're filling up with cops and slowly pulling
away. The water in the gutters and road is reflecting the lights
coming from all the bars and streetlights. There's no sign of
the moon, no sign of any stars, just endless clouds. At least
it's stopped raining, but what rain has already fallen splashes
off the street as cars pass us, and it feels like it's going to come
back. Nobody seems to be able to walk in a straight line. I have
no idea what's happened, and unless it's a call to stop a local
brewery from flooding, none of these people should be allowed
to be involved. If they were sober, they'd know that. I suspect
they even know it drunk. Problem is the police force is under-
staffed, there are no other options, and whatever has happened
is important enough for all of these off-duty detectives to pile
themselves inside the arriving minivans.

"You gonna fill me in?" I ask, leading Schroder back to the
parking garage.

"Christ, I really need to take a piss."

"I'll wait here."

"It's okay. I can hold on."

"Where we heading?"

"I gotta make another call," he says, and pulls out his cell phone. We take the elevator up to the top floor and he leans against the wall of it the entire trip, pulling his cell phone away from his ear and studying it every few seconds or so. "No signal," he says.

We reach my car.

"Does this seat belt work?" he asks, tugging at it.

"I don't know. I've never had any passengers."

"You lose a bet?" he asks.

"What?"

"That why you driving this thing?"

"I'm happy if you want to walk."

"Might be safer. And quicker."

"And wetter. Just tell me where we're heading."

"The retirement community."

"Which one?" I ask, taking the ramps down to the bottom floor.

"What do you mean which one? Oh, shit . . . hang on, let me think a second. It's . . . ah, shit, hang on." He's halfway through composing a text to find out when he remembers. "Lakeview Homes. You know where it is?"

"Listen, Carl, I don't think it's a good idea you going there."

"I've only had a couple of beers, Theo."

"You were starting your fourth. And that's four too many."

"Jesus, I should have gone with the others."

"And what? Lose your job along with the rest of them?"

"No chance of that. Who the hell would they replace us with?"

I get his point. I pull into traffic and one of the taxis loaded up with cops cuts me off, almost taking out the side of my car. I try to toot at him but my horn doesn't work. There is a small amount of drizzle back in the air. I turn on the wipers. The one on Schroder's side gets to its apex with short, jerking motions, shudders at the top, then dies up there. Schroder taps the inside of the windshield.

"Jesus, Tate, you couldn't find something better than this?"

"You want to tell me what all this is about?"

"You already know," he says. "It's why so many of us got the call."

He's right, I do know. "Who's the victim?"

"Guy by the name of Herbert Poole. Apparently he's been all cut to hell."

Traffic has thinned since the drive to Popular Consensus, but it's still moving slow because of the recent rain. The intersection ahead has lost power to the traffic lights, half the drivers treating it like a traffic circle, the other half in too much of a hurry to care much about giving way. The gutters are flooding out into the streets. It's another twenty minutes to Lakeview Homes, a good chunk of that time Schroder sits with his head back against the seat and one hand covering his face, the only sign that he's still awake are his random patches of hiccupping. The rain disappears again. Still no stars.

Lakeview Homes overlooks some meadows and forestry on one side, all of it trailing out of sight into the darkness. Beyond it, and empty at this time of night, is a golf course that costs two hundred dollars a round. On this side of the forest it looks over suburbia with a long driveway heading out to the main road. Despite its name, the retirement home manages to be situated nowhere near any lake. The nearest body of water is a gymnasium with a pool six blocks away. There are already half a dozen patrol cars at the scene and one cab. There's a line of detectives heading toward the field, they're moving behind the big trees and emptying their bladders, the headlight beams helping them find their way.

"Jesus," I say, and Schroder sits up and takes a look. "Every detective on the force is here and drunk."

"It's not our fault. How were we to know this was going to happen today?"

"Statistically, it was always going to happen. You didn't keep anybody in reserve?"

"Jesus, Tate, you may not have liked Landry, but the rest of us did."

"Carl . . ."

"Don't worry," he says, slapping me on the shoulder. "I'm the boss here, and I'm telling you, looking at a dead body has a way of sobering people up."

"And so does losing your job. Best thing for your colleagues right now is to get back into those cabs and get the hell out of here."

"And I'm sure between us we'll all figure that out."

At the moment the detectives do seem to be figuring it out. They're coming back from behind the trees and leaning against the minivan cabs, none of which have left yet. Detective Kent is among them. They're figuring out there's a line here that if they cross will see them reprimanded, or worse, fired. There are old people standing at windows backlit by TVs and dining room lights, they're staring out at the show, all of them hoping they're about to get visitors.

"Jesus, that's disgusting," Schroder says, watching another detective race off behind a tree. "But better than pissing on the front lawn," he adds, and chases off after him to do the same. The uniformed officers don't know what to do. They're caught between telling their superiors to go home and letting them contaminate a crime scene. The residents and staff are just as unimpressed, and it can only be a matter of minutes before the reporters arrive. This is going to end badly for Schroder and for every drunk cop here. In a sober condition, any of them would know being here was a mistake, but that's the problem with drunk people—they make bad decisions. Sober, everybody knows they shouldn't drink and drive, but when you're drunk it never seems such a bad idea. That's what landed me in jail last year.

The retirement community is full of units that are almost small houses but not quite, the roofs all black, the walls painted the same color as Bambi. The creative imagination behind the whole complex could have been shaped by Lego. There are millions of flowers everywhere just the way old people like them, only the flowers are in their final days before the cold weather robs them of life. There's a connection between plants and the elderly—as soon as you turn sixty it must be compulsory to like roses and rhododendrons. The only thing I can see to stop burglars breaking in on a daily basis is the fact there isn't much to steal except record collections and memories and clothes swinging in and out of fashion.

"Sir?" one of the officers asks, walking over to me. He's young looking and nervous and this may or may not be his first crime scene, but it's definitely one he wishes he wasn't here for. "You look to be about the only detective here who's not half-wasted."

I don't even have to think about it. I start nodding. "Tell me what we've got," I tell him.

I follow him to a unit where two other officers are standing outside. There's a front porch and a swing chair and the whole thing is soaking wet. On a nice day maybe the old folks sit out here and sip lemonade and talk about the war, talk about how far Christchurch has slipped, talk about the good ol' days. The officers are talking to a guy in his eighties who looks pale, who has probably sat on this porch countless times in the sun but what he discovered half an hour ago drained the tan right out of him. A second guy, this one thirty years younger, has to keep wiping at the rain dripping from his fringe. He's shorter and rounder and doesn't need a name badge to tell me he's in some administration role here at the home, probably the manager. He's seen dead bodies before—you don't get to work in this kind of place without witnessing your fair share of death—but no doubt what's behind door number one is death of a different variety, death of the sort that requires crime scene tape and latex gloves and people looking for clues. Death like that often comes with the need for a mop and bucket. Best anybody can hope for is it comes with answers.

I follow the officer and duck under the tape and step onto the porch, the wooden decking slightly soft under my feet. Schroder calls out to me but I don't wait. I can hear all the detectives talking back by the cabs, all of them trying to figure out just who should be working, their voices becoming louder as they talk over each other deciding who should stay and who should go, Schroder having the final say over all of them.

"This is exactly how we found it," the officer tells me. He keeps wiping at the back of his neck at an itch that won't leave. "Doors were closed. TV and lights were on."

"You touch anything?"

"Just the door handle," he says. "But the guy who found the body probably touched a whole lot more."

"Somebody needs to get a cordon set up," I tell him. "Nothing coming in from the street, and get some manpower into the fields out there to make sure nobody comes that way either, but tell them to be careful—for all we know the killer may have gone that way and left something behind. Biggest problem right now is the media. If they come here and see that," I say, nodding toward the rowdy mob by the vans as another cab pulls up, "the unemployment rate in this city is going to rise tonight."

"Yes sir."

I step inside. The house is small enough that it doesn't mess around with having a foyer or hallway entrance. Instead the door opens directly into the living room. A man and a woman are on the TV arguing over some food that one of them has accused the other of eating. There's a cutaway shot, the woman sitting in front of a camera now, telling the audience that

Derek is a jerk and just because she slept with him doesn't mean he can eat her cornflakes. Derek comes on to tell us all how lazy the cornflake owner was in bed.

To get to the TV to turn it off, I have to walk around what made the old man outside turn pale. I'm guessing the dead man on the couch was one of his friends. The dead man's clothes are sliced up and stained in blood, and he's stained in blood too, like most of the surfaces in the room. It's hard to tell how many times he's been stabbed. Anything over one is bad, and in his case I'd say *bad* happened at least a dozen times. There are lines of blood on the ceiling, cast off from the knife—the blade slinging it onto the walls and ceilings the way an artist might sling paint from his brush onto canvas. There's blood on the TV, on the coffee table, there's blood over the guy's dinner. From the amount of blood on view and pooled into the base of the couch it's looking like the guy could be hung up from his feet and we'd be lucky to fill a cup. Something has been written on his forehead with a marker.

This isn't a burglary gone wrong or a fight over who should or shouldn't park out front—whoever killed this man invested a lot of rage into the act.

Schroder comes to the doorway and stops. He crouches down and undoes his shoes, which are covered in mud. He takes them off and in the process nearly tips over. He sits them off to the side of the door, then rolls up the cuffs of his pants, which are also soaking wet. Then he comes in and stands next to me. He looks down at his feet, then shrugs. He's chewing on a piece of peppermint gum to mask the smell of beer, but his suit needs to chew on the same stuff to complete the illusion. He spends ten seconds looking at the body before fixating on me.

"Jesus, somebody must have really hated him," he says, then he puts a hand on my shoulder for the second time today and hiccups into his other hand. "Look, Tate, you shouldn't be in here," he says, and before I can say anything he adds "but I'm grateful you are. I just need a little bit more time to get my head in the game. Forensics are on their way, should only be a few minutes."

"And the others?"

"The others are loading up on coffee and breath mints so they can start asking questions. None of them are going to come within thirty feet of this room."

"You should send them home, Carl, and you should go home too."

"I know, but then what? Come back tomorrow and hope for the best? Somebody needs to be here, Tate."

"And you could all be fired if you stay."

"Yeah, then the department would have to hire you, wouldn't they? They'd need at least somebody manning the phones."

"Anything you find will get tossed out in a court of law if anybody gets a whiff you were drunk," I tell him.

"I'm not drunk, and in twenty-four hours this case could end up being as cold as my last beer if we don't do anything about it now."

"You shouldn't be here."

"And neither should you. But I'm a realist, Tate, and right now I know I could do with your help."

"Just saying that proves you're drunk," I tell him.

He crouches down next to the couch to get a good look at the dead guy's face. "Herbert Poole with an *e* has been living here for eight years," he says, and he really does sound sober. Out the door and in the distance one of the minivan cabs is being loaded back up with some of the detectives, including Detective Kent. Could be they're all off to grab coffee and doughnuts. "Lots of friends, no enemies, and even if people here didn't like him this doesn't seem the way they'd show it. More likely they cut his roses or shorten a leg on his walker."

The words on Herbert's forehead say *You didn't care enough.* It even has the apostrophe. "An ex-wife maybe?" I ask.

"He doesn't have one. He's a widower."

"An ex-girlfriend? A son he didn't get along with? It could mean a hundred different things."

The living room is full of the kind of sentimental stuff that in one or two week's time a family member will box up with the intent of putting it on display but will put it into storage instead. There are photos of children and grandchildren, days out at the park, at the beach, at sporting events. If life was more like a Harry Potter novel, the people in those photographs would be crying out and telling us what went on in this room tonight. There's a half-empty tin of beer and a dinner plate resting on the coffee table, and aside from all the blood, the rest of the room seems to be immaculate. In life Herbert Poole with an *e* was tidy.

"He has two children," Schroder says, "according to the manager. And his wife died about ten years ago from a brain tumor. We'll talk to the kids. I don't know, maybe one of them was pissed off with their dad."

We say nothing for a few seconds, letting the tragedy of Herbert Poole and his family settle in.

"Anything taken?" I ask.

"Jesus, Tate, I can't know everything yet."

Herbert Poole's head is tilting back as it rests over the arm of the couch, one arm pinned beneath him, the other in his lap, his body mostly on its side. His face is toward the wall, where a photograph of what is probably him and his wife from forty years ago stares back, though the features in that photo aren't shared with the features on the dead man's face. For Herbert Poole it was probably a good thing to look at while his life was draining out of him.

"Impressions? Thoughts?" Schroder asks.

"Bloody footprints head up the hallway, then head back," I say, looking at the stains on the carpet. "Killer wandered the house for something."

"Then put these on," he says, and hands me a pair of latex gloves.

I step through the living room, careful not to get blood on my shoes, and into the hall. The footprints lead into the bathroom. The shower walls are wet and there is a pair of pants and a shirt wadded up on the floor. I poke at them, lifting a corner until I can see blood. There's a wet towel lying next to them. The killer came in here and showered, he washed the blood off, then changed clothes but wore the same shoes. That could mean he had somewhere to go immediately afterward that wasn't home. Forensics will pull hair from the clothes. They'll find plenty of DNA—and if the killer has a record, we'll find him. Problem is DNA is going to take a few weeks. Other problem is the killer may not have a record.

I head back into the hall. There are more photographs in the bedroom, faces of people yet to be devastated, yet to know a man they knew is no longer with us. I move from one photo to the next, random people with random thoughts, perhaps one of them random enough to have done this.

I open drawers and poke around, an entire top drawer dedicated to packets of unopened underwear and neatly folded hankies, beneath them all war medals that might belong to him or somebody else in his family. There's one gray suit in the closet and lots of old man shirts, old man shoes, and old man ties. I thumb through some receipts. Poole had recently bought a few jazz CDs, some new slippers, a couple of paperbacks. There are letters from the hospital following up appointments—Herbert Poole wasn't a healthy man. With his kidneys and liver shutting down, Poole's murder is putting him into the ground about two months ahead of schedule according to the letters. Somebody just couldn't wait. Which means it wasn't about seeing Herbert Poole dead, it was about being *responsible* for seeing him dead.

I wander back down to the living room. Poole still has a blank look on his face like he can't quite believe he's caused all this fuss. *You didn't care enough.* Care about what? Or who?

Schroder is talking on his cell phone, his spare hand rubbing at his face. There are more patrol cars outside now along with a few station wagons. The cabs have disappeared, along with ninety percent of the people that came here in them. There are forensic techs heading toward the porch. They're wearing white nylon suits so as to not contaminate the scene like the rest of us already have. Another station wagon pulls up and Tracey Walter, the medical examiner, climbs out. She stands next to the wagon and ties her black hair up into a tight ponytail. I stand in the kitchen and listen to Schroder on his cell phone as the newcomers take over the scene. Nobody talks to me or pays me any attention. There's a sense of authority here that was certainly lacking ten minutes ago. People are carrying aluminum suitcases full of forensic tools. Alternate sources of light are being set up, bright halogens chasing away every shadow. Within moments I'm standing in the only living room visible from outer space. Tracey approaches the body carefully, as if scared it's about to jump up and run from her cold hands.

Schroder hangs up. Before he can say anything, his phone starts to ring again. He rolls his eyes and gives an apologetic smile. I head out onto the porch where the crowd has swelled. I learn one of them is Bernard Walsh, the man who found the body. He's wearing a shirt and tie, and either Bernard is magnetic or he loves badges because there are at least two dozen of them attached to the lapel of his suit jacket. I introduce myself and lead him further from the porch, to where there's no angle of the view inside. We stand beneath an oak tree that's three storeys high with a trunk the width of a compact car. It shelters us from the few spits of rain coming down. Walsh is holding a cup of tea that is half gone and looks stone cold. He's shaken up and tells me he hasn't seen anything like this since the war—and he's old enough to be talking about any war in the last century.

"I mean, Jesus, it makes no sense. It just makes no sense," Walsh says. "Herb, Herb was a good guy. A real gentleman. Who the hell would want to hurt Herb?"

"Run through it for me."

"Run through what for you?"

"You finding him. What happened? He didn't show up some-where? Why'd you go inside? You always go inside, or was his door open?"

"This place, don't you for one second think we don't know what this is. I used to be a photographer, came out of the war and needed something to do that didn't involve people scream-ing. I worked for plenty of papers, saw plenty of things. Once I had to do a photo shoot of a slaughterhouse, and the cows were lined up for hundreds of feet, and at the head of that line they were getting shot in the forehead, you know? And the cows, each time they heard that cattle bolt gun go off, they knew. They were braying and panicking because they each knew their buddies were getting killed and they were next to get butchered. That feeling is here too, not in the same sense, and maybe one day in forty years you'll know what I mean. This place, it's like a lottery out here, you know what I mean? All of us gambling on who's going to be the next to go. All of us los-ing our buddies and knowing we're the next to go, but slap me seven ways from stupid, the way Herb went, ah hell, we know we're all cattle facing the bolt gun but this . . .'

He doesn't finish, he gives it a few seconds of thought before moving on, and I let him talk and burn off the tension. "We play chess against each other. There's a few of us—we have an ongoing tournament in the community. We're all about as good as each other, or about as bad as each other depending on who you ask. Mick, Mick was the best, but he don't know it anymore. He don't know much, his mind has turned to mush. Hell, he nearly choked to death a few months back on a pawn. I've seen people lose their minds and I'll keep on seeing it. Herb, see, Herb lost his wife about, oh, going on maybe eight or nine years now." He holds his hand up to his head as if receiv-ing a psychic link, maybe to Herb's wife, because suddenly he goes, "It was ten years. I remember now. Ten years next month.

Or was it last month? Thing is, Detective, when you get to the age we are, time has this way of . . . how should I say this . . . well, time has a way of fucking with you."

"So, Mr. Walsh," I say, cutting in before he moves on to the next thought. "Why'd—"

"Call me Bernie," he says, "everybody else does and I don't see no reason you should be different."

"Okay, Bernie, I take it Herb didn't show up for the chess game?"

"He always calls if he can't make it. We all do. You know, it's just common sense, right? Place like this, it's only a matter of time before we're heading upstairs to chat with the Big Guy. Only I wish He'd picked a different time for Herb, and I sure wish He'd picked a better way for him to go."

"What time was this?"

"Seven o'clock," he says.

I glance at my watch. It's now nine-thirty.

"I got here and started knocking, and when he didn't answer, I let myself in. Normally he'll answer, but when people don't answer in a place like this, well, it gets your mind running, son, it makes you think it's time to dust off your funeral suit," he says, looking at my suit, my funeral suit. "I thought and prayed at the same time, Detective—thought he'd be asleep, prayed I wasn't going to find him as stiff as a board in his bed. I guess . . . I guess in a way the second part of that prayer was answered."

"The door was unlocked?"

"I have a key. It was locked."

"And the lights and TV, they were already on?"

"Yeah, Herb always watches the news, you know? He hated reporters, God, there ain't a single journalist he'd spit on if they were on fire, except for a couple of the girls on the news at night, you know, the ones who can deliver the worst news and still look sexy doing it. Jesus," he says, and he starts to cry, "tonight they're going to be talking about Herb. They're going to look just as sexy and . . . and . . . Christ," he says, and he tips the rest of his tea into the garden. "I feel so old and . . . and . . ." he shakes his head. "And so useless."

I put a hand on his shoulder. "We're going to catch the guy who did this."

He's still looking down at the tea he just threw away, and at the contact of my hand he looks back up. "I've seen a lot, Detective," Bernard says. "I've fought for this country. I've seen men die, good, loyal men have exploded in front of me, their goddamn guts and limbs flying everywhere. One second they're there, the next they're just soup on the ground." He shakes his head. "Let me tell you this, Detective—I sure as shit felt safer in that world than I do in Christchurch."

"When did you last see him?"

His face has gone red and he wipes at the tears. "I see him pretty much every day. It's not like there's much to do around here by yourself except be lonely or die," he says, and then he smiles at the bleakness of the world before his face tightens as the loss of his friend comes crashing down around him. "Shit," he says. "I . . . I . . . ah, shit."

"You saw him today?"

"Huh? What? Oh, yeah, yeah, of course. He came over about four and we watched some horse racing on TV." He smiles. "We like to gamble a little, not that it does us any good. I mean, sometimes we'll place . . ."

"What time did he leave?" I ask.

"What time? I don't know. Probably around five, I guess. He had to get back for dinner. It's an option for us, we can either have our meals provided or we can cook them ourselves. Herb was pretty stubborn that way. He felt a man should always be able to put his own food on the table. But he was getting old and he knew his limitations. He'd let them bring him dinner, but he was adamant on making his own breakfast and lunch. So he had to be back in time for his dinner."

Herb had eaten most of his dinner, which means the person

who delivered it would have been and gone, but they're still going to be somebody we need to talk to.

"You walk with him when he left?"

"Walk with him? Why would I walk with him?"

"So he left around five and that's it."

"That was it, until . . . you know, until I found him at seven."

"You see anybody hanging around yesterday or today?"

"What, like somebody suspicious? People don't tend to hang around here, son. If anything people like to stay away. Herb's kids sure as hell liked to, just like my own do. You give them everything and this is how they repay you, by sticking you into . . ."

"Herb have a run in with anybody? Any arguments?"

"Jesus, what kind of argument would you need to have to end up like that? Anyway, everybody liked Herb. Everybody."

"Not everybody," I point out, and Bernie slowly nods.

"I'll think about it long and hard," he says, "I really will, but for the life of me there's nothing. I don't know why anybody would want to hurt Herb, not like that. There was so much blood in there at first I couldn't even tell it was Herb, but the toupee was his. You see it?" He doesn't wait for me to answer. "It was hanging from his scalp, like it had been unhinged. I used to give him hell over that toupee—it looked stupid, and everybody knew what it was. As soon as I saw it, I knew it was him. Had to be. No chance two people in this small world could have the exact awful taste in toupees," he says, and forces himself to smile.

"And you haven't seen anybody hanging around?"

He shakes his head. "It's like I said, nobody wants to hang around us old folks."

"What did he do for a living?"

"What? Well, he did nothing. None of us do."

"I mean before he retired."

"Oh, yeah, of course you did," he says, and he offers a sad smile. "He was a lawyer."

"What kind of lawyer?"

"I don't know, really. He doesn't talk too much about it. Nothing exciting from what I've always gathered, you know, contract law, dealing with properties being bought and sold, the mundane stuff we get billed about four hundred bucks an hour for."

"When did he retire?"

He shrugs, then starts doing the mental addition. The rest of his body seems to shut down as he thinks about it and he becomes a statue for five seconds. Either he's still got a psychic link to Herb's wife, or he's just gotten one to the man himself because when he starts back up he has an answer.

"A few years before his wife died," he says. "He didn't want to retire, but he got sick. Used to smoke, you know. It's what ruined his lungs. He gave up smoking around the same time he gave up work. Back then the doctors told him he had about two years to live, only it was his wife that died first. Five years ago they told him he'd be dead within six months. Since then they've been telling him three or four times a year that he's only got two months to live, and they'll keep telling him too for another few years yet . . ."

He realizes his mistake and stops mid-sentence. He raises a hand up to his face and wipes at a couple of tears starting to flow, his hands shaking enough to be a danger to his eyes.

"You're going to get the guy who did this, right?"

"Right."

"What will happen to him?"

"He'll go to jail."

He slowly nods, but I can see he's desperate to ask for more. "In the war, we had a way of dealing with things ourselves," he says. "There was one guy, we don't talk about it because . . ." he says, then remembers there's a reason nobody talks about it. "It wasn't good for him," he says. "I wish—Christ, I wish I could have five minutes alone with the man who did this to Herb."

Five minutes alone with Herb's killer isn't going to be a fun five minutes for Bernard Walsh. Forty years ago it might have been, but not now.

"You saw what was written on his forehead?" I ask.

He nods.

"You make anything of it?"

"Herb was a caring person," he says. "Doesn't make sense."

Sometimes it does and sometimes it doesn't, but I don't go down that path with him. I thank him for his time, and he wanders off and joins an expanding group of elderly people who are all absorbing the bad news, people who are used to seeing their friends driven out of here in a horizontal position. Tomorrow some of them won't even remember this happened—maybe Alzheimer's isn't a disease, but the body's natural coping mechanism. Witness statements will be full of descriptions of long-dead husbands and wives they haven't seen in twenty years.

Schroder has a Styrofoam cup of coffee in his hand and is looking steadier as he talks to the other man who was on the porch when we arrived. The man is using his hands a lot as he talks, as if drawing pictures in the air, and Schroder has to keep moving his coffee so it doesn't get knocked. I walk over, interested in the conversation, when Schroder's cell phone starts to ring.

Schroder nods as he listens, and when he hangs up he's looking pale.

The man he was talking to has wandered to the edge of the porch to chat to a younger woman, perhaps his assistant. I get the bad feeling Schroder has just been fired.

"I can drive you home," I tell Schroder. "Forensics can still do their job, and the officers can take statements."

"What? Oh, it's not that."

"No?"

He reaches down and picks up his shoes. "We've got another body," he tells me, and two minutes later we're back on the road.

CHAPTER FIVE

Caleb Cole isn't thinking straight—either that, or he's thinking clearer than he has in a long time. The thing he is certain of is the part of his mind that should be making this distinction died a long time ago, died around the time the rest of him started to decay. He's been a dead man for so long he no longer knows exactly what he is. He knows what he wants—what he wants is the only thing keeping him alive. Dead. Alive. His mind would make that distinction too if he had much of a mind left.

He's tired and covered in blood and he misses his family. It's wrong a dead man should feel so tired. He wants all of this to be over and he hasn't even begun. He has a long night ahead of him, and he has slowed over the years, any youth in him beaten away, stripped down and stomped on, his joints twisted, bones broken, teeth knocked out, every form of punishment rained down on him. He endured it because there was no alternative; he died and kept on enduring, the man he was back then long gone, and the new man he has become—well, sometimes he doesn't even know if he's still human. In the beginning that thought used to haunt him. Not anymore. When he thinks about the reasons he's still alive, he doubts there is any humanity left in him. There couldn't be. The things he's done, the things he's been through, the things he's going to start doing—no, there's no humanity left.

The apartment is small and all he can afford. It smells like rubber from the tire factory a few blocks away where he's worked for the last six weeks, saving up his money so he could buy his car, his phone, using the time to do his homework and rebuild his strength. The phone he bought a week ago. The car he has owned for two days. It was the last thing he needed to get the ball rolling.

Sometimes he'd come home at night and crouch over the toilet, shuddering as he threw up into it, the smell of rubber cooked into his skin. The apartment is on a bendy road made narrow by cars parked along the sides of it, but the narrowness saves the apartment from collapsing—all it would take is one large truck to drive past and his home would be rattled from its foundations. He lives on the second storey, the complex an old state house converted into apartments, each of them small, the walls so thin you can hear your neighbor taking a leak. It's still a castle compared to his last home, and listening to somebody take a leak is sure a hell of a lot better than having to watch. Compared to prison, where he's been for fifteen years, this place is like a dream.

The bed shares the same room with the kitchen and the living room. The only separate room is the bathroom, which is off to the side. He has a window, the view is of a common backyard between several flats, all of it is littered with junked-out automobile parts.

He steps into the shower and washes the old man's blood away. It's the second time he's had to do this. The last shower he took was at the first old man's home, he had to clean up before driving to the second. He couldn't exactly show up on

Albert's doorstep covered in blood and holding a six-pack of beer. He even wore one of the old man's shirts afterward. From the second house he's come straight home, covered in blood again but it's too dark for anybody to notice. He soaps up, the blood is in his hair, he shampoos it out, the lather turning red.

Fifteen years ago becoming a killer felt good. Tonight he felt nothing. There was the excitement and the nerves driving there, but then—nothing. For years he's been dreaming about these moments, thinking all that blood would help bring back some of what he's lost, but it turns out he was wrong. He stood in that first old man's house and felt dead inside, even after the blade had done its work. The second house was the same. This wasn't about revenge, it wasn't about emotion, it was about punishment.

Yet he'd done so much cutting. In those moments he had lost himself, the rage and pain of fifteen years had emerged, taking control of him, and he can remember the first stab but not the others. It wasn't until he found himself staring down at the bodies, blood dripping from his face, that he tried to recall, just how long had he been there? How many times had his arm swung up and down? The dead man in front of him told him it was a lot. He thought then the humanity would arrive, that it would be late to the party and it would come along and cripple him. It stayed away. It didn't even knock on the door.

These people all must pay for their mistakes, just as he has paid for his. The two tonight, it took some memory jogging on their parts to remember him. The others will remember better. The others are all younger. The police, of course, will make the connection. But he's chosen the order carefully, and by the time they make it the night will be over and it will be too late.

He steps out of the shower. The bathroom mirror is fogged over, and that's fine—he doesn't want to see himself. His reflection is too painful to look at. He dries himself down and heads into the bedroom and gets dressed. Then he plays with his cell phone. He uses it to open a news website, and so far there is no mention of the two dead men.

The phone switches off to a lock screen, and he has to slide his finger across it to bring it back to life. He'd never held a phone like this before. Years ago they were much bigger, a lot heavier, and if you didn't look at the screen from the right angle you couldn't see a damn thing. Now they're as thin as his finger and about the same weight, and you can do anything with them. The human race seems to be only a few years away from living like Captain Kirk.

It's creeping up toward quarter to ten. He grabs his keys, his jacket, his knife, and the flowers he bought earlier. He pauses in the doorway and glances at the apartment for only a few seconds. It's the last time he will ever see it. It was never a home. He won't miss it.

The City of Christchurch even at night looks the same after all these years, but it feels different. He read the news when he could—he knew the crime rate was escalating—but now he can feel it. The people in this city have changed. There are more people with shaved heads and tattoos, and people spit as they walk and bump into other and start arguments. Many drive fast cars with loud engines. It's been a long time, but back when he was a member of this world the cars were different but the status they stood for was the same, all men with big egos and small dicks, and he suspects it's the same now. The teenagers are the worst. Fifteen years ago you had guys driving up and down the two main streets in town, big cars that looked one step removed from a junkyard. Now the cars are louder, the colors even louder still, boys cruising all the streets of the city with fluffy dice in their windows and neon lights along the edges of the bodywork, and he doesn't get it, he just doesn't get it. It feels like he's living in some kind of cartoon world with brighter colors where teenagers with shiny cars have gone completely mad.

The people he passes on the street act as if he doesn't exist.

His car is parked half a block away. It's over a quarter of a century old and the only thing he knows about this car is that there's something under the hood that coughs and splutters every few minutes but still manages to get him around town. The guy he bought the car from had stripped the stereo out and replaced it with a piece of plywood that he'd painted black. He drives from the bad part of town to a slightly less bad part of town, networking his way through the suburbs.

It takes twenty minutes to get to her house. Driving a car was just like riding a bike—everything came back the moment he got behind the wheel. His license expired years ago but that's only an issue if he gets pulled over. Drivers are worse these days, no doubt about it, and there must be twice as many of them on the roads. Nobody knows how to use a traffic circle. Nobody seems to remember what a signal light is for.

He doesn't much like her neighborhood. Back when he used to have a family he lived in a pretty good place, friendly neighbors, nice homes. His own house had four bedrooms and two storeys and room for a pool in the backyard if they wanted one. The house he's looking at now looks like it probably has a pool forming on the floor of the living room. The roof has a couple of missing tiles and a tarpaulin is covering part of it. Maybe, just maybe, prison might have been better than this house. He parks down the road beneath a streetlight that doesn't work. He puts his hand on the door but doesn't pull the handle. Instead he sits in the car and stares at the house. He's nervous. For a dead man, that's quite an accomplishment. He isn't real sure what his opening line is going to be to the woman inside.

Maybe he should bring her beer. It's still in the back of the car.

He's still debating how to deal with her when a taxi pulls up outside the house and gives two quick taps of the horn. After a moment Ariel Chancellor steps from the house, glancing at her watch as she walks quickly to the taxi, a dress so short he looks away as she climbs in. She shuts the door and talks to the taxi driver. They talk for about a minute before they pull away from the curb, and he guesses they are negotiating the fare.

Damn it, he's missed his chance. He should have come last night, or any other night since being out of jail.

He starts the car up and begins to follow the taxi.

CHAPTER SIX

Schroder has the passenger window down, and is scraping the mud off his shoes with a penknife and flicking it outside. The rain doesn't seem to be coming back. Traffic is backed up about a thousand feet before the scene. Media vans are cutting each other off to be the first ones to send out pictures. I don't have authority because I'm not in a police car, so can't flash any sirens or honk for people to get out of the way. Both of us continually swear as we inch forward. The inside of the car is cold and the seats feel damp and the backs of my legs are itchy. A passenger plane is soaring off into the distance overhead, the people onboard all with somewhere better to be. We arrive at a cordon manned by four police officers. Schroder shows them his badge and they let us through.

It's quarter past ten and life feels like it's rewound a few hours; similar buildings, similar groups of people standing around watching, similar dead guy to have died a similar death. The only differences are the names of the people and the place and the absence of police detectives running off to take a leak.

The dead man's double is Albert McFarlane. The role of Bernie is being played by a similar looking man in a similar suit, only this one doesn't have badges stuck to it. More lighting is set up, a new group of onlookers, there are different people here but they're thinking the same question—*what in the hell is going on?*

We step out into a night that is dropping a couple of degrees every hour. The air is completely still. There are no birds anywhere. Everybody is talking in library whispers. We move past two officers who nod at us stoically. We step up onto the porch. The deck groans softly beneath our weight. The front door is painted bright blue and is wide open. The air inside isn't any warmer than outside. The view isn't any prettier than the last house. In fact, it's worse. This time the blood has been thrown up onto the ceiling fan. The fan, spinning, has whipped the droplets from the blades around the room, creating a line halfway up the wall like the ring around a bath. It looks like Morse code, lots of dots and dashes, almost like a cry for help. The dead man was stabbed so many times the blade kept throwing more blood up to the fan to redistribute, the law of physics meeting up with the law of creativity.

McFarlane looks just like Herb. Similar kind of position, similar cuts, you could string him up by his feet and he'd have the same amount of blood pour out of him. He's been written on by the same marker across his forehead, same handwriting, only this message is different: *Was it worth it?*

There are a few other differences. McFarlane managed to defend himself a little, as evidenced by the lacerations on his hands. He's attached to an oxygen machine, or was, the tube now lying on the carpet blowing air into it. The long jagged cuts down his body are easily visible because the shirt has mostly shredded away, leaving flabby skin that was pale yesterday, but today is stained red. The cuts are deep and reveal parts of this guy nobody has seen before, except maybe his heart surgeon. He looks like he was raked over by a broken beer bottle.

The retirement home is smaller than the other one but has

the same feel about it, though this one isn't really a retirement home, but a small subdivision of adjoining town houses where the youngest person looks old enough to have test-driven the wheel. The news has gotten out that it's the second homicide of the evening, and there can be no denying the connection, and the media are spreading the story over the airwaves and the gallery of people coming down to watch the show is growing every minute. An elderly lady is walking around carrying a tray, a tea service on top of it, offering drinks of hot tea to the officers on duty.

Police tape has been strung up and only time will tell whether or not the department has enough of it in stock to get us through to tomorrow morning. Each unit, though adjoining, has its own section, with shrubs and small flax bushes and rose plants out front. We head inside. More bloody footprints, hopefully belonging to the same killer. A serial killer is bad enough, but two madmen running around with magic markers and sharp knives is worse. Some of the forensics guys from the first scene have already shown up. They're doing their thing, checking for prints and fibers and DNA. They're working near the body and Schroder is talking to two people.

You didn't care enough.

Was it worth it?

One statement. One question. I stare at a vase full of lilacs on the dining table and think about those words while watching a ladybug climb the stem, going about its day-to-day job but somewhat lost, maybe confused by the amount of light for this time of evening.

I start with the bedroom. There is fingerprint powder over plenty of surfaces. The forensic guys are working fast. Maybe they're keen to get home or back to the other scene, or maybe they're sensing more bodies to come their way tonight. The bed is made up and nondescript, the kind of flower-patterned duvet cover everybody's widowed grandparent would sleep under. There's a bookcase with a wide selection of books. A couple of potted plants, a painting of a landscape, and nothing in here to suggest why the owner angered somebody enough to stab him over and over. There are photographs on the dresser, the victim and his children, of grandchildren, photos this man would have looked at every night going through his bedtime routine. Nothing with his wife.

I put on the same pair of gloves from the last scene, only now they're on inside out. I go through the drawers and cupboards, Schroder joining me a few minutes into the search, the smell of beer no longer as strong.

"Any theories?" he asks.

"Victim one was a lawyer," I answer. "Maybe he upset somebody."

"He hasn't been a lawyer for ten years," he says. "Why wait all that time?"

"Maybe the person he pissed off was in jail," I say, "and just got out."

"It's possible, but our victim wasn't a criminal lawyer, he was a divorce lawyer."

"Some would find that more of a reason to want him dead," I tell him.

"Victim two is seventy-eight years old," he says, "but taught high school for forty years. Retired thirteen years ago."

"Family?"

"Divorced. Two children."

"That explains the photographs," I tell him. "You check out who his divorce lawyer was?"

"It's getting looked at as we speak."

I look through an address book and find no mention of Herbert Poole. "Maybe they were friends long ago. Maybe Albert taught Herb's kids, or Herb got Albert his divorce. You know the reasons for the divorce? Was his wife having an affair? Anything there that can lead back?"

"Jesus, Tate, we've been here fifteen minutes. Cut me some slack."

I breathe out heavily. "Okay, point taken. I'm just throwing ideas out there," I say. "And I'm out of practice. Any prints?" I ask.

"Yeah, lots of them, but we just gotta narrow them down. Could be none of them belong to our suspect."

"Any witnesses?"

"Not yet, but we haven't started canvassing yet."

"What do you make of the messages?" I ask.

He shrugs. "One of them is a question," he says, "and one a statement. Was it worth it? That could be anything. Could mean was his TV worth the thousand bucks he paid for it, or was the hooker he paid for last night worth the hundred bucks? Could reference anything."

"Same with the statement," I say. "You didn't care enough. Probably means he didn't care enough about somebody, rather than some*thing*. Anybody spoken with Herbert Poole's kids?"

"Yeah. It's on the list," he says.

"It's a long list."

"And only getting longer."

"So what do you want me to do? I'm not much help here looking at a dead man, and anything here will be found anyway. Put me to use."

"Look, Theo," he says, and here it comes, the thing that all evening he has only ever been a moment away from saying. It was only a matter of time. "I appreciate all the help, but right now it's best if you just go home."

"So that's it? Thanks, Theo, for the ride?"

He holds up his hand. "Let me finish," he says. "The boss is on his way," he says, and I haven't seen Superintendent Dominic Stevens in a few years and I know where Schroder is going with this. "He'll be here in about fifteen minutes, and if he sees you here . . . well, you can probably kiss any chance of having your career back goodbye, and I can probably do the same for any chance of a promotion. You're a civilian, Theo, he's not going to like you being here, not right off, just let me get him aside and explain the situation instead of him just showing up and seeing you working."

"Yeah, okay, sure," I say.

"I know you're pissed off. Once I've spoken to him, I'm sure we can put you to use, and if we do, you have to follow some rules. You're not a cop, you're a private investigator, but you can't bend the law, not if you want any chance of getting back on the force."

"I'll be a good boy," I tell him. "I promise to behave."

He doesn't answer me for a few seconds, just stares at me long enough to let me know I've just pissed him off too.

"Okay, go home and get some rest. I'll give you a call soon. If you can come back, I'll let you know. Otherwise I'll see you in the morning. And Tate, if you work on this I need you to do me a favor. I'm not kidding here, this time make sure you don't kill anybody."

CHAPTER SEVEN

Caleb follows the taxi into town. If the girl is going to a club or a bar, there are going to be a lot of people around. That's not going to work well. They pass a line of bars, where people who are students and plumbers and lawyers by day double as assholes by night. The music coming from the clubs and the other cars on the street is nothing like he used to hear before he went away.

The taxi slows up when it gets to Manchester Street, coming to a stop at every intersection, timing the red lights perfectly. Then it stops at a green light halfway down the street outside a stereo shop. It pulls over, and Caleb goes through the intersection and pulls over too. He watches the woman in the rearview mirror handing money over to the driver and then waiting for change. When she climbs out she takes a cell phone from her pocket and makes a call. Her short skirt doesn't seem as short in comparison to some of the other girls on the street, the hookers on the street corners that walk past on her way to . . .

She stops walking. She stands on the spot, turning slowly,

and then the cell phone is back in her handbag and is replaced by a cigarette, which she lights up. One of the hookers comes over to her and they start chatting. Caleb doesn't get what's going on. He knows how it looks—it looks like she's standing on the corner waiting to fuck the next person willing to pay for it—but that can't be. Only thing he can think of is she's trying to help these girls. Ariel and her friend start chatting, and they're both shivering because it's so fucking cold and neither of them are wearing jackets. They're smoking and laughing. On the corner opposite a car slows up and a girl over there approaches it and leans into the passenger window. A few seconds later she climbs in and the car disappears.

Another car pulls over to the same corner. It does a U-turn and stops next to Ariel and her friend. Both girls flick their cigarettes into the gutter, and it's Ariel who approaches the car. He can see it all happening and it makes him feel sick. He can't hear what she's saying because the weather and the distance kills any chance of that. He waits for her to walk away, only she doesn't, instead she opens the passenger door, throws a smile and a shrug at her friend, and climbs in. The car doesn't move for half a minute as business is discussed, then it pulls away from the curb, goes through the intersection and past him, then hangs a right at the next corner.

He starts the car and follows.

The trip is a short one. The numbers on his odometer don't even get warmed up. Half a block to the east and the car pulls into an alleyway. The lights switch off and nobody climbs out. The alleyway is so dark there is no room for any shadows, and the car and the people inside it are lost. He parks opposite and tightens his grip on the steering wheel and breathes hard and fast and his head spins and his hands—especially his right one—begin to ache. He lowers his forehead onto the steering wheel. He wants to head-butt it to make himself hurt. He takes deep breaths to try and calm the urge to vomit. The inside of the windshield starts to fog up. He wipes at it with his sleeve.

He opens his mouth and closes it around the top of the steering wheel and bites into it. He wants to scream.

He picks up the knife. Sure, there are people around, not many—another hooker half a block back, a few people driving past, another couple walking the street—but he could probably walk right over to that car and spill a lot of blood before anybody called the police.

He puts the knife back down. It'd be stupid. He can't afford to get arrested when he's not even halfway done. There are teeth marks in the steering wheel. He stares out the windshield at a huge billboard overlooking the car. It's for a travel agency, there are pictures of islands and water and people laughing and it's the life he wants. He focuses on the billboard, staring at all the things he can never have. It only makes him angrier.

The car starts to back out of the alleyway and stops. The passenger door opens and the interior light comes on and Ariel climbs out. She closes the door without looking back and heads back toward the intersection. The car's headlights flick on and it goes the opposite way. Ariel reaches into her handbag and comes out with another cigarette, fiddling around with a lighter as she walks. He can still see the car she climbed out of, it's parked up at a set of lights.

He follows it.

He can't help it. He looks at his watch. It's ten-forty. This is going to throw him off schedule, but he still has all night. He should just carry on with the plan and come back and see Ariel later on tonight, try and time it for when she's finished work.

It's what he should do.

Only he doesn't.

The scenery changes. They leave town and enter the suburbs. Some are nicer than others. He grits his teeth as he drives. They drive for ten minutes, finally pulling into a suburb full of middle-class homes, the streets empty, streetlights cutting circles of light into the darkness. The car slows. It pulls into a driveway. The automatic door begins to open. This is the kind of neighborhood you can't hang around in for too long in a beaten-up car with a knife in your hand and not have somebody call the police.

Best make it quick.

He brings the car to a stop and brings the knife out from under the seat.

CHAPTER EIGHT

Make sure you don't kill anybody.

Schroder's words are rattling around in my mind as I leave the retirement home. He makes it sound like it's become an occupational hazard for me.

The sky is dark with clouds and the night is lit up by the city and the life running through it. I head to the nursing home where my wife lives. I step through the main doors and into the foyer, warm colors and warm air enveloping me. It's eleven o'clock and the nurse behind the reception desk smiles and asks how I'm doing. I tell her I'm doing okay. Visiting hours ended three hours ago, but the nurses know me well enough to let me in most hours unless I'm getting in the way.

I make my way to my wife's room, looking for her nurse along the way, always hopeful that one of these days she'll be there to greet me at the door with some good news. As it stands the news is always the same as the day before—which is no news. My wife's condition doesn't change and never will. When she isn't sleeping, she stares straight ahead, enough synapses in her brain to make her chew when she's being fed but not enough for her eyes to focus on anything, not enough firing synapses for her to smile at me and hold my hand, the vegetative state a permanent one barring a miracle or an advancement in technology, both of which I pray for.

I don't see Nurse Hamilton anywhere, and I head straight to Bridget's room. She's asleep. There is a soft bedside table light and the curtains are closed.

A year ago I'd have brought flowers for Bridget, but a year ago I could afford them. Between the medical bills and my own bills, as it stands I'm only a few months away from losing my house. I don't tell any of this to Bridget. If somehow she could understand I wouldn't want her to worry. The drunk driver who put my wife into this condition should have been responsible for paying all the medical costs, but that's not the way things work in this world. He never took responsibility, not until I took him into the middle of nowhere with a shovel and a gun and made him beg for a forgiveness I couldn't give him. I pull up the chair next to Bridget and take hold of her hand and spend thirty minutes with her.

When I leave I'm hit by a tiredness that makes me aware I've been working since five in the morning, when I was driving around hotels looking for Lucy Saunders. And I'm not just tired either—because the thing keeping me from falling asleep and hitting a lamppost is the hunger pains, a hunger so strong it feels like it's developed claws and is digging its way out from my stomach. So maybe it is a good thing I'm going home now, because I get to concede to the pain and pull into a drive-through at a fast-food restaurant. There's a line of cars ahead of me and I keep myself entertained by trying to stay awake. Eventually I get to order something, and the guy who passes me my food looks like he keeps himself entertained by trying to eat every burger that isn't sold by day's end. I drive to a park and sit in the dark as one day ends and another begins. Mine is the only car around. My midnight snack is in pieces before I

even get to take a bite, the burger also having absorbed some
of the flavor of the small cardboard box. I get through it pretty
quick along with the drink—ten bucks well spent because I feel
more awake. I sit in the car and think about the two dead men,
both retired, certainly a connection between them. These two
might be the only victims or there may be more. Future victims, retirees maybe, the same thing linking them to an event
in their past. The dots are there, but not clear enough to start
connecting.

I leave the park as another car arrives. It comes straight at
me with its lights off. I swerve out of the way and almost hit
a tree. Maybe it's another PI coming here to eat a burger or a
couple of kids wanting to fool around.

I head back out into the wet streets, and as often happens
to me at this time of night, I start thinking about my wife, and
about my daughter, and I can feel my mood darkening. Sometimes, even three years after the accident now, I just start to
cry. I don't feel tired anymore, I don't feel hungry—sometimes
like this I don't really feel anything. I wipe a finger at my eyes
before they start leaking, and suddenly I'm compelled to go and
see my little girl, to make sure she's safe. I drive to the cemetery
and park by the church next to another car. I make the trek
toward my daughter's grave in the misty rain, thinking about
the two dead men and wondering what, or more accurately
who, it was they had in common.

CHAPTER NINE

Caleb's wife won't appreciate the flowers. She hated him in the end, had to, otherwise she never would have left him. She acted like it was all his fault, everything, their dead daughter, all that blood he spilled at the slaughterhouse. He just couldn't help himself, couldn't she see that? It was his job to protect his family, it was his job as a father, as a husband, and as a man. If he couldn't do that, then it was his job to make people pay. It's basic genetics. So there are flowers for her and flowers for his children and God how he misses them, how he would do things differently if he could, how he'd make them safe.

Fifteen years—his son would have been fourteen, his daughter twenty-five. A multitude of possibilities—he could have been a grandfather, his daughter could have been a doctor or an artist, his son a straight-A student in school with dreams of playing in a band. With them dying so young, those possibilities remain timeless, endless.

The cemetery is cold and wet and his feet sink a little into the soft lawn as he stands motionless by the graves. Three graves in total, one of them empty and waiting for him. Then he can lie next to his children, murdered fifteen years ago, his wife murdered too by a bunch of people who didn't care enough to make a difference. They were ignorant and lazy and stupid.

His wife hated him for what he did. The coroner said she took over fifty pills. That's a statistic he has to carry with him, one that shows how desperate she was to leave him. He was no use to her back then. He was in jail when she died, he'd gone there without a trial, having confessed to the police and to the courts, asking for leniency—after all he couldn't control himself. Only he wasn't given any. Instead he was given fifteen years and a week into that sentence his parents came to tell him his wife and unborn son were dead.

His parents. He misses them. Each of them died because of illnesses that are easy to get the more years you see after seventy. They used to come and see him in jail. For the first ten years it was every week without fail. Then age crept up on them and they'd miss a week here or there, then a few weeks in a row. He wasn't there for them when they died. Wasn't there to keep his wife alive. His family has died around him and all he can do for them now is check off names. The first time he even saw his wife's and daughter's graves was the day he came out of jail. He had to ask the priest at the adjoining church for directions.

"It's always harder on the ones left behind," Father Jacob had said.

"You couldn't be more right," Caleb had answered.

The cemetery could double as a maze. There are trees and hedges cordoning off sections of graves, plots cut off by archways and stone pathways. The church is hidden from the cemetery behind a horseshoe ring of trees, only the very top visible over them, though more becoming visible as autumn takes away the foliage. He looks at the gravestones and wonders how many people out here have similar stories to his own and comes to the conclusion none of them do.

"I'm sorry," he tells his wife, and he truly is, and if he could take it all back, he would. There's a cool wind whipping rain off the grass and from the trees into him and he begins to shiver.

"I really am," he repeats, and he doesn't know what else to say. She can't hear him. Coming here was pointless, really. The dead can't talk, they can't listen, they can't hear, not in this state anyway. But he does have a message for them—one he can't give them after he dies. For what he's done, when all of this is over he won't be able to join them. He knows he'll be going somewhere different from them. He has to tell them how sorry he is. And he wants them to know he can't make up for it, but he can hurt those who let it happen. Including himself.

And he must admit, he wants them to forgive him. They won't—he knows that—and it's painful when the psychics toy with that emotion.

"I just wish that . . ." he says, but no other words come. There are many things he wishes for.

He walks away from the grave, his shoes soaking up more water, the maze slowing him down, his body heavy with thoughts of the past as he trudges through wet grass and gardens on his way back to the parking lot.

CHAPTER TEN

I'm not alone when I get back to my car from seeing my daughter's grave. There's a guy sitting in the car I parked next to, trying hard to get his car started. The engine isn't quite turning over but he keeps giving it a go. He looks up at me and there's not much light coming from the street and none coming from the church, so it's hard to get a good look at him, but what I can see doesn't look good. There are scars on his face, and his nose looks like it's been broken several times. He sees me looking and there's nothing I can do except offer to help, whereas what I'd rather do is get into my car and get the hell out of here. Then I figure for this guy to be out here at this time of night he's suffering a loss, maybe a similar loss to my own.

"You need a hand?" I ask him.

"I don't know much about cars," he tells me, climbing out of it. He must be around fifty, with a thick head of gray hair that is flattened down.

"Nor do I," I admit, "but I've got a set of jumper cables that might do the trick."

I open the trunk of my car and fish out the cables. We pop the hoods and attach our respective ends. I think if there was a competition to see who had the worse car, we'd both win. I start my car and my engine barely turns over, and for a second I think we could both be stranded here, but then it catches and I put my foot on the accelerator a few times.

I walk around my car while the other guy climbs into his. It takes a couple of tries, but then his engine starts. He guns it a few times, then climbs out and from the light of the cars I can get a better look at him. He looks like he's been beaten up, not recently, but a long time ago, and many times too. We unhook the cable and I wrap it up and throw it into the trunk.

"I appreciate it," he says.

"No problem," I say, and instinct kicks in, and next thing I know I'm offering him my hand.

He looks at it for a few seconds. He seems unsure what to do, and I'm starting to feel like an idiot, but then he reaches out and shakes it. I shake his back, and he winces a little.

I quickly let go. "Sorry," I tell him.

"Not your fault," he says, massaging his fingers. "Just an old injury."

"Well, don't be surprised if you have to return the favor in the next day or two," I say, looking at my car.

"I'm not even sure the car is going to last another day or two," he answers.

The moment is over, and it's nice to have met a stranger who wasn't a jerk and who, at this time of night, wasn't trying to steal my wallet. We both acknowledge the moment and climb into our cars. He gives a small wave as he drives away, then I'm back on the street, feeling good about helping somebody.

It's one o'clock when I get home. I kick off my shoes and

put them next to the radiator hoping they'll be dry by morning. I fire up the computer and heat the remaining half of a supermarket pizza from a few days ago because the burger only helped out for a few minutes. I make some coffee. I haven't eaten anything healthy since coming out of prison and see no reason to break the tradition. I lost eighteen pounds behind bars and none of them seem to be coming back—without my shirt on I look like a corpse.

I sit down in my study, where articles about Melissa X are pinned to the walls, photographs of her when she was Natalie Flowers. There are crime scene reports filed around the room in chronological order. Her icy blue eyes stare out at me from different images, they are the only thing identical between the two personalities, the rest changed with makeup, hair colors, and three years of killing.

I turn my back on Melissa and search for today's victims online. The stories have hit the news, but not their names, although victim one, Herbert Poole, comes up from cases in his past, and victim two, Albert McFarlane, has a story of when he retired from school, students thanking him and wishing him the best. Schroder has already confirmed the lawyer victim two used for his divorce wasn't victim one. The connection must be somewhere else.

I shut the computer down and head to the lounge. I lie on the couch and watch the news. I have the beginnings of a headache that I don't think is going to take hold. I rub the side of my head and it fades a little as I watch a woman in her early thirties with a big smile and straight hair look into the camera and open the proceedings. Two old people murdered on the same day, and the media are throwing around the *serial killer* label. They already have a name for him—*The Gran Reaper*. I grimace at the name, wondering who the hell comes up with them so quickly, whether the media machine churning out the doom and gloom have some geeky guy stashed in a basement office earning minimum wage just for these occasions. If they do, then with his latest effort they should be paying him less. There is footage from the scenes, but there's no mention of drunk detectives showing up. I'm grateful, but not as grateful as Schroder and the others will be—he and his work buddies seem to have dodged a bullet and kept their jobs. At least for now.

Knowing the media, it may only be a matter of time.

CHAPTER ELEVEN

Caleb's next stop is two suburbs over, a house on a dead-end street where the neighbors seem to be making the best of what they have: old homes with tidy yards, cracked windows but all of them clean, patchy paint but none of it hanging in flakes, the bare wood sanded back. He parks outside the woman's house and even though nobody would want to steal his car, he locks it anyway. Hell, they'd have to get it to start first. He leaves the knife under the passenger seat.

The pathway up to the doorstep is lined with broken sunflowers, their thick stems bent from the last strong wind, some of them missing except for the stumps, others still attached and lying limp on the lawn. A dog next door is running the length of the fence, its paws scrabbling against it, but it doesn't bark. He reaches the front door. He rings the doorbell and is unsure if it's broken or if he just can't hear it. Just when he's getting ready to knock, a woman swings it open, offering him a large smile painted on in bright red lipstick.

"Right on time," she says, smiling at him. "Come on through."

Right on time is one o'clock in the morning, and he guesses she thinks that makes her readings more authentic. He follows her into a room darkened by thick purple curtains. The house smells of whatever was cooked for dinner, some kind of chicken dish. The woman is wearing a scarf over her hair, a velvet dress that reaches the floor, and has tattoos on her hands that he can't make out. In her early fifties, he knows thirty years ago she could have been quite beautiful. Except for her hand—her right hand is disfigured, the fingers all pointing back at her body, looking like a claw. He's not sure if she was born that way, had an accident, or if she's faking a disability to add to her persona.

"Sit," she tells him, and points to a chair.

The room is illuminated by two lamps from opposing corners. There is a bookcase jammed with titles, words like *afterlife* and *spirits* adorning many of them. The table they sit at is a card table with black cloth draped across it and nothing else. There's a couch against the wall and a cat sitting flat along the arm of it. It stares at him, as if reading his mind, something he hopes he doesn't have to pay for at the end of the session. There's a vase full of incense burning by the window.

This is his first time here, but his fourth time in a similar environment. The other three psychics he's seen all did readings from their homes, outfits the same but different shades of dark, books by the same authors, and lighting just as dim. They had similar ways of contacting the dead. He is hoping this woman will be more genuine.

"Give me your hands," she says.

So far it's the same. He reaches over the table, his left hand somewhat hesitant as her clawed one embraces it.

"There is a lot of pain inside you," she tells him, but she isn't summoning a spirit to tell her that, it's written and scarred in his features. "I sense," she says, then cocks her head slightly, her eyes closed, and he can tell she's trying hard to listen to something. He stares at her, wanting to believe it's real. "I sense you have lost somebody close to you," she says. "Is that right?"

He nods, then realizes she can't see him. "Yes," he says.

"Your wife?"

"Yes," he says again, hoping she isn't just guessing.

She scrunches her eyes tighter. The other psychics had stopped with the wife. They didn't figure out his children were dead too. This one is focusing . . . focusing. . . .

"I sense there is more pain," she adds. "You loved your wife very much. Was there . . . somebody else too?"

It's an open question, but he takes it because he wants to believe. "Yes."

"I'm sensing somebody younger," she says, and when he says nothing she tightens the grips on his hands, the good hand stronger than the claw, and thinks for a few more seconds. "Somebody quite younger."

"My daughter," he says, then feels stupid for supplying her with that information. He's overeager.

"Yes, yes," she says, "I sensed a young girl. Very beautiful. Your daughter."

He nods, knowing she can't see him but keeps nodding anyway. "Yes," he says, and doesn't mention his son.

"It was some time ago," she says. "Is that right?"

"Yes," he answers, still eager but more suspicious now. The way she says things, it's like she's fishing for information more from the living than from the dead.

"And you've come to me to try and talk to them," she says.

She opens her eyes and looks at him. "A lot of pain," she says, "for everybody involved. No?"

He nods.

"And you have come here for what reason?" she asks. "To talk to them? To tell them you miss them?"

"I want them to know how sorry I am," he says. "I let them down. Can you tell them?"

She smiles at him. "You can tell them yourself," she says.

"There is somebody here," she says, and she looks over his shoulder. It's so believable that he glances back, but all that's there is the couch and the cat and the door to the hallway.

The woman closes her eyes again. "Yes, I definitely sense somebody here," she says. She tilts her head to the other side now, and he's not sure which part of the room the spirit—if there is one—is in.

"A woman is here," she says. "I . . . I can't quite see her clearly. A beautiful woman. Your wife. She . . . she is sad she left you. It was sudden, sudden for both your wife and daughter."

"Yes."

"Some kind of accident," she says. "I can't . . . can't quite make it out."

"Something like that."

"There was a lot of pain there."

"I miss them," he says.

"She can hear you," she says. "She says she misses you."

"Can you . . ."

"Wait," she says, tightening the grips on his hands. "Wait, she is telling me something. She has to go, but there's something she wants me to tell you. Yes, yes," she says, nodding and listening enthusiastically, and then, "yes, I understand. I'll tell him."

She opens her eyes. "She's gone," she tells him.

"Gone?"

"Gone. But she gave me a message. She wants you to know that her pain is gone, that she and your daughter are together, that they love you, that she wants you to be happy."

He pulls his hands away. The woman flinches, her eyes widening as she realizes she has said something wrong. "Sometimes the messages can be vague," she tells him. "Sometimes it can take a few attempts."

He hands over the eighty dollars she told him over the phone that it would cost and it disappears into her claw. She walks him to the front door. He didn't see them on the way in, but on the way out there's a set of suitcases packed next to the door, on top of them a pair of passports and a set of tickets. Later tonight or tomorrow she's leaving the country with her husband or partner and he remembers the holiday with his wife twenty-five years ago, lots of sun and great food and nice wine and nine months after that they had a daughter.

"My wife," he tells her, "would never want me to be happy. She blames me for what happened—she always will."

She nods slowly, and he guesses that's what being a psychic is all about—learning from your mistakes. He expects her to defend herself, to tell him he's wrong and his wife does want him to be forgiven, wants him to be happy, but she says nothing and slowly closes the door.

He should have known.

The car starts up on the first try. He pulls away from the house without glancing back. Playtime is over. It's time to move on to the next victim. She's going to be the easiest—after all, she's the only one on the list who's in a coma.

CHAPTER TWELVE

My phone goes off and it's the first I've realized I've fallen asleep on the couch, still dressed in my funeral suit. I look at my watch. It's two o'clock. I've only been asleep for ten minutes. The news has ended and there's an infomercial on TV, some new piece of must-have fitness equipment that folds down and slides under your bed so you don't have to feel embarrassed about it when the neighbors come around. The woman displaying it has more abs than I have nutrients floating around inside my body. I check the caller ID. It's Schroder. Either he's ringing to tell me I can work on the case, or I can't.

"I've spoken to the powers that be," he tells me.

"And?"

"And I reminded them when it comes to serial killers, you have a knack for looking in the right places, even if you do go about it the wrong way."

"And?"

"And they reminded me that your success rate comes with a homicide rate."

"The first was an accident," I say, "and the second one killed himself." The first one is partly true and partly not true. The latter is also made up from the same parts. Schroder knows this, can't prove it, and wouldn't want to even if he could.

"You're on the case," he says. "Not as a cop, but as an official consultant."

"That's all I was hoping for at this point."

"Yeah. If it goes well—hell, maybe this is your chance to get back on the force."

"Yeah, sucks that my chance comes about by two people dying."

"Three," he says.

"What?"

"That's why I'm calling you now and not in the morning, and this is why we need all the help we can get. We've got a third victim."

"You're kidding me."

"Christchurch hospital. He's hanging on. Could go either way. Meet me there five minutes ago."

The traffic is sparse, ninety percent of it made up of taxis ferrying the drunk. It thickens around the hospital where there's been an accident outside the main entrance, a boy-racer has jumped the curb and knocked down a lamppost, pinning somebody inside his car. The parking lot is mostly empty and I don't drop any coins in the meter. I head to the emergency department and it's full of people who have fallen over drunk and hurt themselves. I call Schroder and he comes through the security doors to meet me.

"Nice shoes," he says, looking down at my running sneakers.

"You too," I say, looking down at his running sneakers, which, like mine, are probably the only thing he had that was dry. He's also changed into a new shirt. "We can be shoe buddies. So, does being a consultant come with a wage?"

Schroder shrugs. "It does, but don't ask me what it is. Hell, maybe it'll be more than what I make."

We head back through the doors. There's a series of intersecting corridors and people have probably died in here looking for the right place to be. Doctors and nurses are walking about in a hurry, patients are in cubicles behind curtains, voices and tears and laughter coming from different ones.

We follow the corridor to a small foyer with chairs where two women are sitting down, one doing the crying, one doing the comforting. The first the wife, the second a neighbor or friend. We stop thirty feet short of them so we can talk without them hearing.

"It's bad," Schroder says. "Lots of internal damage, lots of blood loss. Doctor ten minutes ago said if the guy has a priest, now would be the time to call him."

"What happened?"

"According to his wife he came home, parked the car, then didn't come to bed. She got up after ten minutes to go look for him. Found him in the garage next to his car, he was holding his guts in with his fingers. He was in so much pain he couldn't move, couldn't even call out. By the time the ambulance arrived he was already unconscious."

"She see anything?"

"Just her husband." Schroder lowers his voice even though nobody can hear us. I can still smell beer on him. "Different type of victim, just the one stab wound and nothing written on him, but it's our guy."

"Yeah? What do you have?"

"Killer walked across the front lawn and dragged some mud with him. Matches up with the bloody footprints back at the retirement homes. I mean an exact match, right down to gaps in the tread. It's our guy."

"Well, if it is him, why is this scene so different?"

"Theory is he panicked and fled."

"What else have you got?"

"From victim three, not much. From the first two he drank coffee at each of the scenes, but he's wiped down the cups.

He's wiped down all the surfaces he may have touched, including the bathroom. So no prints. DNA, well, we got plenty of that. Just that's not going to be any good until the results come back."

"Jesus," I say, "three people within, what, six, seven hours?" I nod toward another big set of doors, which lead to another corridor and operating rooms where right now our victim is on a table with somebody's hands inside him. "What if he's not our last?"

"Victim three is Brad Hayward," he says. "Forty-one years old, an accountant, wife with two children, all of whom were home when it happened."

"The kids see anything?"

"The kids were in bed."

"So the extra people at the house could be why the killer didn't hang around to make sure the job was complete."

"That's the theory," Schroder says. "So far no links to either of the other victims."

"So a teacher, an accountant, and a lawyer—"

"All walk into a bar," Schroder says, then shakes his head. "Does sound like a setup," he adds.

The wife has been staring at the doors the entire time, but now she looks over at us, whispers something to her friend, stands up, and comes over. She clutches at the bottom of her jacket and tugs it down, straightening it, then brushes away the tears from the front of it. Schroder introduces me but doesn't give me a title. She nods an acknowledgment but doesn't offer to shake hands. I feel like I'm not wanted.

"Do you know anything yet?" she asks, directing the question at both of us.

"We're certainly building up a picture of what happened," Schroder says.

"Was it the Grim Reaper?"

"It's Gran Reaper," Schroder corrects her.

"What?"

"It's Gran Reaper."

"Gran?"

"As in Grandparent."

"Cute," she says, but doesn't sound like she means it.

"We don't know for sure it's him, but it's possible," Schroder says.

"Which firm does your husband work for?" I ask.

"Goodwin, Devereux, and Barclay," she says.

"They interact with lawyers?" I ask.

She shrugs. "You'd need to ask them, but I assume so."

"Have you heard of Herbert Poole or Albert McFarlane?" I ask.

"Your partner asked me that already," she says, "and the answer is no. Are they the two men killed earlier today?"

"What can you tell me about your husband?" I ask. "Was he well liked? Having any problems? Any strange phone calls, any late-night meetings, anything at all?"

"Brad's a great man," she says, frowning at me. "Nothing like that at all, and everybody likes him. Everybody. I hope you're going to have better questions than that."

"What time does he normally finish work?" I ask.

"It varies. He aims to finish at six most nights, but most times he doesn't finish till seven or eight. Sometimes, like tonight, he doesn't finish till much later. It's not unusual for him to get home after midnight."

"And he calls first?"

"He called around five and said he wouldn't make it home till around eleven. He has a lot of work at the moment. One of his colleagues was arrested for murder and is in jail now," she says, "so Brad has to take on the extra workload."

"So finishing late is a recent thing," I say.

"He would finish late in the past, maybe once or twice a month, but now it's almost every night, and of course much later too. Midnight is about as late as it gets. I don't complain because he's under a lot of stress at work. I mean, it came up, sure it did, I was sick of having to take care of the house and the kids and I didn't want to become a widow to an accountant firm, and . . . and . . ."

She stops talking. The word *widow* has registered with her and her face is changing shape around the thought, I can see it in her features, in her eyes, she's mapping a future with her husband no longer in it, no more phone calls, no more arguments, no more being unsure of when he's going to arrive home. No more of anything—just an emptiness in her life that one day she may fill with somebody else or won't.

"He's going to make it," she says. "He's . . . he's lost a lot of blood," she says, "and the doctors . . . they still don't know if . . ." she stops talking. Her friend stands up and comes over and puts an arm around her. She gives us a dirty look, like everything is our fault, like we're being intrusive with all the questions even though we all want the same thing.

"How long has he worked at the firm?" I ask.

"Five years, going on six."

"Before then?"

"Before then he used to work for Inland Revenue."

I glance at Schroder and he returns the look. The Inland Revenue thing is a problem. That means we can start throwing darts at the phone book and each time we'd find somebody with a motive. I know it means that I hate Brad Hayward, and Schroder hates him too. We're out there putting our lives on the line every day just to give a third of our wages to the government, and it's not like the government's taking one-third of the risk. And if Schroder gets shot, Inland Revenue isn't going to send flowers and wish him the best and thank him for all the tax he's paid.

"Any problems back then? Any threats?" I ask.

"No, nothing," she says, and Schroder's cell phone goes off. He excuses himself and steps back.

"Why'd he leave?" I ask.

"Oh, well, he just wanted a change," she says, her eyes looking down.

"That's all?"

"That's what I said."

"Would he tell you if there had been any threats?" I ask.

"Brad tells me everything."

I've never known whether girlfriends and wives really believe that.

"I know what you're thinking," she says.

I don't need to prompt her to carry on.

"You're thinking with all the late nights, that Brad was having an affair. Well, he wasn't."

I wasn't thinking that—at least not seriously, but now I certainly am. "Listen, Mrs. Hayward, were people suspecting your husband of having an affair? I need to know everything. Anything you hold back could be vital, it could help us find who did this."

"I'm not holding anything back."

"Why did he leave Inland Revenue?"

"I told you, he just wanted a change," she says, and this time she holds my eye for a few seconds before looking away and, combined with what she said about her husband being faithful, I know she's lying to me. I've been doing this for too long to let somebody like Mrs. Hayward fool me. "Better money, better conditions, plus nobody wants to work for the tax department," she says.

I nod. That's true. "I'm going to ring them first thing in the morning and talk to his old boss and find out anyway," I say, "so you might as well tell me."

"Is this necessary?" her friend says.

"It's okay," Mrs. Hayward says, and then she holds my look. "It was nothing. Just, you know, problems with another woman. She said he was harassing her when he wasn't. Stupid stuff. She didn't like Brad so she made up stuff about him. It was easier to move on than to follow it up. So that's it, Mr. Policeman, and now you think Brad was cheating on me and he wasn't, he'd never do that, he's not the cheating kind," she says, only I think he might be and she thinks he might be too. The late nights, the extra hours at work—you don't have to be an accountant to see what that adds up to.

I thank her for her time and wish her husband the best. Schroder wraps up his phone call.

"Get anything?" he asks. "You looked like you were giving her a hard time."

"Her husband was having an affair. It's probably why he was late home tonight. Maybe he was messing around with the wrong girl. Maybe that's the connection."

"She tell you that?"

"Not in as many words," I say.

And on that note a doctor, looking dejected, comes out from behind the doors, and before he can even say a word we all know what he's about to say, and the two women break down and cry and the Christchurch homicide rate marches on.

CHAPTER THIRTEEN

We're not dealing with a serial killer. We're dealing with a spree killer, and that's not something Schroder or myself or anybody else in the department has had experience with. A serial killer takes his time. A spree killer is running around killing who he can in as quick a time as he has. You're dealing with one victim and at the same time our perp is creating another.

At three in the morning we leave the hospital and the city's most current grieving widow and drive to the crime scene in our own cars. We drive past the journalists who, like vampires, never sleep and, who, like vampires, suck the life out of people. The world would be a better place if vampires were real and reporters were not.

The neighborhood suggests accountants get paid well and there must be more of them living on the street. They probably have accountant parties every few months and swap the latest lawyer jokes and write everything off as an expense. Reporters shout questions at us and I can feel dozens of lenses zooming in on my face. We park behind a patrol car, which has somebody locked in the backseat, somebody wearing a press ID hanging around his neck and a pair of handcuffs around his wrists. Resting on the roof of the car is an expensive camera with one side scratched up and gouged from a fall.

The house is a four-bedroom, single-storey place with a very small front lawn. The interior smells like dinner. There are a few other detectives already here, including Detective Kent, who is talking to one of the neighbors. She gives a friendly nod toward us as we walk past. There's blood all over the garage floor and the side of the car, Brad having fallen backward and slid against it. There are handprints on the concrete and streaks of blood. It looks like Brad tried to drag himself forward before his body gave up on him. The garage door had been left open by the killer, but nobody had seen poor Brad as he lay waiting for his wife to help him, or one of the neighbors. Well, the neighbors are here now—and plenty of them. They're all standing outside their houses and watching, fascinated by the goings-on of death, addicted to the drama. They can't look away. The amount of blood here means the doctors didn't have much to work with.

I step over the blood and through the internal doorway into the hallway. The house is ten degrees warmer than outside. There's a heat pump still blowing warm air in the living room. It's working hard to combat the cold air coming through the open door. There's a big-screen TV showing a live news report. The sound has been muted, there's a reporter at the scene and in the background I can see my car. Maybe a viewer out there will feel sorry enough to donate a later model with more working parts. The car is coming through in HD, as is the reporter, as is every line and wrinkle on her face. The camera is adding ten pounds to the reporter and twenty years to my car.

One of the bedrooms has been turned into a study. There are photos on the wall of family with various degrees of happiness on their faces. There's a framed poster-sized movie print on the wall with an alien holding a woman in his arms, the background full of 1950s tanks and 1950s soldiers acting the way they all did back in B movies when army tanks never solved problems but added to them. I figure nothing has changed. I switch on the computer and while it loads up I go through the drawers and the desk and start stacking things on top of it, an address book, folders containing work, a list of bank accounts and social networking sites all with passwords written next to them. The computer comes to life and I spend time going through the history folder, bank accounts, all websites this family has visited and find nothing useful. If Brad was having an affair, there isn't any evidence of hotel room charges or flowers. The names from the address book and the shop receipts will be cross-referenced with anything found from the first two scenes.

I head back into the garage. Brad's keys are still hanging in the ignition. It's a much nicer car than mine and I wonder if the wife would mind me borrowing it since I'd be using it to help find her husband's killer. I figure if I asked I'd be adding to the body count in the morgue. I open the door and can immediately smell perfume. It's strong, and even stronger against the passenger seat. There are some dirty blond hairs caught in the fabric of the headrest, about twice the length of the wife's hair and a different color. I go through the glove box, the trunk, and check under the seats. There are plenty of gas receipts tossed about, two empty drink bottles, a pair of socks, and some candy bar wrappers. I close up the car and head into the bedroom. I look through the wife's cosmetics, sniff the perfumes, and don't find anything to match.

"Looking for a new fragrance?" Schroder asks, holding onto his phone.

"Can't a man just want to smell nice?"

"So what are you doing?"

I tell him about the car.

"And?"

"And none of these match. Add that to the hairs I found, and—"

"And somebody else was in his car."

"Perfume's still strong. Had to have been tonight."

"Could be he dropped off a colleague," Schroder says.

"You spoken to his boss?"

"Not yet. Look, Tate, this is crazy, completely fucking insane, but . . . but a fourth body has just shown up," he says, shaking his phone as if trying to rid it of the bad news.

I feel like throwing the perfumes over my shoulder and slapping my arms against my sides, and just saying *Well, I guess that's it then*, because all we're doing is chasing some psychopath across the city and the night still has a bunch of hours left in it, and we got no way of knowing the killings are even going to stop by morning light. This time tomorrow we could be neck-deep in bodies.

"No," I say, shaking my head, trying to refute his statement.

"Four bodies," he says. "It's like . . . hell, I don't know what it's like."

"It's like the world has gone mad." I put down the perfume and something turns inside my stomach. "Jesus," I say, my voice sounding weak. Four people. At least four families. Dozens and dozens of people about to have the world pulled out from under them, parents, friends, family—that's a whole lot of pain.

"It'd go easier if He were on the case," he says.

"So who's our new victim?"

"Her name is Victoria Brown," he says. "She's a lawyer and, shit, get this," he says, shaking his head and letting me know it's going to be bad, "but she's been in a coma for seven years."

"What? Did you just say—"

"A coma. Yeah, I know. It's fucked up. Listen, I'm heading there now. I want you to go and talk to Brad Hayward's boss, see what you can learn."

"You don't want me to come with you?"

"Here's the thing. Look, Tate, I don't want you to react badly, okay?" he says, and now my mouth goes dry.

"Carl . . ."

"Reason I don't want you coming with me is because you're going to overreact. But your wife is okay."

I actually shake my head, the movement brief, as I pull back at the same time. "My wife? What?"

"Our fourth victim is a patient at your wife's nursing home, Tate, but Bridget is fine. Absolutely fine."

I take a step forward. "What the fuck are you telling me? Somebody tried to hurt her?"

"No, no, nothing like that. She just happens to be at the same nursing home as our victim."

"I'm going there."

"Tate . . ."

But I move past him and race outside to my car.

CHAPTER FOURTEEN

All the killing is making Caleb tired. It was always going to be a long night. He just has to stay focused. Stay strong. Stay positive. Dealing with the next victim is going to be harder, and more draining, because it's not just one victim but four—the doctor and his wife and their two children. It's going to be tricky. The coma victim, she was easy. No effort at all—she didn't even know he was there. But the doctor—he's the key. What he has planned for the doctor will be more punishment than any one man can take.

He's covered in blood. He doesn't have spare clothes with him but he'll get them soon.

The doctor lives in an expensive neighborhood that every morning is full of maids and gardeners and children being driven to school by soccer moms in cars way too big. There aren't any lights on in any of the windows. It's after three o'clock already and he's tired, so beat that he just wants to crawl into a hole somewhere and take a nap, so tired that what he wanted to do in one night might just take two, but doing everything in one night gives the police no time to figure out what's going on. One night was the goal. Only he made a mistake following that asshole home earlier. That used up time and energy and he could have been caught. It was stupid.

He parks right out front. There's a bunch of different ways he can make his way inside, but there is one simpler than any other. He keeps ringing the bell until a light comes on in the hallway.

"Who is it?" A man's voice, sounding tired.

Caleb hopes the wife has remained in bed. "Dr. Stanton?"

"Yes."

"It's me, James, from further up the road," Caleb says, trying to sound frantic. "It's my daughter, we've had an accident. Please, please, you have to help me," he says, and before he even finishes his sentence he can hear the locks being twisted open.

The door swings open.

He's never met Dr. Stanton, but he's seen pictures from the trial seventeen years ago, when Stanton got up on his soapbox and said not everybody can be held accountable for their actions. He was wrong. He's put on weight and his hair has gone completely gray and receded a few inches since then, and for some reason it makes Caleb happy to see that.

Stanton looks him up and down, sees the blood, and looks shocked. "Where is she?" he asks.

"You don't recognize me, do you?" Caleb asks.

Stanton is halfway out the door and comes to a stop. He can tell the doctor senses something, his psychiatrist radar starts pinging at the danger only a few feet away, only it's pinging way too late.

"Recognize you? No, no I don't," he answers, hesitant now. "Do you . . . do you have a daughter?" he asks, his follow-up question proof he knows that something is wrong.

"Yes."

"Where is she?"

"She died."

Stanton pauses. He takes a small step backward. He reaches out to put a hand on the door. "What did you say your name is again?"

"I said it was James," he says, "but it isn't."

"Listen, James," Stanton says, missing the point while taking another step back, "I don't know what kind of game you're . . ."

The sentence ends, the following word taking a different shape as Caleb's fist connects with Stanton's nose. Then he falls inside, cupping his face with his hands.

Caleb follows the good doctor inside and shuts the door behind him. He tries to shake the pain out of his hand. He's used his right when he should have used his left, instinct taking over, and now he has to pay for it. His hand is locked in a fist and it's going to take a few moments to straighten. He puts his foot into the doctor's stomach. He uses his good hand to reach into the waistband of his pants and pulls out his knife just as the doctor hits the floor. He looks around, they are in a foyer that leads through to a lounge to the left and what might be a living room ahead. To the right is a staircase. There is nobody around.

"You see this?"

"You roke I ose," Stanton says, looking out from behind his cupped hands.

"I'm going to break the rest of you if you don't stop complaining. Where is your wife?"

"What?"

"Your wife. Is she in bed?"

"Oh."

"What?"

"Ooh are you?"

"Roll over," Caleb says, annoyed at how complicated this is becoming. "If you don't I'm going to bury this knife right into your chest. Then I'm going to do the same thing to your kids."

"Dote urt I chil-den."

Shit. He doesn't have time for this. The wife could already be on the phone to the police. He brings the knife down as hard as he can, the doctor flinches but can't escape what happens next—the handle crashes into his head and makes him go quiet for what should be quite some time.

"Daddy?"

The voice comes from upstairs. He tucks the knife into the back of his pants and makes his way to the stairs. There's a girl standing at the top, a little girl with messy brown hair hanging to her shoulders. She's wearing pink pajamas and there's a teddy bear tucked under one arm, the finger of her other hand in her mouth as she bites down on it. Her eyes are wide and her face is pale. He makes his way toward her.

"Who are you?" she asks.

He glances at Stanton in the hall and decides the girl can't see her father from there.

"It's okay," he says, using his calm voice now, but he can tell she doesn't think so. He can tell she's about to scream. "Really, it's okay," he says, and sure enough her mouth opens but when she tries to scream, she sobs instead and the scream gets caught. He closes the distance between them. He crouches in front of her so he can look her in the face, one hand on her mouth, one hand on her chest, pushing her against the wall, the bear being crushed in the process. She's struggling to sob around his hand and he's careful not to cut her. He feels confused as he looks at her. He needs to feel nothing, otherwise none of this would work, but he's feeling something.

"I'm not going to hurt you, I promise. I'm an old friend of your dad's. Where is your mother?"

The little girl shakes her head.

"I need you to help me out, because I'm trying to help your parents," he says. "If I take my hand away from your mouth do you promise not to scream and talk to me like a grown-up?"

She nods. He takes his hand away from her mouth, ready

to replace it in a second if she screams, but she doesn't. She doesn't say anything either. Doesn't shake her head or nod.

"Your name is Katy, isn't it?"

"With a y," she says.

"And how old are you, Katy?"

"I'm nine years old next week."

"Wow, so you're going to be a big girl."

"That's right," she says. "Who are you?"

"My name is Caleb," he says. "I know your dad."

"Where is he?"

"He's downstairs waiting for us. Where is your mommy? Is she in bed?"

She nods.

"Is she asleep?"

"I don't know. She doesn't live here anymore."

"What do you mean?"

"Mommy and daddy don't love each other anymore, and mommy moved out to live with somebody she does love."

"But you said she was in bed."

"It's late," she says. "Everybody is in bed when it's late."

"Do you live here all the time?" he asks.

She nods.

"You don't live with your mom?"

She shakes her head.

"Okay, okay, right. Listen to me. I'm going to go on a trip with your dad," he says, "and it wouldn't be very responsible of us to leave you here with your sister, so we're going to take you both with us. Now how about you show me where she is, huh? Good girls don't get hurt if they do good things," he tells her, but of course nothing could be further from the truth. "You don't want to get hurt, do you?"

She slowly shakes her head.

"Okay, Katy with a y, why don't you take me to your sister?"

"Which one?"

"What you mean which one?"

"Which sister?"

"Melanie, of course," he says, but her question worries him. "Katy, how many sisters do you have?"

"If you were friends with my dad, wouldn't you know?"

"I've been away for a long time, Katy, but how about you tell me?"

"Two."

Two. Jesus, just how much did he get wrong? No wife, three daughters, what else?

"Katy, are there any other adults in the house?"

"No."

"No brothers?"

She shakes her head. "You seem mean," she says.

"I'm not mean," he tells her.

"Are you going to hurt anybody?"

"No," he says. "Tell you what, you can make sure nobody gets hurt by making sure everything I say gets done. You can be my special helper."

"I don't want to be a special helper," she says.

"Your older sister is Melanie," he says.

"Yes."

"And the other sister? Is she younger or older?"

"She's only one," she says.

So he's dealing with an eleven-year-old, an eight-year-old, and a one-year-old. He thinks about how it's going to change the plan, and realizes it doesn't. It might tweak how things are done, it'll give him some more leverage with the doctor, but the end result is going to be the same.

"What's her name?"

"Octavia. What about Dad? Are you going to be mean to him?"

"Your dad did a bad thing," he tells her.

"My dad helps people."

"Sometimes he helps the wrong people."

"What did he do?"

"It's a grown-up thing, Katy. You wouldn't understand."

"I'm grown up," she says. "Remember? I'm talking to you like a grown-up would."

Despite the situation, despite the man bound on the floor and all the blood and the years in jail, he can't help but smile. It feels good, for the first time he feels something, and it's dangerous.

"Maybe Dad can help you," she says. "Are you one of his patients? Are you a crazy man?"

His smile disappears. "No," he tells her. "I'm a friendly man."

Her eyes narrow as she stares at him. "I don't believe you."

"Well, the thing is, Katy, it doesn't matter if you believe me or not, because you're going to do what I say. If you don't, you're going to get in trouble, and the last thing I want is to see you or your sisters getting hurt because you wouldn't do what I say," he says, reaching into his pocket for the duct tape. "Now, how about you show me where they are," he tells her, "before you make me mad," he adds, and she shows him, not saying another word on the way.

CHAPTER FIFTEEN

From out of nowhere the rain comes back. I have to increase the speed of the window wiper that works. It makes a strange grinding sound, making me worry it's going to fly off the window and get lost in somebody's front lawn, but then, just as quickly, the rain disappears again, just a thirty-second assault on the city. I have to drive carefully even though I have the urge to speed, scared that if I take my car over thirty miles per hour the engine will turn into a jigsaw puzzle. There are patrol cars and lots of vans with sleepy looking reporters beside them at the nursing home, and even though I managed to leave before Schroder he's beaten me out here.

Schroder is standing in the foyer next to Nurse Hamilton who, for the moment, looks nothing like Nurse Hamilton, but more like a woman wearing a Nurse Hamilton suit that's been stuffed under a couch for the last twenty years. She starts to come over, then thinks better of it. Schroder leads me up the stairs to the second floor and in the opposite direction of Bridget, but I can't follow him, not straightaway, not until I check on my wife. I head to her room and there is enough light from the hallway to see her sleeping peacefully.

"She's okay," Schroder tells me. "What happened here has nothing to do with her."

I'm not sure what to tell him. I try to grab hold of my thoughts to calm them down—I want to move Bridget to another home. I want to hunt down the man who violated this place.

"Come on, Theo, we've got work to do," he says, holding up a thin file in front of me. "Look, I know you're pissed off, but you need to focus on what's relevant here, and what's relevant is that Bridget hasn't been hurt but somebody else has been, and we need to make it as right as we can for that person because that's what we do."

I take a few seconds to listen to what he's saying. I try to absorb it. I realize he's right.

"Theo, are we on the same page here?"

"We are," I tell him.

"Good." He turns around and I follow him into a part of the nursing home I haven't been in before, but it looks the same as the rest of it—rubber plants potted along the corridors, landscape paintings, views from the windows out over the gardens. We pass rooms along the way, other patients in similar states to my wife, some in better shape as they turn and look toward us as we walk, others in worse shape, hoses and tubes connecting them to a form of artificial life.

"Victoria Brown," Schroder says. "She's forty-nine years old, married, no children. She's been here for seven years after being assaulted in a shopping mall bathroom. She had her head smacked into a sink and never woke up," he says. "Never got the person who did it," he adds.

"There's a lot of blood," I say, stopping outside the room and looking in.

"He stabbed her like he stabbed the first two."

"So whatever pissed our guy off happened at least seven years ago," I say.

"Has to be. I don't see her making anybody angry since being here. And he must have been angry," he says. "She put up no fight and he just kept stabbing her all the same."

"What did she do? Before the attack?"

"Here's the thing. She was a criminal lawyer."

A small chill rushes down my spine as a connection is made. "So that gives us two lawyers and one teacher and one accountant. He leave a message?"

"It's on her forehead. Same as the others. *You were complicit.*"

"In what?"

"In whatever made victim one not care enough and was or wasn't worth it for victim two."

I look up and down the corridor. "And nobody heard or saw anything?"

"No, and it's not like the victim was making a sound."

"You talk to the husband?"

"He's dead. He killed himself a couple of years ago. Hung himself."

Does every story in this city have a bad ending? Does everybody have a sad tale?

There are forensic experts inside and outside the room. There are plastic markers next to blood drops on the floor and bloody shoe tread prints that are dark near the body but lighten with every step until they disappear near the stairs. The dead woman's arms are still by her side and there is no expression of horror on her face. Her eyes are closed, her face perfectly relaxed. It's the first time either Schroder or myself have ever seen a murdered coma victim. Maybe it's the first time anybody has. We've seen them get pregnant and contract diseases, but not this.

"You okay?" Schroder asks.

"I'm not sure," I tell him.

"You look like you could do with some air."

The handwriting across the dead woman's forehead is a match for the others.

"Two lawyers and one teacher and one accountant," Schroder repeats.

"Doesn't seem like the setup to a joke anymore," I tell him.

"No. But it never did." He pushes his hands into his back and stretches it out, his spine popping softly. I once saw a guy do that and throw out his back. "The staff say you were here earlier," he says. "You didn't see anything?"

"I did see somebody walking with a bloody knife but didn't think it was worth mentioning."

"Hey, look, I'm just asking."

"I'd have told you. Who found her?"

"One of the nurses was doing a routine check. She saw the bloody footprints and just figured one of the patients had had an accident. Followed them into here and started screaming. Woke up the other patients and brought the rest of the staff running. It's pretty obvious these aren't random victims," he says. "Random doesn't bring you into two retirement homes and one nursing home. Our killer is working from a list. Question is, how many people are on it?"

It's a good question. The room has a similar view over the grounds as my wife's does, and the two women enjoyed it about the same. The layout is the same too, the bed in the center with walking room all the way around it for the nurses. There's a vase full of flowers so fake they wouldn't even have fooled the coma patients. There is not much emotion in this room, not until a madman came in here and filled it with rage.

"Victim three doesn't fit the list," I say. "The killer went to a lot of effort to sneak in here and stab this woman lots of times and leave a message, he could have made the same effort for Brad Hayward. He could have waited for him in town by his car, or pulled up to him at a set of lights, or waited till the wife was asleep. He could even have tried to sneak into his workplace."

Tracey Walter steps into the room behind us. The medical

examiner looks tired. She's spent a long day examining the dead, and now she has to spend a long night cutting them open.

"Let's get this done," she says in the way of a greeting. She puts her case on the floor and pulls out a thermometer with a skewer on it. I look away as she stabs it into the woman somewhere around the liver, then look back to see her checking the temperature. She takes another look around the room as if figuring out how hot it is in here. She takes down some notes, seems to do some sums, then comes over.

"Preliminary guess is death was ninety minutes ago," she says, looking at her watch, "which puts death around two-thirty."

"I was here around eleven thirty, maybe quarter to twelve," I say, thinking that things could easily have been different if I'd come here later, or if the killer had come here earlier. I could have been pulling in as he was leaving, or pulling out as he was arriving. I could have seen him, maybe I'd have gotten a sense of what was going on, maybe what was left of Victoria Brown could still be alive.

"Body is fine to move," Tracey says, and heads back down the corridor toward the stairs.

"We've been running background checks on the victims," Schroder says.

"And?"

"And speeding tickets are as bad as these people ever got."

Forensics takes over the scene. It's time to go and see John Morgan, Brad Hayward's boss. It's already four o'clock. Schroder hands me a slip of paper with Morgan's address. His handwriting was bad when I met him back at the academy, but it's gotten worse over the years. The letters blend into a mess and he has to point out what he's told me.

"If it helps," he says, walking with me past the bloody footprints that peter out the closer they get to the stairs, "I'm feeling the same thing you are."

"Which is?"

"Helpless," he says.

"Not hopeless?"

He shrugs. "Take your pick," he says,

I go to say goodbye to my wife before leaving. I enter her room and Bridget is standing by the window and the curtains are open. I flinch at the sight of her there, so much in fact that I have to take a step back to balance myself. "Bridget?" I say, and I wait for her to turn around and smile at me, only she doesn't. I quickly cross the room, I take her hand and look into her face but she doesn't see me, doesn't react to my touch, she's just staring out at the police cars in the parking lot, the red and blue lights reflecting off her skin.

"Bridget?"

I turn her toward me, expecting her to focus on me, praying for it, but it doesn't happen. Other than standing up, she doesn't look any different for all the excitement that's been going on. She hasn't noticed my recent absence of four months in jail, nor my return. Outside the window the media are gathering to report the story of a woman who died, a woman Bridget never knew even though they were only a hallway apart. Maybe Bridget saw the killer leave. Maybe she watched him climb into his car and drive away. Nurse Hamilton has told me sometimes they'll find Bridget has gotten up during the night to sit in her chair. Sometimes they'll find her standing in the hallway clutching a photograph of our daughter. I take those moments and turn them into hope.

"Bridget," I say, and I take her hand and lead her back into her bed. I sit down with her, I need to because seeing her standing filled me with so much shock and excitement that my legs can't seem to handle the weight of it all. I spend fifteen minutes with her, I close the curtains before going downstairs, and when I leave I tell Nurse Hamilton what I saw. She nods slowly, a sad smile on her face, a real one on mine. "The first time I saw her standing outside her room I almost had a heart attack," she says. "I've never seen her standing by her window, though."

"Maybe she wanted to see what was happening," I say.

The sad smile is still there, and I can feel mine slipping away. "Maybe," she says. "With brain injuries, you just never know."

Only she does know, and I know too, and when I walk out of the nursing home I keep running what could have been through my head, the could-have-been of Bridget turning toward me and smiling, the could-have-been of her coming home with me, of the doctors scratching their heads and saying it must have been a miracle, the "you never know" of brain injuries making an appearance.

When I reach my car I look back up at the window, a small part of me expecting to see my wife there, the bigger part knowing I won't, so when I see her face staring out and the curtains drawn I almost jump. Her pale features and white pajamas are lit up by the red and blues of the patrol cars as she stares down at them. I stop with my hand on the car door and I watch her, hoping to see movement. Nurse Hamilton appears next to her, she puts her arm around Bridget's shoulders and looks out at the scene below but doesn't see me. She leads my wife away.

My hands shake on the way to see John Morgan, and I'm not sure what from. The excitement of hope, or that spooky feeling I got when I saw Bridget staring out the window like a ghost, or because I need a coffee fix, or because of the case. It's five o'clock when I finally get to John Morgan's house. I can't stop thinking of Bridget's face as she stared down at the cars. I could swear it looked like she was focusing on them and not through them.

Or maybe that's just what I'm hoping I saw.

CHAPTER SIXTEEN

The doctor has a nice house and if Caleb could stay here he would. He'd love to be able to head out and kill the last few people on his list, then come back and deal with the good doctor and his family in comfort. He could spend the night. Make himself a big breakfast. Relax on the big soft couch downstairs and watch some TV. Only the doctor's house isn't the location he has in mind for the end.

His eyes are getting heavy as he slams down the trunk on Dr. Stanton and moves around to the driver's seat. His body is sore. It's the beatings. Jail broke him. Over the years his left leg has been broken four times, his right leg only once, as if the men who hurt him learned early on they had an aversion to symmetry. His left arm has been broken twice, and his right arm never broken at all. Most of his fingers have been crushed and snapped and he can't make a fist in his right hand without agony. In his former life, he used to be a math teacher. He knew a lot about statistics. One statistic was that there are two hundred and eight bones in the human body and eighteen of his had been broken.

The beatings in jail came about because the inmates were told he'd raped and killed his daughter. The cops told them that. It was because Caleb had killed a cop. He took what they gave, and the more they gave the more he died inside, and he let that happen. They stripped away his humanity, and when you take that away from a man you're unleashing a world of possibilities.

He has loaded up on blankets and has filled a bag of food from the fridge and pantry. He spent a few minutes reading news articles on the Internet with his phone, seeing what was already being written about him, only they're not about him, not specifically. The media is calling him the Gran Reaper on account of the first two victims being old. They mention victim number three, but not by name. No mention of victim number four.

Victim number three. Caleb had strayed from the list and that was a mistake. What if the guy hadn't been alone? What if there had been kids there? What if one of them had come into the garage? Would he have walked away?

He goes upstairs. Katy and Melanie are in the same bedroom, where he made them wait with the assistance of duct tape and plastic ties. Before tying them up he made them change into warmer clothes, both girls selecting jeans and shirts and jackets. Melanie, a little over two years older than Katy, hasn't stopped complaining. She has the same hair and the same eyes as her sister, but her face is rounder and meaner.

"This is stupid," Melanie says. "My hands hurt and the police are going to come and arrest you. And I'm tired."

"You can sleep later," he tells her. "But the police aren't coming."

"I want to sleep now, and yes they are. And who are you again? You didn't say."

"His name is Caleb," Katy says.

"Don't be dumb," Melanie says, looking at her sister. "That's not what I meant. I meant, who is he exactly."

"Oh," Katy says.

"I'm not going to hurt you," he tells them.

"You already have," Melanie says. "My dad would say you're deluded. He uses words like that to describe people like you all the time."

"Shut up."

"Deluded," she repeats. "You see that, Katy? I struck a nerve."

He pulls out the duct tape.

"Don't make him mad," Katy says, and starts to cry. "Please don't hurt us."

He rips off some tape and puts it across Melanie's mouth as she twists her head and tries to avoid it. He does the same for Katy too, not prepared to risk her screaming on the way out to the car. He carries them downstairs one at a time and puts them into the backseat.

Then he gets Octavia.

The bedroom has been painted pink, there is a mobile hanging from the ceiling with pictures of unicorns and princesses on it. The baby is asleep. He picks her up and she murmurs. He rests her on his chest so her head is over his shoulder, and bounces her up and down a few times, shushing her and she stops making noises. He carries her gently downstairs. He has taken the car seat out of Stanton's car and put it into the passenger seat of his own, turning it around so she is facing the seat and not the windshield. He tucks a blanket around her.

The car won't start.

He keeps turning the key, the engine whining but failing to turn over, making less of an effort with every try. He pushes his foot on the accelerator, he throws his weight backward and forward as if rocking the car will help, but none of it does, and after thirty seconds the only sound the engine makes when he turns the key is a small click.

It's closing in on five in the morning. Soon the birds will be awake.

Octavia starts to cry.

"Shush," he says, slowly rocking the seat, but she won't shush, instead she just cries louder. "Goddamn it," he says, "I said shush."

The two girls in the back start fidgeting around. He climbs out of the car, undoes the car seat, carries it inside with the baby still attached, and rests her in the hall. He brings the other two girls inside.

"What's wrong with her?" he asks. "She hungry?"

The girls don't answer. They can't, because of the duct tape.

Damn it. He's running out of time. He drags the girls into the living room so they don't have to see their father, which he then hauls out of the trunk a minute later and takes through to the garage. He jams him into the trunk of his own car. He gets the girls into the car too, then grabs a jar of baby food from the kitchen.

"Here," he says, and shoves a spoonful of food at Octavia's mouth. She twists her head away, still crying. "Come on," he tells her, "eat this or I'm going to leave you here," he says, but of course Octavia is crying too loudly to hear him, and wouldn't understand him even if she could. He uses his other hand to hold her head, then jams the spoon into her mouth. She sucks at the food, chews at it, then swallows, then cries again. He looks at the duct tape, wondering if it wouldn't be an easier way of keeping her quiet, and decides that it would be. He peels off a strip but just then the baby burps and goes quiet. She smiles, closes her eyes, then drifts off to sleep all in the space of ten seconds.

He gets her settled into the doctor's car, then heads back out to his own. He leans in and releases the hand brake. It's simple to push as the car rolls down the driveway, then becomes difficult when it levels out. He stands inside the driver's door and twists the wheel and pushes as hard as he can, his knees and hips aching madly, his shoulder sore, but he pushes hard, needing to get it done. The car starts to move. It's slow but steady, and he pushes it past one house, then another, and the momentum builds and two minutes later he's put half a dozen homes between his car and the doctor's place. He doesn't have the strength or the time to push anymore. A couple of the houses have lights on inside now, but nobody else is on the street. He wipes down the surfaces he's touched. He's never been in the backseat but wipes it down anyway. He wants the police to find him, but not yet, and his car breaking down like this complicates things.

He walks back to the garage. Pushes the door opener button and drives out with the nuclear family, minus mom, all jammed into the back of the car. Christ, it's already after five o'clock, and he's becoming more certain things are going to take two nights now instead of the one. He starts rubbing his knees, the left one is worse than the right, and as he massages it his hand hurts too. The road is blurrier than it was earlier. The world loses all the sharp edges as the two lanes seem to merge into one, and rubbing at his eyes doesn't help that much. He's driving toward the judge's house. Kill him, then Mrs. Whitby, then head on out to the slaughterhouse to finish it.

He pulls over. Yawns. And closes his eyes for a few seconds, leaning his forehead on the steering wheel. It was always going to be a tough task finishing everything in one night. Impossible even. Ten years ago he would have had the strength. But not now. It's disappointing, but he always knew it was a possibility. It won't change the end result, and it's why he's killing in the order he chose. The police can't make the connection. He's spent hours Googling his victims and doing his homework, and the three he's killed that matter, none of them ever appear in the same story. After all, it was seventeen years ago—back then the news wasn't as available online as it is now. Back then there wasn't even much of an online to begin with. He knows the cops will be working with more than just Internet search engines, they'll have criminal records and courts transcripts, but all of it is useless until they know where to start looking.

James Whitby's mother—once Caleb cuts her to pieces, that's when they'll figure it out.

Hell, maybe it's even better this way. This way he has tomorrow to decide what he's going to do about Ariel Chancellor. He can still see her standing on the street corner, her dress short, the car pulling up beside her . . .

He changes direction, heading away from the judge's house and going north. He turns on the radio and listens to the news. The fourth body has been found but no name has been released. That's good. The longer they keep that information to themselves, the less chance there is of somebody from seventeen years ago figuring it out. Twice he finds himself nodding off, the first time falling asleep for less than a second and veering toward a lamppost, the second time for a little longer and almost hitting a tree. Then there is a sudden stench from the baby that doesn't disappear, even when he winds down the window. It helps keep him awake.

It takes twenty minutes to get to the slaughterhouse. It's been fifteen years since he came here. The night is wrapped tightly around it, letting go only where the headlights wash across the front of the building. He parks outside what used to be the office door. He has to step carefully to avoid twisting an ankle. He unloads the bag first, taking it deep inside where his footfalls echo through the rooms. It's colder in here than outside. He lays down the blankets in the corner of one of the offices, then heads back out to the car. The air has that wet early morning feel to it that you get in April. Every day for the next few weeks can either remind you of summer or remind you of winter.

"There's your bathroom," he tells Melanie, cutting her binds and nodding toward the edge of the driveway where Melanie can choose from one of dozens of trees, "and make sure you don't get lost. The forest is a week's walk in every direction," he says, not that it's true. "And if you get lost I'll end up punishing your family."

She reaches up and pulls the duct tape off her mouth. "How am I supposed to see anything?"

He hands her a flashlight.

"Why can't I use one of the bathrooms inside?"

"They don't work."

"There's no . . ." her voice catches in her throat, then she manages to get herself under control. "There's no toilet paper," she tells him, her voice firm. "You think of that too?"

"You'll have to do without it."

"But that's gross."

"No, what's gross is what might happen later if you don't go now. This is going to be your last chance for a while."

"Are you going to watch?"

"Why would I do that?"

"I don't know, maybe because you're some kind of perv. That's why you got us tied up right? For that kind of thing and worse."

He shakes his head, wondering, *What the hell is wrong with people these days?* "Just hurry up before I lose my patience."

She points the flashlight ahead and rushes over to the trees and behind one. It takes her two minutes and then she returns. He leads her inside and hands her the blankets.

"Make yourself comfortable," he says.

"What? On the floor? You have to be kidding."

"Just hurry up."

"No."

"What?"

"I'm not sleeping on the floor."

"There's nowhere else."

"Yes there is. There's my house. Take us back there," she says, frowning. "And what happened to your face? Why's it all gross?"

"Tell you what, Mel, do you mind if I call you Mel?" he asks, and he shows her the knife. "I know you're a brave girl, and I think you understand things are quite bad for you and your family right now. I know you're trying to be tough, and I respect that. The thing is, if you don't shut up I'm going to hurt Katy. You get me?"

Melanie's frown disappears and her mouth sags at the edges. "You wouldn't," she says, but she doesn't sound sure.

Caleb nods. "Of course I would," he says, annoyed at her, "and it'll be your fault. The floor," he says, "get yourself comfortable."

She gets bedded down, and then he secures her with plastic ties and puts duct tape over her mouth. He goes back to the car and frees Katy. He tells her the same things and she asks the same questions and they come to the same understanding, the only difference is her face is covered in tears. She goes to the same tree and is gone a similar amount of time, and when she comes back her face is covered in flecks of dirt. He hands her her teddy bear, then puts fresh duct tape over her mouth. Her eyes are wide and both girls are looking scared and still there is nothing, no humanity, only the memory of Jessica, his daughter, bloody and torn on the same floor these girls are lying on.

"Don't try to escape," he tells them. "It will only make things worse."

They can't answer him, only with their tears. He leaves them a battery-powered camping lantern, the light turned low enough to make the edges of the room dark.

He goes out to the car and picks up Octavia. He twists his face and holds her away from him at arm's length and carries her inside. She has woken up and is smiling and laughing.

"What's so funny?" he asks her.

"Hello," she says.

"Why are you laughing?"

"Hello, hello," she says.

"Hello," he answers. "Do you know how to be quiet, Octavia?"

"Hello-zies."

He leaves her on the floor and goes back for the car seat, and when he comes back she's bum-hopped herself to the other side of the room and is playing with a rusty nail. He snatches it off her and throws it deeper into the slaughterhouse.

"Goddamn it," he says to the other girls. "Why the hell would you let her play with that?"

The girls can't answer, and of course it's not their fault. They couldn't have stopped Octavia playing. He should have left one of them untied to look after her. He looks down at the baby, who's starting to cry.

"Don't," he tells her, but it does no good. "Great," he says, and then lays her down on the blanket.

God, it's been ages since he's done this.

He holds his breath, looks away, and undoes her diaper. Changing his own daughter's diaper was bad enough, but changing somebody else's . . . he sees what's in her diaper, gags, then looks away. He gags again, then has to jump to his feet. He makes it to the door to the office, leans out, retches once, twice, then throws up into the dark. He should have gotten one of the sisters to do it. Next time he will. When he comes back he can't even look at Octavia. He pulls the diaper away and stuffs it into a plastic bag, then uses some wipes to clean her up while looking in the opposite direction. She stops crying.

"I should have stayed in jail," he says, then stuffs the wipes into the plastic bag with the diaper. He swings it around and knots it, then throws it in the same direction he threw the nail, decides it's not far enough, then goes and retrieves it. He puts it outside instead.

He puts a fresh diaper on Octavia, pulls her pajama bottoms back up, then sets her back in the car seat and clips the straps into place.

He puts her between her sisters. "Hello," she says again.

He gets the duct tape and cuts a strip for her mouth and finds he can't bring himself to place it.

"Bufwiffy," she says, then giggles. If she doesn't fall asleep soon, he'll have to duct tape her. Then her little face scrunches up, turns red, and then she smiles again. The room smells.

"Goddamn it," he says.

"Bufwiffy."

He reaches into the bag and grabs another diaper along with the duct tape.

CHAPTER SEVENTEEN

John Morgan is awake and has a coffee ready for me in his lounge. The smell perks me up a little, which is a bit of a surprise because I hadn't realized I was starting to fade. I apologize for having to interview him so early, but he doesn't seem to mind. We sit down in opposite couches with a coffee table between us with magazines squared up in a pile in the center, a mixture of fashion and architecture topped off with a *TV Guide*, which has recently been used as a coaster. His wife is in bed, either asleep or trying to fall asleep. The coffee is hot and pretty good and couldn't be any more appreciated. Morgan's salt-and-pepper hair is sticking up on one side from hours buried in a pillow and his right sideburn is bushier than his left for that same reason. He's wearing a robe with pajamas underneath.

"Brad was, well, he was a great accountant," John says, "and will be hard to replace. You heard about Edward Hunter?"

Edward Hunter was an accountant whose family was killed, and who wasn't happy to let the police find justice for him.

Instead he found it himself, and now he's in jail for it. He's the man Brad's wife mentioned earlier.

"I've met him," I say.

"Nice guy. Really nice guy," he says, "but you know, crazy people often are when they know how to hide the crazy."

That's as good a way of putting it as I've ever heard.

"There was always something . . . something odd about him, I suppose," Morgan says.

"It was Edward's workload that Brad had taken on?"

"Not all of it. We split it up, but Brad certainly had a share of it."

"So he was working extra hours."

"We all are," he says.

"Was Brad, to your knowledge, seeing anybody at the firm?"

"Seeing? He saw people every day."

"That's not what I mean."

For two seconds he looks confused, and then he slowly shakes his head, surprised at how slow he was to get my point. "You mean was he sleeping with anybody?"

"That's what I'm asking."

"Not that I'm aware of."

"He work late tonight?"

"Yeah. We all did. We left at the same time."

"When was that?"

"Probably around ten thirty."

"He give anybody a lift home?"

"No, we were the last two to leave."

"When you hired him, you were aware he was having problems where he last worked?"

He blows at his coffee, then sips at it slowly, taking a few seconds to think about his answer. "I heard about it," he says. "But nothing was proven, and Brad was a great accountant and didn't deserve to be judged on rumor. In his time with us he's never put a foot out of line. I've been doing this for a long time now, Detective, and people in the workplace are always making shit up to get other colleagues into trouble. It's nothing new. What I do know is nobody at our firm has made any kind of allegation like that."

"What else can—"

"Is it true, the way they say it happened?" he asks, leaning forward as if ready to receive a secret. "That somebody just knocked on his door and killed him in front of his wife?"

"I can't discuss any of the facts at this stage," I tell him.

"Jesus, I mean . . . Jesus," he says. "Tomorrow we're going to be . . ." He shakes his head. "How can he be dead?" he asks. "It just doesn't make sense."

"It never does," I say, but that's not true. Sometimes it makes perfect sense. "What else can you tell me about him? Was he happy at work? He have lots of friends? Was he well liked, hated, did he steal stationary and take long smoke breaks?"

John Morgan leans back into his chair, and for the next thirty minutes we talk about Brad Hayward, and most of what he says sounds like a eulogy, only good things making it into the final cut of John's summation. I don't doubt any of it. I also don't doubt that somebody out there will say all the opposite things about Brad Hayward. I listen close and take notes and try to figure out how or if Hayward's cheating ways made an impact on what happened to him tonight.

When we're done he leads me to the door.

"Are you going to find the man that did this?"

"Yes."

"Is it related to the Gran Reaper?"

"Possibly," I tell him, wondering if the media already knows.

"And I heard on the radio before you got here that there's been another one. That's four already," he says. "What in the hell is going on?"

I don't have an answer for him.

I head back to the car, the people in this street tucked into their safe little world. The temperature has stabilized around a crisp forty-seven or forty-eight degrees. The nights will stay that way for a few more weeks until getting down to thirty, then below thirty over the winter. Either way this will be over by then—either we'll have this guy in custody or he'll have run out of people to kill. I pull out my cell phone and call Schroder and tell him I'm done with Morgan and he rewards me by telling me there haven't been any further homicides—at least that we know of. I lean my head against the headrest and close my eyes, then just as quickly open them in case they stay closed for six or seven hours. I wipe my face with the hand not clamping my cell phone to my ear and the stubble scratches at my palm. A quick look in the mirror and I notice I'm looking like shit. That happens to me a lot these days.

"I got something for you," he says.

"Yeah?"

"Breakfast. If I don't eat something I'm not gonna last much longer. Meet me at Froggies."

I drive into town, glancing at the cell phone on the passenger seat, waiting for it to ring, waiting for Schroder to tell me there's a change of plan because victims numbers five and six have just showed up. I reach town without the call coming, and reach Froggies Diner on Hereford Street about two blocks down from the police station.

Froggies Diner has only been around for five years but feels like it's been here forever. Within days of it being built it became a second home to every cop on the force, most of us spending at least five hours a week there. The hours between seven and nine in the morning you're sometimes lucky to find a seat. It's styled on a cliched roadside diner, a long Formica counter with bar stools, red vinyl booths running along a length of windows, posters of old New York hanging up on the walls. There's a jukebox in the corner that plays CDs and MP3s, the early morning sunlight coming through on a low angle and reflecting a full spectrum of colors off the plastic and glass casing. The door swings open into a bell that dings when I walk in. I'm thinking at six in the morning Schroder is going to be the only one inside when I get there, but he's not—the diner is about a quarter full of tired cops who all look just as bad as Schroder, who looks about as bad as me. Detective Kent is sitting in a booth nursing a coffee and staring out the window while talking animatedly on a phone. I watch her for a few seconds and she turns and catches me, then smiles. I smile back, hold her look for two more seconds, then walk over to Schroder who is at the counter.

There's a plate of bacon and eggs and mushrooms in front of him, next to him a plate with the same thing waiting for me. I haven't stepped in here in three years. There's a coffee for him and a coffee for me, both of which are steaming hot, and it's the temperature that's stopping me from knocking them both back. I sit down next to him. There's a short-order cook out the back working away at his own breakfast. One waitress is carrying out an order while another is wiping down the counter. The waitress carrying the order has a tight T-shirt that fits her extremely well, it has $5x5=25$ on it, and beneath that it says *Good times*. She catches me staring and she isn't sure whether I'm doing the addition or looking at her breasts, wondering what those good times are. She turns around. On the back her T-shirt says $4x4=15$ and then *Bad times*.

"What did you get from Morgan?" Schroder asks.

"Hayward was a model employee. He left work alone at around ten thirty. That time of night it's a fifteen- to twenty-minute drive home tops. Wife called the police at eleven thirty-two. She guesses he'd been home ten minutes before she went to check on him. That gives him a good thirty unaccounted minutes."

"Maybe not that unaccounted," Schroder says, his words softened by the mouthful of bacon. "I've just spoken to the ME. I told her your theory. She's given the body a preliminary look and found traces of lipstick on the victim's penis."

"So either he was having an affair," I say, "and could only spend thirty minutes on it, or he saw a prostitute."

"Or maybe he just really, really liked lipstick," Schroder says.

"You got something you want to confess?" I ask him.

He laughs. "Even if he did see a hooker, there's nothing illegal about that."

"There is if she isn't paying her taxes."

"Yeah, maybe Hayward was giving her accounting advice in exchange for her services."

Now it's my turn to dig into the bacon. It has that crispy texture you get when bacon is burned just a little, which is what I like to call perfection. I eat one slice and can't stop. I jam a second into my mouth, some egg, some mushroom, and the flavors are starting to wake me up. I reach for my coffee but it's still too hot.

"We should fingerprint his belt, and also the car. Maybe we'll get a match. Maybe she's in the system somewhere for shoplifting or drug possession," I say, not wanting to stereotype all prostitutes, but at the same time knowing the odds of her having a conviction are pretty good.

"Yeah. Good idea."

"I asked John Morgan about where they park. They use a nearby parking garage, which would have provided a much easier location to murder somebody. He'd have had time to write his message too. Why not just wait there? It sure as hell makes more sense than following him into his garage and running away from his house."

"Yeah. Doesn't make sense," Schroder says. "Listen, I got something else for you too," he says, and he stuffs his last piece of bacon into his mouth, leans back, and reaches into his pocket. "This is yours," he says, and he hands me my badge and ID, two things I gave up three years ago when I resigned.

"I'm back on the force?" I ask, barely containing my excitement.

"It's temporary," he says, then starts in on the eggs. "But should be permanent if you don't screw it up. Just follow the rules and do what's asked of you and no more."

"Does it come with a car?"

"Don't push your luck," he says. "But you do have your driver's license back, which means all that driving you keep doing is now legal."

I run my thumb over the metal badge. I remember the last time I saw it, laying it down on my office desk and walking away. I turned my back on the job because everybody in the department suspected I was the reason my daughter's killer had disappeared. I thought quitting my job was the best way to keep a low profile. It worked. At least until I killed again.

"A lot's happened," Schroder says, pausing with the food to test the coffee temperature, which he tries to cool by blowing on it. "You haven't earned it back, but circumstances dictate the situation, Theo, and you can do some good here."

"Thank you," I tell him, and I slip the badge and the ID wallet it's enclosed in into my back pocket.

"You can thank the superintendent. He's the one who made the decision. And the best way to thank us both is to make neither of us look like idiots."

I remember him running through the field yesterday to take a leak behind a tree. "I won't," I tell him.

"Hurry up with your breakfast," he tells me, "because we've got a briefing at seven."

CHAPTER EIGHTEEN

Dr. Stanton is awake. He tries to cower deeper into the trunk when Caleb opens it. Caleb has never seen a man look so panicked. He has the look of someone who doesn't know if his children are dead or alive. He should warn him that this is the easy part, that with what's coming up this was the wrong time to be scared. There is a lump on the side of his head the size of a golf ball—he'll have one hell of a headache, but he'll live. His arms are bound behind him and his pajamas are all wrinkled to shit and his ankles are tied together.

"Your daughters are okay," Caleb tells him. "But if you don't do what I ask, I'm going to hurt them. I'm going to cut off their faces and mix them all up so you won't know who the fuck you're looking at. Do you believe me?"

The doctor nods but says nothing. Caleb can see he's very much believed.

"See, that's the thing, Doctor, in the past you've believed the wrong people, but it's good to see you've learned from those mistakes. Do you know who I am?"

A shake of the head.

"No, I didn't think you would. Life has moved on and I look a little different, I suppose, from when I was in the papers back then. But we've never met. I've been watching you over the last few weeks and learning even more about you over the years, but there are some things about you I didn't figure out. I see your wife left you. That's a shame," he says, "because it would have been fun to kill her in front of you. In jail, it's been hard to learn things, but sometimes we have access to the library and the Internet. It's amazing how much shit there is on the Internet," he says, and it's true. It's one of the things that has surprised him the most since coming out of jail—just how far the boundaries of privacy have eroded. People put their life stories online. They update their friends about how they are feeling. His update would say *Caleb is angry.*

The world was bat-shit crazy.

"Dote hurt eye chilren."

Since arriving here half an hour ago, the scene has started to change. The slaughterhouse is a little more lit up than it was before, it's soaked in the early morning misty light that is a hundred shades of gray, the trees look cold and foreboding, as if among them hide the creatures from any one of a thousand nightmares. Then he realizes that he is one of those creatures, that he is the boogeyman Dr. Stanton never dreamed about. He reaches in and grabs the doctor's nose. He twists it without any care or hesitation and there's a clicking sound and the nose springs back into shape. Blood drains out of it as the doctor thrashes about. It flows down the side of his face and past his ear, but he's going to be okay. When it comes to banged-up noses, Caleb has had plenty of experience, and this one was dislocated, not broken. After ten seconds he's sick of watching him.

"Get on your feet," Caleb says.

"What do you want?" he asks, looking up from the trunk, the blood still flowing, but way slower now. He's been crying and dirt has gotten stuck to the tear trails on his face.

"Get on your feet," Caleb repeats, showing him the knife.

Dr. Stanton, with his hands behind him, tries to climb out, and ends up rolling out of the trunk and falling onto his side on the ground, the wind knocked out of him.

"There's nowhere to run, and nobody to hear you scream for help."

"Who are you?" Stanton asks, and he sniffs, then spits out a wad of snot and blood. He gets to his feet, puffing and swaying a little.

"You still haven't figured it out?"

"No."

"You remember James Whitby?"

"James Whitby? No, who the hell . . ." he starts, then stops, and Caleb can see that it's coming to him. "But . . . he's dead."

"That's right."

"He was . . . was murdered," Stanton says, frowning.

"Come on, you're almost there."

"You're . . . you're the man who killed him. You're . . . you're Caleb . . . Caleb Cole?"

"You got it."

"Oh Jesus, Jesus," he says, shaking his head, sending drips of blood from the end of his nose into the dregs of night. His eyes are wide, his face full of an awareness of the past and of his immediate future. "None of that was my fault," he says, his voice getting high. "I was just doing my job, and I did the best I could with the resources I had. I promise you that, and what he did—I'm sorry, I'm truly sorry."

"Sorry?" Caleb says, amazed at the word. "Sorry? That's all you have say? That you're sorry? Where were your apologies when I was in jail for the last fifteen years?"

"I—"

"Shut up," he says, and he punches the doctor in the stomach as hard as he can, the impact making both men double over, Stanton winded, Caleb clutching his hand against his stomach and cradling it. When he's able, he pulls the duct tape out and slaps it over the doctor's mouth. Stanton draws ragged breaths through his damaged nose. Caleb is tempted to cut a small hole in the tape to help him breath, but he's so angry that he'll keep on cutting and next thing he'll be left with three useless kids and one dead doctor. Instead he grabs him by the hair and pulls him toward the slaughterhouse, leading him inside.

So one day is going to turn into two. No big problem. And like he thought earlier, it gives him time to figure out what he's going to do with Ariel Chancellor. Right now, the only thing he needs to figure out is how best to get comfortable. It's going be tough when all he has to deal with are concrete floors and the occasional leftover piece of furniture.

He tosses Stanton onto the floor next to his daughters, then ties up his feet, then bunches up some blankets against the wall and lies down. He can feel the cold ebbing up from the concrete. The girls are all looking at him. He can hear them sniffling, crying, he can hear every time they move against the floor. For fifteen years he's dealt with the sounds that others have made, the snoring and crying and taunting of others. Only thing that would stop him falling asleep right now would be a tank rolling through the front door.

He thinks about turning off the light, but he leaves it on for the kids, not wanting to frighten them any more than necessary. Stanton is staring at him too. There are equal parts confusion and fear in his eyes, and a whole lot of anger and hate too. That's good. Caleb wonders which of those will shine through the brightest when he makes the bastard choose the order in which those little girls are going to die.

CHAPTER NINETEEN

The city is full of good and bad things, and this morning is a classic example. Good thing—the rain has completely gone, the sky looks pretty clear, and when the sun comes up we might just have blue skies in every direction. The temperature is around forty degrees but should go up to almost sixty by the afternoon. The icy wind from yesterday is now somewhere over the South Pacific, blown there by a wind that is still cool, but nowhere near as chilling. Bad thing—the air feels damp. I'm tired again and my tongue got burned drinking the coffee, so it feels numb. My car looks worse the lighter the morning gets, and there are already reporters hanging about outside the main entrance to the police station. They're floating around like bottom-feeders, desperate to snack on any little piece of information, and the worst of them is a local psychic with slicked-back black hair and ultra-white teeth by the name of Jonas Jones. He's wearing a pin-striped suit with a silk tie that makes him look like a well-paid lawyer. The reporters fire questions at me and I don't answer them, and Jonas follows me into the foyer and I put a hand into my pocket to make sure my wallet doesn't disappear. Schroder is ten minutes ahead of me, wanting to change into his third shirt for the day and tidy up a bit before the briefing.

Good thing—Jonas starts with a joke. "I sensed you were going to help," he tells me.

Bad thing—just when I start to laugh, I realize he's not joking.

Jones used to be a used-car salesman before going bankrupt and figuring out a new way to screw people. He's been success-ful at it too, appearing on reality psychic shows and writing books about his communiqués with the dead. So far he's been instrumental in solving the case of who's the most annoying psychic living in the country, and I bet he loses his keys around the house just as much as the rest of us. Over the years he's been a pain in the ass to the department. Yet his books sell and people watch his show, suggesting the book and TV industries make about as much sense as the rest of the world.

I ignore him and keep on walking.

"I can help," he says, flashing me the same smile he used to flash his customers back before he ran his business into the ground.

I'm only two inches taller than Jones, but I use them both to look down at him. "Listen, Jones, just get lost, okay?"

"He's going to kill again."

"You think?"

Jonas's psychic abilities are way off because he doesn't sense that I don't want him to follow. He doesn't sense that I'm get-ting close to breaking his legs.

"He stabs them nineteen times," he says, "and I know why."

I stop walking and look back at him. "Who told you that?" I ask.

"So it's true," he says.

"No comment," I say.

"Ah, I see, you really don't know. Well, you will soon. I just happen to know already."

"Because of your psychic link?"

"It's a gift," he tells me.

"One that keeps on paying." I push the button for the elevator. I press it a couple of times hoping it's just an urban legend that pushing it repeatedly doesn't really speed it up. "So why nineteen times?"

"It's easy," he says, "but if I tell you, I want to be kept in the loop. You're not a cop, but you must be a consultant because you were at all the scenes yesterday and you're here now and I know you need the money," he says, keeping his voice low. The officer behind the desk is watching us. "I don't need to be psychic to see that," he says, but if he were psychic he'd know that I am a cop and not just a consultant. "I give you the info, you keep me updated, and this can be the start of a useful partnership."

I go with what didn't work before, but will hopefully work now. "Like I said, Jones, just get lost, okay?"

"I want to help people," he says. "And you want to help people. There's no reason we can't help each other."

I push the button again. The elevator doesn't speed up. "And no reason you can't profit from it."

"A man needs to eat," he says. "And none of you are different," he says. "Everybody in this building profits from people being hurt, Tate, or is everybody in this department doing this job for free?" He hands me his card. "Call me when you need help."

The elevator doors open and he walks away, leaving me pissed off that he's made a good point. I look down at his card—*Jonas Jones* is written in silver letters raised against an ivory background, beneath his name in bold letters is *Psychic*. It's a typo—the *ic* should have been an *o*. With no garbage bin in the elevator, I tear the card in two and store it in my pocket. If the two halves of the card rejoin by the time I reach the fourth floor, then I'll admit that Jones does have some magical abilities. I wonder if he really does know why the victims were stabbed nineteen times. I should have grabbed him by his shirt and dragged him upstairs and questioned him. The thing is, psychics may be full of bullshit, but they can have a unique way of seeing things, and they can offer a theory that, though inaccurate, can branch off a new train of thought that can lead somewhere.

I'll call him after the briefing.

The doors open at the fourth floor and it's a different world from downstairs. Dozens of people all looking hungover and tired. The floor smells like cheap bourbon. Things aren't as clean around the station anymore on account of their main janitor going to jail last year after it turned out he had a taste for killing people. Schroder is wearing a new shirt and he's back in his original shoes, which have dried out, but he's still wearing the same pants. He smells like he's had a beer and followed it with a toothpaste chaser.

The briefing room is much bigger than the last time I was here. It used to be a conference room that could sit a dozen people with perhaps standing room for another ten, but now the wall has been knocked down and rebuilt further out to double the size of the room, the Christchurch crime rate demanding the modification. There used to be potted plants in the corner and a couple of prints on the wall of landscapes, but that's all gone now. There's a large aerial shot of the city taken last year, and in that moment when the camera shutter flicked open, it would have caught a hundred crimes going on, each of them too small to see.

The window overlooks a city that at the moment has a glow far out to the east, where the sun is breaking the surface. I can see the Avon River snaking its way alongside Durham Street, the banks still green and lit up by the streetlights. A few people are jogging by it, their heavy breath forming clouds in the air. The morning is still, not many other signs of life, not even any birds.

On the main wall of the room is a map with pins locating

the crime scenes. There are photographs of the victims on the wall. Photographs of the crime scenes. Within twenty-four hours that wall has almost run out of space. Tomorrow more builders might need to come along and double the size of the room again, maybe even put on an extension that goes out over the side of the building. There are seats set out in a chessboard formation, all of them facing the front. I take one near the back and Schroder takes one near the front. More people file into the room. Many of them are yawning. Many are carrying coffees that weren't made in the station. Most of them recognize me and do a double take.

Seven o'clock passes and the briefing doesn't start. Most of us stay in our seats, knowing it'll just be a matter of minutes. The sky gets lighter outside, the glow of the city becomes stronger. At quarter past seven Superintendent Dominic Stevens walks in. He's the least tired looking person in the room. Everybody goes quiet and we all watch him take his place at the front. Stevens is barely on the good side of sixty and, according to Schroder, these days on the bad side of irritable since giving up smoking. His head is neatly shaved and his face is stained with old acne scars. His voice is grave and he's decked out in his well-pressed uniform.

"Four victims," he says, in way of a *good morning,* "and I don't need to tell each and every one of you that you need to be giving one hundred percent," he says. "And if any of you ever show up to a crime scene again stinking of booze I swear it'll be your last day with a badge," he says, his words even and calm and the threat sounds very real. "If I could spare the manpower," he says, "I'd fire a few of you now just to prove how pissed off I am at you all. That goes for everybody in the room," he says, focusing his gaze on Schroder for a few seconds before casting a general gaze over the rest of us.

"Now, I don't want to sound like an asshole by storming in here and busting your balls, but it's for your own good because obviously you need it. I mean, I sure as hell never thought

I'd have to explain to a group of such competent people that showing up drunk at work is a bad idea, but maybe it's my fault for overestimating you all."

Nobody in the room is holding his gaze. For some, the desks are the most interesting desks they've ever seen; for others, so are their shoes, or the window, or a spot about six feet to Stevens's right.

"Okay, I can see I've made my point," he says. "Now, I know you're all tired. Nobody here has ever been through something like this, but some sick fuck is out there killing our citizens, and today we're going to nail this son of a bitch," he says, "and when we do then you can all go home and get some sleep. Now, I didn't want to have to come in here and give you all a pep talk, but you need it," he says, and then does it, breaking down the routine, stressing the importance of us not messing up, and going over every detail in detail. He looks at me during his final part of the speech, where he says none of us can afford to let the department down, and more than ever this city needs us. I couldn't agree more.

"I know emotions are running high," he says. "We buried one of our own yesterday and we're hurting," he says, and he looks at an empty chair near the front of the room that I'm guessing Landry usually sat at. We all look at it, and I wonder if last night Stevens watched the latest cop drama to get tips on what to say. "We're low on numbers and help and for all we know we could have another four dead bodies by this time tomorrow."

There's a murmur across the room and I contribute to it. Four more bodies today, maybe a few more tomorrow. It's hard to be optimistic when there's a pattern forming and you don't know the shape of it.

"The results are in on our two oldest, and first victims," he says. "Multiple stab wounds each," he says, the number echoing in my head in Jonas's voice. "Victim number one has nineteen," he says, "victim number two we'll know later on.

Victim number three has the one stab wound, no defensive wounds, and we have a preliminary report for victim number four, which also states at least a dozen wounds and no defensive wounds. Victim number three falls outside of the scope in what appears to be a disorganized attack compared to the others. Our killer was able to sneak into two retirement communities and one nursing home without being seen, yet he chose to stab victim number three in his home while his wife and kids were inside. One stab wound and no message and two possibilities—Brad Hayward isn't part of the pattern, or he is part of it and the killer wasn't able to follow through. We have a dead accountant, a dead teacher, and two dead lawyers—one a criminal lawyer, one a family lawyer—and so far no connection. Somebody must have seen something, somebody must know something. People don't just start killing people without a reason," he says, and it's true. People kill people for money, for love, for revenge. They kill people because they like the way it feels or because they're hearing voices from God. Those are all reasons. So is killing somebody for their watch. They're just not always reasons we understand.

He turns toward the board and points at an enlargement of the first victim's forehead with the note written across it. The marker isn't fluid across the skin—it's broken up by the wrinkles, an occasional hairline or two of ink missing. There is blood on the forehead, streaks on one side where it's been wiped off with a sleeve or a rag to make a cleaner writing slate.

"'You didn't care enough,'" he says. "Somebody was angry at our victim, he felt let down by him, he felt like something in his past could have not turned out the way it did because of Herbert Poole."

He points to a similar photo, this one of victim number two's forehead. Same handwriting, same tiny patches of missing ink where the felt has bounced over a wrinkle, same streaks of cleared away blood. "'Was it worth it?'" he asks. "Complete with question mark. Was what worth it? The same thing that let him down with Herbert Poole?" Then on to victim number four, similar photo, same handwriting, less wrinkles in Victoria Brown's skin so the handwriting is neater. "'You were complicit.' Whatever victims numbers one and two did to our killer, he felt victim number four allowed them to do it." He turns back toward us. "Listen up, people. There's pressure from the media, from the citizens, and from the victims' families, and I've promised them all we're going to provide them some answers, and I'm sure as hell going to keep that promise, and you're all sure as hell going to work your damn hardest to make that happen. We're drawing the line. No more of this shit anymore in this city. You're all familiar with the case, I want to hear some feedback. Questions? Theories?"

Nobody says anything. It's like being back at school and nobody knows how to answer the teacher. We're all back to looking at these really interesting desks and shoes, and that spot to the right of Stevens.

"Don't be shy," he says, then slowly shakes his head, disappointed in all of us. Then we make eye contact and I know it's a mistake. "Tate?" he asks.

Everybody turns to look back at me and the world stops. I wasn't expecting this and feel myself turning red. I do my best to meet all their eyes.

"Many of you will remember Detective Inspector Theodore Tate," Stevens says. "He's been assigned to help on account of his track record, the good part of it anyway, which, as we know, lately has been outweighed by the rest of it."

Detective Kent is giving me a sympathetic smile, and perhaps it's part relief too—if I wasn't here she'd be the newest team member and the one facing the question.

"Many of you have worked with Tate before so you know what he's capable of, and now you all have the chance to work with him again. He's asked repeatedly to be a part of this force because over the last few years he's believed he can do a better job than us, isn't that right, Detective?"

"I just want to help," I tell them, "and work with the best there is."

The answer doesn't win anybody over.

"Well, how about you take this opportunity you've been given, and prove how clever you are by offering something we'd all like to hear?"

Now I feel even more like I'm back at school, being screwed over by the teacher. I look at Schroder. He's expressionless. I hope he had no idea Stevens was going to pull this on me. "So, any theories?" Stevens asks.

I have lots of theories. One of them is that Superintendent Dominic Stevens is an asshole even though five minutes ago he said he didn't want to sound like one. I can't share that because it's not really a theory, it's a fact, and he wants theories. I could theorize that my life would be better off if somebody had beaten the shit out of him in the parking lot before work. I could theorize life might feel a little better if it happened after work too.

"The stab wounds," I tell him, my hand in my pocket sliding the two pieces of Jonas's card against each other. It's magic time.

"What about them?"

If Jonas can figure it out, so can I.

"The first two victims—what if they were stabbed the same amount of times?"

Stevens looks at Schroder, then back at me. "What are you saying?"

"We need to find out from the medical examiner exactly how many times victims two and four were stabbed."

"Because?"

Because a psychic knew the first two had nineteen stab wounds, and guessed the last one had the same.

"Because at least a dozen times could also mean nineteen times, which would give three of our victims an identical amount of wounds."

"But not the fourth," he says.

"Which goes to what you were saying about victim number three falling outside of the pattern. Same killer, but different reason for killing. He's not part of the pattern."

"Carry on."

"Well," I say, everybody still staring at me and my mind racing, "well, if three of the victims have been stabbed nineteen times, then it must mean something."

Nobody says anything. I can tell I have everybody's interest now.

"What kind of something?" Stevens asks. "Like a year for example? Or a person? Is that what you're saying?" he asks, working with me.

"Exactly. Whatever annoyed our killer may have happened nineteen years ago. Or it happened to him when he was nineteen."

"There may be nineteen people on his list," Schroder offers.

Most of the people in the room take a collective gasp at that thought. Some of us probably think we might be lucky if he stops at nineteen.

"Yes, yes," Stevens says, nodding now. "Or it could be they hurt somebody he loves who is nineteen, or even killed them."

"Or cost him nineteen years of his life," I say, "or nineteen could even mean a monetary thing since we're dealing with dead accountants and lawyers," I say, not wanting to follow that up by saying dead lawyers and accountants are normally the best kind. "Could be they cost him nineteen thousand dollars, or a hundred and ninety thousand dollars, or nineteen years in jail."

"Okay, it could be nothing or it could be something," Stevens says. "Detective Schroder," he says, turning toward Carl, "I want you to get hold of the ME as soon as this meeting is over and find out if Tate's theory has any merit."

Then Stevens turns back toward us, nods once in a gesture I don't quite get, then steps off to the side of the room and hands the floor over to Schroder. Schroder coughs into his hand, focuses on me for a second, then on everybody else. The sun finally joins the rest of us in this early morning nightmare, it comes in through the window and hits Schroder just as he's about to start talking. Another detective stands up and pulls one of the blinds.

Schroder breaks down what we're doing. Patrol cars are out on the streets. They're doing what they've been doing since the second body showed up, and that's patrolling every neighborhood and looking for anything suspicious. It's about all they can do until we can make a connection. So Schroder fills us in on these facts, and then he fills us in on what we know, which unfortunately isn't much. He divides us up to work different crime scenes or different witnesses. Detectives are sent to work the lawyer angle, two of them looking through the case files of victim number one's past, two of them through the case files of victim number four. It will involve getting warrants. Law firms don't like to give up information. They're also the hardest ones to present warrants to, because they argue everything. Details have to be exact. If the answers are in the files of clients these lawyers have dealt with, they're going to be hard to get. Perhaps even impossible because of attorney-client privilege. It's going to be a day full of interviews, of detectives digging into people's pasts to find what connects them. Detectives are going to go through student files of Albert McFarlane and cross-reference them against criminal records. Everybody in the room is eager for a piece of the action. Schroder doesn't give me an assignment. When it's over, everybody stands up and heads for the door, but then pauses as Schroder starts back up.

"One more thing," he says. "We've heard that tonight there's going to be gatherings of boy-racers around town," he says, and everybody groans. "It means the streets are going to be clogged. It means patrol responses may be slow, it means getting from A to B may end up taking longer. It's estimated there are going to be over two thousand of them," he says. "Two thousand vehicles deliberately being a pain in the ass, making some kind of point only adolescents are likely to get. For the love of God, don't shoot them," he says, and nobody is sure if he's joking. "Just keep it in mind," he says, "and allow for it."

Then everybody is on the move again. Some of them pat me on the shoulder and the rest nod toward me as they head for the door. I stand up and approach the wall of death and look at the photos.

Stevens stares at me for a few seconds, then comes over. I'm expecting the warning, the *don't mess up* warning, followed by the *you shouldn't be here* warning.

"How's it going, Theo?" he asks, and puts out his hand. I reach for it a little hesitantly, as if he's going to pull it away and all the offers that have been made. I shake it. "Listen, I appreciate your help yesterday."

"Thanks," I tell him.

"You were the only sane one out there, and I've heard if you hadn't taken some control all of my detectives might have made the front-page news and be scouring the back pages for new jobs. That's why you're getting this chance. You earned it. But it's a short leash. A very short one. Listen, I know I acted like a bastard ten minutes ago, but at least everybody is on your side now. If I'd stood up there and said what a privilege it was to have you back, they'd all have hated you because it'd have made it sound like they needed your help. This way they feel bad about how I treated you, and it'll help them warm up to you."

I'm not so sure it's worked the way he thought it would, but I get his point.

"Plus what you came up with, if you're right, it could be a good lead. Carl really thinks you can help," he says, then nods at Carl who has come over to stand next to me. "People keep telling me you're a loose cannon, but my way of thinking suggests maybe that's exactly what we need, huh?" he says, and claps his hands together. "I mean, Jesus, this nutcase is a loose cannon, right? Time we fight fire with fire."

"I appreciate the . . . compliment, I guess."

"Well we're not paying you to waste time doing that," he says, still smiling, "we're paying you to help catch this son of a bitch. Good luck," he adds, leaving me confused about what he really thinks of me. Then he turns toward Schroder. "A word?" he says, and Schroder follows him out of the room. I walk over to the window and stare out at the view, shielding my eyes from the sun. Still blue skies in every direction, but the south can't be seen from this angle. At ground level people are walking about, some with purpose, some aimlessly, some heading to the parks that make up the Garden City. They're pushing strollers and throwing Frisbees in what are the dying sunny days before winter.

I move over to the wall when Schroder comes back in.

"Was it bad?"

"Was what bad?" he asks.

"The warning Stevens gave you about me."

"Like he said, you're on a short leash."

"Yeah? What else did he say?"

"He said nobody would file a complaint if I had to shoot you."

I'm not sure if he's joking and don't ask in case he's not. "So what's my assignment? You want me to follow up with the stab wounds?"

"I'm on it. I want you to run with this," he says, and he hands me a folder.

I open it up. Inside is a rap sheet belonging to a woman named Ariel Chancellor—a photograph of a twenty-two-year-old woman—who is now twenty-five according to the date of birth—stares back at me. She looks like she hasn't eaten anything thicker than a potato chip since her teens. Her face is hollow and pale, her blond hair straight and lifeless, the ends of it frayed. She's frowning at the photographer, the sense that if you could see her hand maybe she'd be giving the finger too. There are pictures of her fingerprints and a brief bio. She's been arrested on drug possession and shoplifting. I look from the photo up to Schroder who, aside from the makeup and long hair, has a similar look on his face as the girl.

"Looks like a friendly girl," I say. "She's who was in Hayward's car last night?"

"According to the fingerprints on his belt and in the car, yes. It's your lead, Tate."

There is no mention of prostitution in the file because the only crime in prostitution is the failure to declare your income. Whether you're being shot in the line of duty or faking an orgasm for cash, Inland Revenue wants their share. There's a last known address, which hopefully is still current.

"Jesus," I say, "if she was in the car with him and she's a prostitute, then Brad Hayward picking her up may have nothing to do with his death. It's not like the other victims were picking up prostitutes."

"It's a lead," Schroder reminds me, "likely a dead end, but it's yours to follow."

"And the stab wounds?" I ask.

"Look, I'm meeting the medical examiner down in the morgue in . . ." he glances at his watch, "just over an hour. You're welcome to meet me down there if you're done in time. Until then, go and talk to this woman. Get her statement. Every line of inquiry needs to be wrapped up, Tate. That part of the job hasn't changed."

CHAPTER TWENTY

We head downstairs together, taking the stairs instead of the elevator, either to save power like we're all supposed to be doing all over the world to save on resources, or for the exercise. We get to the bottom. Schroder goes out a door to the parking lot and I head into the foyer and down the front steps to the street. There's a crowd of reporters forming a semicircle, and in the center of it is Superintendent Stevens, shaved head gleaming in the sunlight. He has the attention of everybody there, except for Jonas Jones, who breaks away from the group. I don't hang around for the speech and the questioning. Jones follows me. I figure I could try and lose him, but a man of his abilities will already know where I'm parked.

I reach my car half a block away and somebody has backed into it, the front left headlight is busted and there's glass on the ground and no note left behind. I sweep the glass into the curb with my foot. Traffic is backed up from traffic light to traffic light, people flocking to start the workday.

"Let me guess," I say, turning toward Jonas, "you woke up

this morning knowing somebody was going to damage my car?"

"That's funny, Detective. Do I have that right? You're a detective inspector again?"

"You tell me."

"I can help you, Detective. We can help each other. I have a gift, and you're wasting time by denying that."

"You're unbelievable," I tell him. "Twice in a morning. You must be desperate."

"Don't dismiss me, Theodore. I can help. There is an opportunity here for us both to do some good."

"And you'll write a book about it?"

"You would get some credit. And paid, of course, and looking at your car I can tell getting paid isn't something you're used to."

"No, thanks," I tell him.

"I can help you, Theodore."

"Yeah? Then why don't you help me and tell me what the stab wounds mean?"

"Why don't you help me, and tell me about the case? Whether you think I'm a fake or not, we can help each other. I know how people think. You must at least know that's true."

"Then you must know what I'm thinking right now," I tell him, and I pull away, leaving him to stare at my car for a few seconds before he turns back the way we walked.

The day is still warming up. I take my jacket off at the first set of lights I stop at. My body clock is a little out of whack from daylight savings—for some reason every year daylight savings feels like we're jumping forward or backward six hours instead of just the one. I stop off at a café and grab another coffee, figuring I can afford it now, figuring if I don't take a few minutes to do this I'll end up falling over in a gutter. I get the feeling I'm going to need two cups an hour just to stay alert through the day. I sit at a table and watch the city through the window, people passing by, cars doing the same thing, and everything looks normal and now, right now in this moment, Christchurch is the city it used to be.

The clouds from the south creep over the top of the café and start to cover the city. Somebody toots at another car and there's an exchange of hand gestures and obscenities. A teenager in a hoodie walks past the window and sees me looking out. He takes the time to inhale a big wad of snot and spits it at me. It hits the window and slides down slowly, mostly green but with a bit of blood in there too, and he carries on looking angry at the footpath ahead of him. A man in the café behind me calls the waitress a whore and tells her coffee should be cheaper before storming out, and Christchurch is back.

I finish my coffee and drive to Ariel Chancellor's house. It's the kind of neighborhood I'd certainly never want to live in, with houses looking near collapse and gardens that have been eaten alive by bacteria. The street has potholes every thirty feet. The sidewalks are cracked and broken from pushed up tree roots. I park outside Ariel's house safe in the knowledge nobody will think I'm a cop because of my car, safe in the knowledge my car isn't worth stealing. The house is in rough condition, with a tarpaulin over part of the roof. I walk up the pathway to the front door, where paint is peeling off the walls and resting in flaky puddles on the porch. I knock, half expecting my hand to disappear, that the door will be full of rot and held together only by termites.

A woman answers, squinting at the bright light and holding her hand up to her face. Her skin is pale and there are cold sores around the sides of her mouth. It takes me a few seconds to come to the conclusion that it's Ariel because this version is different from the photograph. She's older and thinner and looks as though six hours ago she may have been strung out on whatever it is that made those needle holes in her arm. She's holding onto a glass half full of golden fluid and ice cubes. She has dyed her hair black and it's about half the length it was before, coming down to the top of her neck.

I hold up my badge. "Ariel Chancellor?"

I can see in her features that once, before life crushed her, Ariel Chancellor was an extremely attractive girl.

Her voice sounds like a cigarette butt is jammed down her throat. "Who are you? What do you want?"

"I'm Detective Inspector Tate," I say, introducing myself, and it's good to say those words again and not be lying about it.

. Her eyes snap into focus. "You don't look like a cop," she says, hooking her hair over her ears.

"No?"

"No. Cops wear cheap suits. Your suit is worse than cheap."

"You recognize this man?" I ask, holding up a photo of Brad Hayward.

"No," she answers, without even looking at it. She starts to close the door, and I put my hand out and stop her.

"You want to reconsider?"

"Not really, no. You want to get the hell off my porch?"

"Your fingerprints were found in his car."

"My fingerprints have a way of getting found in lots of cars," she says. "He say I took something from him? If so, he's a liar. You can't trust men who pay for sex."

"So he was one of your clients."

"If that's the label you want to give them, sure."

"He was murdered last night."

"And what, I'm supposed to care? You think your buddy there would give a shit if I showed up dead in an alleyway?"

"He had a wife and two kids."

"And they're better off without him." She lets go of the door, conceding she's going to have to talk to me. She reaches into her pocket for a packet of cigarettes.

"You're wrong about that," I tell her.

"Am I? You have a crystal ball? He could have turned into a bad father, a drunk, somebody who'd hit his kids."

"Please. He was killed in front of his children," I tell her, which is close enough to the truth.

She lights one of the cigarettes. She holds the packet in my direction and I shake my head. "They're better off without him," she says. "They just don't know it."

"You may be right," I say, doubting that she is.

"I am right. I'm good at reading men, Detective, it's what I do."

"At least help them get some closure and talk to me."

She looks up at the sky and squints against the glary light, staring up for about five seconds as if that's where the answers are. "It's going to rain," she says. "Business is always slow when it rains." She looks back at me. "Fifty bucks," she says. "Give me fifty bucks and I'll talk to you."

"I don't have fifty bucks," remembering the guy at the hotel yesterday morning with his baseball bat.

She looks out at my car. "No, I don't suppose you do," she says.

"But if you like, I can arrest you, throw you in a cell for a few hours, and let you sober up a bit. Now that I can do for free."

"I suppose you could," she says, and takes a sip at her drink. "Fine, you may as well come in." She rattles the ice in her glass and holds it up to eye level. "Fix you a drink?"

"It's too early."

"No, it's not that, I can tell," she says, smirking at me. "Remember what I said about reading men? I can see it in your eyes. You're battling a demon."

"Maybe it's too early for you too," I tell her.

She shrugs. "It's always happy hour somewhere," she says, and I can't imagine the last time she spent an hour being truly happy.

CHAPTER TWENTY-ONE

Caleb Cole can barely move. His chest aches when he lifts his arms, the joints in his elbows and shoulders feel like they're on fire. He massages his fingers deep into his neck just so he can start looking around. He might have been better off sleeping in the car, but he didn't want to be away from Stanton in case he tried something. He's had—he looks at his watch—shit, ninety minutes' sleep. He can't believe that's all. Ninety minutes and the baby is crying. Somehow she has managed to pull the tape off her mouth and it's dangling on her chin.

He's cold. The slaughterhouse is the kind of building that would only get above fifty degrees if on fire. He hates it here. He has to wait until tonight to finish what he had wanted to finish last night, but he can't face spending the entire day here.

He puts his hands on his hips and stretches out his back. He limps for the first few paces until the feeling comes back into his legs. This was supposed to be over by now.

"Quiet down," he says to Octavia, but she doesn't—instead she just gets louder. He unclips her from her seat and picks her up in both hands and holds her out. He could shake her, he supposes. It'd probably work. And how the fuck are the other two kids still asleep? He guesses they must be used to the noise like people living near airports. He bounces Octavia up and down a little and pulls the rest of the tape away and her crying quiets a little, but not enough to stop annoying him.

"Hungry?"

Her crying turns into a series of hiccups, and then she stares blankly at him before nodding. "Yes," she says, her mouth holding on to the y much longer before snapping out the other letters like a gunshot, so it sounds like *yyyyyyyyyyyyyes*.

"I'll get you some food."

"Yyyyyyyyyes."

"You don't talk much, do you?"

"Yyyyyyyyes."

"Do you know any other words?"

"Cat," she says.

"Cat," he repeats. "That's really useful."

The doctor is watching him. He's straining against the plastic ties, but stops struggling when he sees Caleb watching him. Caleb opens up the bag of supplies and finds another jar of baby food. Both of the other girls are awake. He frees Katy and gives the food to her.

"Feed her," he says, nodding toward the baby.

Instead of feeding her, Katy runs over to her father and wraps her arms around him. She starts to cry, and Stanton starts to cry too. Stanton muffles something around the duct tape. The words are indistinguishable but the tone makes the message clear. He's telling her everything is going to be okay. He's telling her not to worry. Caleb takes a step toward them, ready to grab the girl by the collar and drag her away but decides to give them their moment. After all, the amount of nice moments in these people's futures is very limited. He lets them have this one—but after thirty seconds, when it looks like they may never part, he changes his mind.

"Come on," he says, and Katy doesn't let go. "Come on," he repeats, "or you're all going to go hungry."

Katy lets go. She sniffs back some tears and wipes her jacket sleeve over her face. "Okay," she says, and she puts out her hand for the food.

She takes Octavia out of the seat and sets her between her legs and wraps her arms around her the same way she did her father, then puts her back into the seat and opens the jar. Spoonful after spoonful Octavia races it down. While she's eating, Caleb tears open a packet of cereal. He eats a handful, looking at the container of milk and wondering if he should add some to his mouthful. He moves on to the loaf of bread instead. Katy finishes up, then hands Octavia a plastic cup of water. She drinks from it while staring at her sister. There is baby food all over her face and she's probably filled her diaper back up and he can't face doing anything about it either.

Octavia drops her mug and it rolls across the floor, she reaches out for it but can't reach and starts to cry. This is what a turtle must feel like, he imagines, when it's lying on its back. Katy picks it up and hands it to her. Her crying stops.

"There you go," Katy says.

"Cat," Octavia says.

Katy rubs Octavia's arms as she drinks. Caleb washes down the cereal with an orange juice.

"I need to use the bathroom," Katy says.

"Okay," he says, because he needs it too. She puts Octavia back into the seat then he leads her outside. "Same tree," he says, and she goes over and disappears behind it. He moves to the car and pisses on the hood.

In the full morning light the slaughterhouse has lost none of its creepy feel. It should be nothing more than an abandoned building, harmless, just a bunch of walls being climbed over by nature, but it's not. This is the building where his baby girl died, and inside there are ghosts. There are dark rooms with large meat hooks. There are nightmares. The slaughterhouse is a home to all the misery in the world.

He stands with the sun on his face. His clothes feel a little damp, but fifteen minutes out here and that won't be a problem anymore. There are no clouds, just blue skies. A beautiful day that could stay the way it started, or just as easily shower the city with rain. He closes his eyes and there's a moment, a brief moment, when he asks himself whether he can walk away from all of this. He doesn't have to go back into the slaughterhouse, doesn't have to deal with the doctor and the children, and nobody has to die. He can walk away, find a beach somewhere and sit in the autumn sun, soak up the atmosphere, and things can end differently. He can swim. Just pick a direction and go for it. See how far he can get before the tiredness sucks him under. He used to be a pretty good swimmer. There was a time he could go length after length without fatigue, his breathing would stay calm, his arms slicing through the water effortlessly. Before he got married he used to swim three times a week, normally for an hour at a time. It was the only exercise he got. He'd go before work started, when the only people at the pool were keen swimmers like himself. When he got married life got busier, then his daughter arrived, then swimming became one of those things you cut adrift as you get older and responsibilities change.

Only he can't do that. His family is dead because of the doctor, because of these other people. He hasn't finished getting justice for his family.

He finishes up. So does Katy. Back inside he looks through the bag and opens a tin of tuna. The smell hits him like a bullet and he almost gags, he throws the can through the doorway into another room, it lands on its side and rolls out of sight. If the rats can stomach the smell, then good luck to them. Katy picks Octavia back out of the seat and walks over to Melanie, her arms around Octavia's chest from behind. It's like watching a large princess doll carrying a smaller princess doll. She settles down beside her older sister with the baby between them.

"Are you hungry?" he asks the doctor.

The doctor mumbles something else from behind the gag that he can't make out, but the tone suggests it isn't about being hungry. The tone suggests a whole lot of *fuck yous* mixed in with a good ol' fashioned *go to hell*.

Octavia is staring at him again while she sucks at her drink, a line of drool hanging from the bottom of it that creeps him out. Katy reaches up and removes the tape from Melanie.

"I need to use a bathroom," Melanie says.

"Okay," he says, and cuts through the plastic ties. "Don't stop holding her," he says to Katy, and nods toward Octavia.

"I wasn't going to."

"And don't try to free your dad. You've got nothing you can free him with, and if you try, I'm going to be mad. If I get mad, then bad things are going to happen, and I'm going to have to punish you, and Melanie, and Octavia. Okay?"

She nods, her mouth turning down at the edges. "Okay," she says.

He takes Melanie outside. She keeps scowling at him. "You don't have any idea how to look after a baby, do you."

"You're wrong."

"I'm never wrong."

"You are this time. I used to have a daughter."

"Where is she? You tie her up too and bring her out here?"

"No, but somebody else did. And he killed her."

"Oh," she says, and she opens up her mouth to say something else, and he waits for it, knowing she won't know what to say, and that's exactly what happens. "Oh," she says again, then looks down.

"Toilet's over there," he says, and points at the trees. "Don't try to run away. I'm not going to hurt any of you, I promise," he says, "as long as you do what I say. You just have to trust me. But, if you try to run away," he says, then inhales sharply and scrunches up his face, "well, do I need to tell you what will happen?"

She shakes her head.

"Good. Now hurry up," he says.

He stands next to the building drinking orange juice as she runs into the trees for a few minutes before coming back. Most of the trees are skeletons now, a few of them still clutching on to handfuls of leaves, and the sun coming through them looks cold. The ground is soft from yesterday's rain, there is a trail of muddy footprints leading back and forth from the car, and a set of handprints too where Stanton fell over. The car has at least a dozen wet leaves stuck to the body, and the windshield and windows are clouded over with moisture.

"You know the police are looking for us," Melanie tells him. "The police can track people. They do it all the time."

"On TV they do," he tells her, "but this isn't TV."

"No, not just on TV," she says. "We had this girl at school and she ran away. The police found her within a day. And there was another girl who—"

"Melanie," he says, "I don't want to hear you talking anymore, okay? And I don't want to hurt you, I really don't, but you're making me feel as though I want to."

He leads her back inside. She goes over to her father the same way Katy did earlier and wraps her arms around him. Caleb leans against the wall drinking orange juice staring at them. He remembers his own daughter holding him that way.

"That's enough," he says, and unlike Katy she lets go right away. "Octavia needs her diaper changed."

"Yeah? So why don't you do it?"

"Because I'm telling you to. Your sister can help."

They lay Octavia down on the blanket. Katy starts humming. He doesn't recognize the tune, but from the sound of it he guesses it's her own tune, something she's making up as she goes along. The doctor is crying. It's pathetic.

"What's it like having no control?" he asks, but of course Stanton can't answer. The girls all look over at him but say nothing.

"Not much of a man, are you," Caleb says.

Stanton looks directly at him. He muffles more of the *fuck yous* and struggles against the ties, but really, what does he expect to happen?

"We're done," Melanie says.

Katy stops humming and starts singing. "A, b, c, d, g, f, g . . . g, f, g," she says, over and over.

He realizes she has a beautiful singing voice, but he's not in the mood for it. "Stop that," he says, but she gets louder. "I said stop that."

"She can't," Melanie says. "When she gets really sad she starts doing that."

"Why?"

"Because she's sad, weren't you listening? She didn't used to do it."

"A, b, c, g, c, g . . ."

"Why did she start?"

"She started when Mom left."

"G, f, g," Katy says.

"And when was that?" he asks.

"Why should I tell you?" she asks, handing Katy's teddy bear to Octavia. Octavia smiles and grabs it tight. Katy stares on, still singing, her sweet voice echoing through the room.

"Because I asked nicely. If you like, I can ask not so nicely."

"Six months ago. She's a bitch."

"What?"

"She's a bitch. A fucking bitch."

"Whoa, slow down," he says, showing her his palm. "Don't use that kind of language."

"Why not? You use it."

"But I'm an adult."

She shrugs. "Doesn't change the fact my mom is a bitch who walked out on us. A fucking bitch. That's what Dad says when he doesn't think we can hear him."

More sounds from Stanton. More struggling. Maybe he should knock him out again.

"Sounds tough," he says to Melanie.

"Tough? No, what's tough is you. You're a tough guy, right? You must be since you're keeping my dad tied up and walking around with a knife. Bet your mom and dad would be proud."

Octavia pulls away and starts tracing her finger back and forth across the floor. He's thinking he may have to gag Katy. It's distracting. Gag Katy and knock Stanton out—his to-do list is building up. He points toward the bag and looks at Melanie. "Help yourself," he says, "and feed your family too. They're going to need their strength. And no more swearing."

"So I can take off Dad's gag?"

He nods. Katy is still singing, and there are tears on her face and a long string of snot hanging like a spider web between her nose and her hand. She wipes it over her top as Melanie walks over to her father and slowly pulls the duct tape from his mouth, the front of which has drips of dried blood on it.

"Don't you fucking hurt them," Stanton says, then spits a wad of mucus onto the floor.

"You swore," Katy says.

"Don't hurt them," he says, then he looks at his girls. "It's going to be okay," he says, changing his tone. Melanie hugs him again.

It's obvious he wants to hug her too but can't. She holds him tight and his next words of assurance toward them is muffled against her shoulder. She steps back, and Katy carries Octavia over so they can hug too, and it's such a sweet moment in which Caleb imagines different scenarios, all of them involving the knife that is still owed a lot of blood. The good news is that Katy stops singing. Both Melanie and the doctor are trying to look strong, and both of them fall short. Katy is the only one who's really showing her emotions. Octavia is too young to have any emotion other than *I'm happy* or *I just shit myself*.

"I'm scared," Katy tells him.

"It's okay, honey, it really is," he says, then coughs for a few seconds. "We're going to be fine."

Caleb says nothing. They can believe what they want—he'll prove them all wrong soon enough.

The father looks past his daughters and over at Caleb, then tries to clear his throat again. "Listen, Caleb, I've been thinking about why you've been doing this, and I, I . . ." he says, but his throat blocks back up and he has to clear it again. "I understand why you hate me," he says, and the look in his eyes says something else, his eyes are saying he's thought about it, doesn't understand what's going on, and wants to kill Caleb. "I really do, and I can't blame you for that, Caleb, I really can't," he says, his words almost running together. "You deserve to hate me, but not my children. You've made your point. For the love of God, leave them be."

Caleb shakes his head. "No, Doctor, I haven't made my point. I haven't even started. And your kids, they are part of this, just like mine were."

"No, no they're not. Listen to me, they're not responsible for what happened."

"You're responsible," Caleb tells him. "My children are dead and so is my wife and I've spent fifteen years in jail getting the shit kicked out of me every day, and what have you been doing, huh? Buying a nice house, raising your kids, laughing and smiling and making a family and pissing off your wife and . . ."

"It wasn't my fault what happened," Stanton says, then can't carry on as Melanie tips a glass of juice toward him. He gulps it down greedily. For the first time Caleb realizes how much Melanie looks like her father. Katy does too, but not Octavia. At one year old, Octavia doesn't look like anything other than a generic baby. All babies look the same except when they're your own.

"You killed my daughter."

"No, no I didn't," he says, spluttering on the juice.

"Yes you did," Caleb confirms. "You and the others."

"I can see how you see it that way, Caleb, I really can, but that's not how it was."

"It's exactly how it was. I want you to experience what I went through."

"What?"

"The loss and the blame, I want you to live what I lived, and I want you to die how I died."

"What does that even mean?"

"I think you know," Caleb says, looking at the pain on Stanton's face, looking at the awareness dawn on him. "Do you have any idea what it's like to lose a child, let alone two of them?"

Katy moves over to Octavia and starts singing again. Melanie stays with her father, but suddenly she's not looking as brave as she's trying to be. Stanton is doing an even worse job now of trying to look strong. Octavia is drawing a circle on the dirt floor with her finger, looking confused as to why the circle keeps disappearing.

"I . . . I don't understand," Stanton says.

"I think you do," Caleb says. "See, I lost two children, and if you were to lose two children at least you'd still have a spare."

Stanton starts shaking his head. "No, no, you can't. You can't. Please, don't hurt them."

"You hurt me."

"I'm—I'm sorry," he says, his voice dry again. "I'm truly sorry."

"What does he mean?" Melanie asks.

"He doesn't mean anything," Stanton answers, then, in a lower voice even though all his children can hear him, he says, "Caleb, you can't do this."

"You have a debt to pay, Doctor."

"There's no debt!" he shouts, spittle flying from his swollen lips.

"You say you're sorry, but that's only because you're here

where my daughter died, and because you're desperate. Were you sorry fifteen years ago? Were you sorry for taking our lives away? No, you weren't, because if you were you would have come and seen me, you would have come to tell me how bad you felt."

"Is this what you want? To be just like Whitby? Is that what your wife and children would want?"

"What they want is to be alive again."

"You're dishonoring them."

"No, I've honored them. I've kept them alive in here," he says, touching his head, "and in here," he says, touching his heart. "I'm the only one who has. The rest of the world has moved on. You moved on. You're still a doctor, you still treat people. If there was any guilt inside of you, you would have become somebody different, you'd have given up your job fifteen years ago when you saw what you had done. Instead you feel nothing, except now, because right now you feel remorse because I'm here to punish you. This is the moment in your life, Stanton, where being a bad person catches up with you. It's the moment where you have to be accountable."

"You're wrong. I think about what happened to your family all the time. I use it to make people better. Please—"

"Melanie, go and sit over there with your sisters," Caleb says.

"No. I'm not leaving my dad."

"It's okay, Munchkin," Stanton says, and his nickname for his daughter makes Caleb's heart jump. On occasion he'd called his daughter the same thing. Munchkin. Pumpkin. Princess. Sometimes it'd be Princess Munchkin or Princess Pumpkin.

Melanie is starting to cry.

"Do what he says," Stanton begs. "All three of you, go to the other side of the room."

They do as he asks, Katy and Melanie carrying Octavia between them. Caleb moves in close, he crouches in front of the doctor. He lowers his voice. "It will be different for you, I promise," he says.

"Please, please, don't hurt my kids," Stanton says, matching the volume of Caleb's voice. "They haven't done anything to you. I'll do anything, anything, don't hurt them."

"What are their nicknames?" Caleb asks.

"What? Why?"

Why? He doesn't know. He doesn't need to know either, or at least he shouldn't. But right now it's important to him. "Tell me," he says.

"Munchkin and Kitten," he says. "Munchkin Mel and Katy Kitten."

"And Octavia?"

"Huh?"

"Octavia."

Stanton shakes his head. "She doesn't have one."

"Why?"

"Don't hurt them," Stanton says.

Caleb shakes his head. Fuck it. It's time to move on. What does he care who is named what? "It's too late for that."

"No, no it's not. There's no reason why it's too late. You haven't hurt them yet, you don't have to, you can do what you want with me, but you don't have to hurt them. Please, I'm begging you."

"Begging. My daughter begged for her life," he says, knowing she would have. She would have begged and cried and called out for him and his wife. "We also used to call her Munchkin," he says, and Stanton winces and Caleb knows why—suddenly it's all become a lot more human to him. Suddenly Stanton's imagining what it would be like to lose his own daughter. Well, he isn't going to have to imagine for long. "I'm going to let you decide which one of your kids dies first," Caleb says. "I never had that choice." The sun is coming into the office, highlighting a beam of dust in the air. He knows the girls can't hear him, because if they could they would be doing more than just crying, they'd be bawling their eyes out and screaming. "You're going to be with them when they die," Caleb says, carrying on. "My daughter was all alone out here with the man that killed her," he says, and he's seen it play out in his mind a thousand times a day since it happened. It's always there on repeat, an image he can't shake, an image that has defined him. "He stabbed her and raped her in the middle of winter. It was thirty fucking degrees out here and that didn't slow him down. Stabbed her over and over in her chest and her stomach. Before that he stripped her naked and pressed her tiny body against concrete as cold as ice, and during that time you were sitting in your warm office drinking coffee and offering bullshit advice while having no fucking idea at all about how people tick."

"I . . ."

"You killed her, you fucker!" he yells, and now comes the sobbing from the children, and small brief screams too, and here comes his emotion, here it comes racing through him and if he doesn't dial it back he's going to ruin everything by gutting the doctor where he lies, and the doctor, well, he's flinching at every word, as if they're punches being thrown down on him. "You, you and your fucking skewed way of seeing the world, you and your arrogance, your vanity, you and all your importance because you just had to be the man, right? You had to be the fucking man who knew better! You only thought about your career, about making a name for yourself."

Katy Kitten and Munchkin Mel are in full cry mode now as they clutch the teddy bear between them. They are low to the floor so they can clutch Octavia too. He looks at them, he sees the fear, but they don't know what fear is—unless he undresses them and presses them into the floor they'll never understand it.

He pulls himself back from losing control. He shakes his head and lowers his voice. "James Whitby, he couldn't help himself. He was damaged goods, he was a bad guy, but it's who he was. You say you were only doing your job, but that's what the others were doing. You were doing more than that—it was your word that Whitby could be helped. Your word that his lawyer argued to the judge. You were the one in that stand seventeen years ago who convinced those twelve people that James Whitby was a stand-up guy, that he . . ."

"I never said that!"

"No, and you never said we'd all be better off with him in jail. Instead you said he needed help, that medical help would help him. You said he could be cured and the jury and the judge, they believed that."

"I . . . I am, I'm truly sorry, I'm . . . oh, Jesus, don't hurt my kids."

Caleb leans in and slaps him as hard as he can. The sound is louder than the crying from the girls. It echoes across the room and out the door and into the heart of the slaughterhouse, out past the can of tuna and the rats who are probably nibbling at it, outside past the plastic bag full of shit and the car with piss on the hood. For a moment it's the only sound in the room, the girls stop crying, and then they start back up, the youngest slaps her palms against the floor.

"Think about what it is you want to say to them," Caleb says, his voice still low but a lot more forceful now. "You've got the day to decide, because tonight I'm going to do to your family what was done to mine."

"Please—"

"And I'm giving you the chance to comfort them, you son of a bitch. That's a whole lot more than my daughter ever had. They don't have to die out here alone."

"Don't do this."

"Are you a religious man, Doctor?"

"What? No, no . . . why?"

"Because now would be a good time to start praying. An eye for an eye, Doctor. It's in the Bible. Symbolically, it sums up what we have here."

"You don't have to . . ."

"Don't waste your words on me," Caleb tells him, getting

out new plastic ties to bind the children. "They're useless. Use them on your children. Talk to them, be with them, tell them goodbye, but make no mistake, tonight out here in this God-forsaken place I'm going to start killing your family and there isn't a goddamn thing you can do about it."

CHAPTER TWENTY-TWO

Ariel Chancellor's house smells of wet cat and wet dog and I stay away from the walls to keep my clothes dry. I look down at my shoes to make sure they're not squelching into the carpet and bringing up water. We walk through to the living room, where there are large stains in the ceiling with plaster and paint flaking away, the center of it bowing outward with the weight of rainwater trapped in the roof, a bucket on the floor collecting the drips. The light has no bulb in it and with all that moisture up there it must be a fire hazard. Ariel doesn't offer me any tea or coffee or heroin. She sits down in a couch that tries to swallow her and works away at her drink, getting through half of it. I stay standing, wanting to get out of here quickly, hoping she can tell me something useful before I leave.

"How long's it been since your last drink?" she asks me.

"I had coffee a few hours ago."

"Huh, that's good," she says. "Really funny."

"How long have you been doing this?" I ask, looking around the living room.

"Doing what?" she asks. "Fucking men for money or having nothing to show for it?"

"Both."

"Since I was thirteen."

"Jesus," I say.

"You almost look sorry for me." She lights up a cigarette, then offers me one again, and I am sorry for her, who wouldn't be? I shake my head at the proffered cigarette. "Life is what it is, right?" she says, the end of the cigarette catching her attention for a few seconds. "This may look bad, but others I've known have gone through worse."

There are pictures on the walls, prints of white tigers, posters of muscle cars and horses, a vase on top of the mantelpiece with a long-dead rose in it. The TV has buttons and dials to prove how old it is, and if I checked the back the serial number would probably only be two digits long. There are photographs of friends with blank looks, but there are other pictures too—her as a child, her face full of innocence, family or friends in the photos, her dad or uncle in them too, family snapshots of a normal looking family with normal looking smiles, and I wonder where they are now, what they did wrong for their daughter to want to take this path.

"You're wondering how?" she asks.

I turn back toward her.

"You're wondering how I became this way," she says.

"Yes."

"The universe fucked me," she tells me, "it fucked me for free. So ask me what you came to ask and let me finish my drink and get to bed."

I get the photograph of Brad Hayward out. It was taken two months ago. His wife has been cropped out of the picture. He's happy and that could be because he's had a good summer, or because he has a coupon card and he's nailed ten prostitutes and his eleventh one is free.

"You saw him last night."

"Yes."

"Have you seen him before?"

She shrugs. "They all look the same," she says. "What I remember more is whether or not they are a showerer. This guy—he didn't shower beforehand. Then again, nor did I," she says, holding eye contact with me.

"What time did you see him last night?" I ask, hoping she just sticks to the facts.

"I don't know. I don't keep a schedule."

"Did he seem like he knew what he was doing? Was he nervous? First-time user? Experienced?"

"I can't remember. All of that I guess. None of it. Whatever," she says, losing interest in the questions.

"It's important."

She takes a drink and swirls it around in her mouth for a few seconds before swallowing it. "It wasn't his first time with a hooker," she says, staring at the ice cubes. "I doubt it was his second or third either."

She sucks on the cigarette and blows the smoke into the cold air, where it hangs in front of her face and doesn't go anywhere, her face behind it like a mask. I get the feeling I could come back in an hour and that mask would still be there. I have the urge to shake her. Every few seconds or so when she blinks, her eyes seem to open a little less than the time before.

"Where do you work?"

"Normally corner of Manchester and Hereford."

"That's where you were last night?"

"Pretty much."

"And you got into his car. Where did he drive you?"

"About half a block away. There's an alleyway further up Hereford Street."

"That's where you normally go?"

"You have no idea what normal is in my kind of work," she says. "But yeah, the alley is a favorite spot. Driving is the last thing they're thinking about."

"How long were you with him?"

"I don't know. Why does all this matter?"

"It matters because somebody murdered him and it's my job to find out."

"And I should care?"

"Yes. People ought to care when somebody gets murdered."

She shrugs. "Whatever. I don't know. Five minutes. Maybe ten. I've told you everything I know. I'm tired."

I'm tired too. "Just another couple of questions. Two minutes and I'm gone."

She sighs, like I've just told her she has to help me move next weekend.

"Make it quick," she says.

"How long were you with him?" I ask again.

"Five minutes."

"You recognize any of these people?" I ask, and I show her photographs of the other three victims. They're all *before* shots—no need to traumatize any witnesses with photos of bloody corpses. I lay them out on the coffee table side by side.

"Nope."

"You want to take a closer look?"

"No."

"None of them were clients?"

"I don't do chicks."

"The other two?"

"I don't do men who look like they might die in the process. I don't need that kind of trouble."

I run their names by her and she keeps shaking her head. "I don't know. Maybe. Are they famous?"

"No," I say, scooping the pictures back up.

"The last one, isn't she a lawyer?"

I pause with my hand on the photographs. I slide the one of Victoria Brown back out and put it on the table. "You know her?"

"When was this photo taken?" she asks.

"Ten years ago," I say, the hint of a connection forming, a hint of excitement growing inside me.

"Jesus, I can't remember anything from ten years ago. I got into some trouble with some drugs three years ago, which I'm sure you know about and the fines are the reason I'm living in this shithole and not the slightly better shithole I used to live in. I think she was my lawyer."

My excitement fades. "She was in a coma three years ago."

"That'd explain the job she did."

"You must know her from somewhere else. Take another look," I say, tapping the picture.

"You said this was only going to take a few minutes."

"Please."

"I don't know," she says, and I'm losing her again.

"What about these other two men?" I ask. "This one, he was a lawyer too," I say, showing her the first photograph again.

"Never seen him," she says.

"You sure about that?"

"No, of course I'm not sure. I go out. I buy stuff. Clothes and food. Maybe I've walked past him in a supermarket or on the street. How the hell would I know?"

"And this one?" I ask, back to victim number two.

"I don't remember him."

"But you remember her," I say, pointing toward Victoria Brown. "She's been in a coma for seven years. It means you remember her from before then. You ever need a lawyer before that?"

"Needed one, sure, but could never afford one."

"This guy here wasn't your teacher?" I ask, pointing at Mc-Farlane.

"What? I don't know. I can't remember my teachers."

"He taught at Papanui High School, you go there?"

"Of course not. You must really think my parents hated me."

"You knew she was a lawyer," I say, tapping Victoria's picture again. "You have to know her from somewhere."

"Jesus, enough about the lawyer, okay? I don't know where I know her from." She yawns and makes no effort to cover her mouth, then finishes off her drink. "Maybe I saw her on TV. Maybe she had some big case that made the news. You think of that?"

It's a good point.

"You see anything suspicious?" I ask her. "Anybody follow you? Anybody watching?"

"What? When, last night?"

"Yes, last night. Or any other night."

She shrugs. "Nothing like that."

"What can you tell me about your other clients last night?"

"About as much as I told you about that one," she says, and nods toward the photograph of Hayward on the coffee table next to the other three. "You show me some photos and I can tell you who did and didn't shower, but that's about it."

I thank her for her time, scoop up the pictures, and replace them with my card.

"I thought you were a cop," she says, looking at the card.

"I am," I tell her. "But that's my number," I say, looking down at the card, which says I'm a private investigator.

"I don't get it," she says, and I get the idea there's a lot of things she doesn't get. Simple logic, for one. A maid, for another.

"Call me if you can think of anything, okay? We're trying to get a killer off the streets."

"And I'm trying to get through this," she says, holding up an almost empty bottle of vodka, "before going to bed and living the dream all over again in about nine hours."

I leave her to her drink and her dreams. I drive to the hospital hoping to still meet Schroder in time. Half of the parking lot has been shut down due to construction, the workers all on a coffee break and not one of them without a cigarette in his hand. It seems like some smokers do it just to have something to do with their hands in social situations. I park in a section for staff parking where they have dedicated a few spaces for the police department, right next to Schroder who is sitting in his car on the phone. He looks over at me and nods. A couple of doctors are standing outside and smoking, chatting to a nurse with long blond hair who looks like she just stepped off the set of porno. She keeps flicking her hair over her shoulder and laughing at everything they say, and I get the idea she would flutter her eyelids and laugh all through surgery too to keep their attention. I step past a dumpster with a biohazard sign on it, which might be full of needles or, just as equally, full of body parts. I have to sign in to get past a security guard with no neck who gives me directions to the only elevator in sight, and I wait for Schroder before stepping in.

"What's wrong?" I ask him, when he catches up, his face creased into a frown.

"Maybe I should drink more," he tells me. "That way I can get fired, and getting fired is probably the only thing that's going to stop my wife from leaving me. You know," he says, looking at me with a thoughtful look, "I'm always telling her things are going to get better, but then another case comes along and . . . and I'm gone. She said it's like being married to a ghost. And with the new baby . . . things are just stressed, that's all."

"I'm sure it'll be okay," I tell him, but the only thing I'm sure about is how lame that sounded.

"Yeah, well . . . fuck it," he says, and stabs at the button to take us down into the bowels of the hospital.

The one thing reliable in life is this—the feeling in a morgue always stays the same. People come and go—staff, medical examiners, cleaners, victims—and the equipment is updated ever so subtly over the years, probably handpicked out of catalogues brought to the hospital by sales reps. The atmosphere is one thing that can't be upgraded—it's bleak, it's depressing, every time you catch the elevator here you're taking a ride down to a well of misery.

The morgue is full of shiny surfaces that look cold, they reflect the harsh white light and make the sterile environment look even more sterile. There are gurneys with bodies lying on them—four of them I can identify, two more I can't, all of them with the same look on their faces.

Normally there are two medical examiners who work here, but the second, Sheldon, is away. His daughter is getting married in Fiji on a beach, so he's away with his family soaking up the sun and drinking cocktails and all of us, including the dead people in here, would much rather be with Sheldon than with Tracey, even though Tracey is the more attractive and lively of the two. Her current caseload has aged her since seeing her a few hours ago.

"Come on, guys, give me a chance," she says, not even looking up at us, she's so preoccupied with a file in her hands. "I know you're desperate, but unless you want to join these people," she says, nodding toward the victims, "you need to give me some time."

"Just your general impressions," Schroder says, trying to sound calming.

"Sure, my first impression is that I need to get paid more. Second impression is Sheldon chose the right week to go on holiday. And, if you like, I can do a really good impression of a really short-tempered medical examiner who snaps and attacks one police officer and one . . ." she looks at me, "just what the hell are you now anyway?"

"Your impression of a medical examiner going nuts would have to include two police officers," I say.

She looks at Schroder, and Schroder nods. "It's true," he says, then he reaches out and puts a hand on her arm. "Look, Tracey, I know we're asking a lot, and I wouldn't be here if it weren't important, but please, what do you have?"

Slowly she nods and for a moment there is a small smile. "Okay," she says, "this way," and we gather around the body of Victoria Brown. "First of all, you were right about the stab wounds," she says, looking at Schroder. "Nineteen exactly," she says. "Three of them into the same wound, each taking different angles beneath the surface. But our man over there has only the one," she says, nodding toward Brad Hayward, who doesn't react to the sound of his name.

"I can confirm the same knife was used on each victim," she says, "and that victim number two also has the same amount of wounds."

I feel a chill run up my spine. Three victims with nineteen wounds. That has to mean something.

"Victim number one was dying anyway—lung cancer had been toying with him for years," she confirms. "Victim number four wasn't dying, but she wasn't really living either. And like I said a few hours ago, there are indications victim number three had just had sex. And his wife should get tested," she adds. "For syphilis."

That's not a conversation that is going to go well.

She hands over an impression of the blade used to kill these people. She's isolated one of the wounds and poured thick liquid into it that's taken the shape of the wound and then hardened. It gives us the dimensions of the knife. It looks like a kitchen knife, something a chef would slice onions with, or something Hitchcock would put into the hands of a madman. Knowing what kind of weapon it is doesn't bring us any closer to knowing who's using it, especially when there's a million identical knives out there, but the nineteen stab wounds does. How it does, we don't know—not yet.

"I'll call you when I know more," she says.

Catching the elevator to the world above ground doesn't reverse the feeling of misery and depression I caught when catching it down, it just gives it more contrast. It always takes a few minutes to shake that bleakness away. Coffee break is over and we stand in the parking lot surrounded by the dust of construction and roadwork, construction workers yelling at each other over the pounding of equipment and engine noise. The doctors and nurse are off playing doctors and nurses. The day is bright and I yawn into my hand, go to say something to Schroder, then yawn again, this time into my other hand. I don't like to play favorites. Schroder starts to yawn too, then he reaches into his pocket and pulls out a small white cardboard box with *Wake-E* stenciled across it in orange letters.

"Caffeine tablets," he says, and chucks one into his mouth. "Want one?"

I do want one, but what I don't need is an addiction. Aside from the one to coffee . . . which is one I need to break anyway. I shake my head. We walk over to our cars. Schroder looks at the addition of the broken headlight on mine, seems about to mention how it just adds character, or some other joke, but can't come up with anything.

"Something happened to me last year," he says, "which could have ended me up in there," he says, nodding back toward the doors. "Down in the morgue. Not many people know about it. I mean, I had to get checked out by some doctors, but there wasn't any damage."

I want to ask him what kind of something, but I let him take his time.

"You think it's going to rain?" he asks, looking out at the clouds.

I shrug. "Maybe. Ariel Chancellor sure thought so."

"Yeah, I think it might too," he says, his thoughts still somewhere else.

"You wanna talk about it?"

"Not really," he says. "It was just before Christmas, back when I came to see you in jail to help me out with that Hunter case. I was in a house and a perp came up behind me. I thought he was going to shoot me. I thought the last thing I was going to see was my chest all over the bathroom wall. Anyway, he didn't shoot me, but he made Hunter push me into a bathtub full of water and keep me in there until I died."

"Jesus."

"Yeah, exactly. It gets worse too. The thing is, I did die. I was under that water and I was panicking and I'm thinking whoever the fuck said drowning is a peaceful way to die didn't die from it, didn't have his hands cuffed behind him and his head stuffed into a bath full of water. When you're sucking water in instead of air, it's the worst thing in the world. Every-thing burns. Everything goes dark. Then there's just nothing. Then I was just gone. Thing is, a few minutes later Hunter pulled me out of that bathtub. He breathed life back into me and pounded on my chest until I started coughing up water. I remember lying on the bathroom floor with no idea what in the hell was going on, I remember being pissed off that somebody had just done that to me, and I remember being scared because from the three or four minutes I was dead, I remember nothing at all. All this work we put into making the world a better place, I don't know . . . I mean, I don't re-ally believe in God, but I like to think that there is one, you know? And for four minutes I was closer to God than I've ever been and got nothing. So maybe my wife is right, maybe it's time I move on."

"You want me to argue with you? You want me to tell you what a loss that would be to the department? To the people of this city?"

"Not as big a loss as it would be the next time if there's no-body there to breathe life into me," he says.

"So what are you saying?"

He looks up at the sky, then wipes a hand over his face. "I'm not saying anything," he says. "I'm just tired, that's all. Tired and mad and just . . . just nothing. You nailed it with those nineteen stab wounds," he says, moving on, but he's wrong—it was Jonas who nailed it, not me, and we'd have known soon anyway; Tracey would have made the connection. How the hell did Jonas know? Even Tracey didn't know, so nobody tipped him off.

"Carl . . ."

"Look, Tate, I'm fine. Let's just focus on the case. How was your visit with Ariel Chancellor?"

"It was interesting," I tell him, then fill him in on the details.

"And she has no idea how she recognizes Victoria Brown?" Schroder asks when I'm done, talking loudly to be heard over a jackhammer that has just fired up.

"That's what I'm saying. She might have seen her on TV. We need to check if she had any high-profile cases. If she did, that could be how Chancellor knows her. If she did, maybe that high-profile case is related to what's going on. If she didn't, then Chancellor knows her in some other way. She was no help though, she was still high from something and drinking something and was remembering less the longer we talked. It's looking like she was just a random prostitute Hayward picked up on his way home and has nothing to do with what's going on."

"We'll have the warrant for Brown's caseload soon," Schroder says, "but I can already tell you we've checked the news archives and found nothing with her name in it. That doesn't mean she hasn't had a case in the news because more often than not the media focuses on the suspect and victims and rarely mention the name of the lawyer. We're in the process of checking court records but, like any government-run department, nobody has really heard of the word *efficient*. Between that and the law firm she worked for, we should have something by the end of the day, but it's frustrating—you'd think everybody would be wanting to work together to catch this bastard."

"I'll take another run at Chancellor later on today when she's fresher. How are the criminal records panning out?"

"Nobody recently released has been in jail for nineteen years," he says.

"What about nineteen months?"

"We have something there—the list is about a hundred names long for people who have been released this year alone. But jail may have nothing to do with it," he says.

"All of this is revenge motivated. Where's our guy been all these years? Why not kill these people a long time ago? Victoria Brown couldn't have pissed him off in the last seven years, so where's he been if not jail?"

"Hospital? Overseas? The army?"

"It's jail," I say, and Schroder nods.

"It's what I'm thinking too," he says. "He just hasn't been inside for nineteen years. It must mean something else. We'll go through all released prisoners from across the country in the last six months and start there, and if we get nothing, we'll work our way backward until we do."

CHAPTER TWENTY-THREE

I listen to the radio on the way back from the hospital. For the last few months the media and politicians have been discussing capital punishment. Some want it brought back—it was abolished in 1961, and there is certainly an argument for its return. Some are disgusted at the thought—they say it's murder, that it can never be justified. The debate comes and goes, always strongest during a murder investigation, strong support for each side—one of those debates where there is no middle ground, where everybody has an opinion. If they asked me, I could tell them it's a permanent way of keeping killers off the streets. It's actually the only way. The public is asking for a referendum—they want to be heard. But in this world the victims remain dead and the killers are set free and the people aren't listened to. I don't see that ever changing. Well, maybe, if the apes really do take over.

I stop in at a café and grab a coffee and a bagel. The woman behind the counter is in her mid-twenties and gives me a huge smile and asks how my day is going. I tell her it's going well and

I don't tell her about the bodies I just looked at or the fact that my day started nearly thirty hours ago. I ask her how her day is, and she tells me it's going great, but doesn't elaborate either, which, I hope, is for different reasons. The café is quiet down the back, and I make my way to one of the booths. There's a newspaper on the table, the Gran Reaper is the headline, but the thing with newspapers is they're out of date before the ink even dries. I turn the paper over so the headline doesn't have to stare at me, instead looking at the sports section where a woman in a bikini is about as thin as the surfboard she stands next to. Somebody has added a moustache and a penis in blue pen and a speech bubble with letters inside too roughly crafted to make out. I'd have thought they'd have added them to the woman and not the surfboard. I slide the paper to the opposite end of the table and take out my cell phone.

I call my wife's nursing home. It takes a minute for the receptionist to get Nurse Hamilton on the line.

"I know what you're thinking, Theo," she says, before I get the chance to even start telling her, "but she was only missing for five minutes and she hasn't hurt herself."

It turns out she doesn't know what I'm thinking. "What? Bridget is missing?"

"No, not *is*, but *was* . . ." she says, drawing out the *was* so it lasts a few seconds. "Isn't that why you're calling?"

"No," I say. "I was calling about last night, about how she kept going to the window."

"Oh, oh, I see. Well in—"

"What do you mean she was missing?"

"It was nothing, so don't panic yourself," she says, trying to sound casual, but I am starting to panic. "She just wandered off, that's all. She was perfectly safe the whole time."

"My wife is catatonic, and she's wandered off?" I say, and the woman who made the coffee looks over, her smile faltering. I lower my eyes and my voice. "How did she wander off?"

"She didn't wander far. But she did make it outside."

I struggle but manage to keep my voice down. "Outside? How the hell did she make it outside?"

"Please, Theo, calm down."

"I am calm," I say, staring at the surfboard's penis. I slide the paper even further away. "But I don't get how she made it outside."

"She made it outside because of what happened here last night," Nurse Hamilton says, her voice authoritative now. "Poor Victoria, her death hasn't been easy to deal with, Theo, not at all. You might be used to seeing that kind of thing, but I assure you, nobody here is. We're short three staff today, Theo, three people couldn't face coming back so soon and they probably won't be here tomorrow or the day after either. There are still police here asking questions, so yes, there are some cracks today that things can fall though but we have her, Theo, we have Bridget and she is unharmed and that's all that matters."

I close my eyes. I should be angry, but I'm not—Nurse Hamilton is right, and Nurse Hamilton isn't the kind of woman prepared to lose an argument. The fact Bridget is okay is all that matters. In fact, how can I be angry with the fact my wife somehow made her way outside?

"What was she doing?" I ask.

"She was doing nothing," she says, her tone less defensive now. "We found her outside staring at the garden pond, nothing more. We took her back inside, and she's in her room and we're keeping an eye on her."

"Was she looking at the pond? Or looking through it?"

"I know what you're asking, Theo, and no, she wasn't looking at it—the sun was reflecting so brightly off the water there's no way she could have seen a thing."

"I'm going to come and see her," I say.

"You can't afford to get your hopes up. It's not like this is the first time she's walked anywhere."

"I know," I tell her, rubbing at my head where there is a slight throbbing behind my right temple, "but like you say, it's the first time she's made her way outside. She went out there for a reason."

"No, Theo, it's the first time we've had a homicide here and been short staffed. That's how she got outside, and if we'd been short staffed in the past she probably would have gotten outside back then too."

"I'm going to call her doctor," I say. "I know you think it's a waste of time, but I'm thinking it couldn't hurt to have some tests done, you know?"

She says nothing for a few seconds, and I get the sense she's either nodding or shaking her head. "It can hurt," she says. "Not Bridget, but it can hurt you."

"If there's a chance . . ."

"I know, trust me, I know. My job is based around knowing. Every day I deal with patients like Bridget, and I deal with their husbands and wives and loved ones. I see the pain and the hope, the tragedy of it all, that's what my world is. Theo, you're in that world with me, and I'm telling you this as a friend who cares about you and as a nurse who's seen it all before, I'm telling you that you need to let go. You need to move on."

"I can't."

"I know," she says, "and that's what makes you *you*."

"I'm going to call her doctor," I tell her. "I want him to take another look at her."

"That's fine, Theo. I hope he finds something that can help, I really do."

I hang up and run my finger up and down the handle of the coffee cup, wondering if the path I'm about to take is going to rip open all the wounds from three years ago. I haven't moved on, but I have started to heal.

I ask the waitress if I can borrow a phone book, then sit back down in the booth. I find the number for the hospital and ask to be put through to Dr. Forster. It's been a long time since we've spoken. In the beginning I was in touch every day with more questions. I divided my time between looking for revenge on the man who did this to us, getting that revenge, and looking for answers on the Internet. Then I started calling him less, and then not at all.

My coffee has cooled enough that I can drink half of it within a few seconds. The call goes through to an answering machine. I leave my details and ask him to call me back hoping he will—I haven't spoken to him in over two years. I finish off my coffee and head back out onto the street.

When I get to the station I'm a little wired on caffeine while the entire fourth floor seems to be wired on methamphetamines. People acknowledge me as I walk through them, yesterday's comments at Landry's wake about how I was part of the problem and not part of the solution seem to have been forgotten. One detective is imitating playing a guitar as a few of them discuss getting together to play Xbox on Friday night, while another one plays air drums.

I find Schroder in the conference room staring up at the board. There are stacks and stacks of folders on the table next to him, at least a few hundred in total.

"Files of everybody released from prison this year," he says, putting his hand on them. "This pile here," he says, and he taps the pile at least twice the size of the second biggest, "are criminals with violent prosecutions behind them."

"You've started looking?"

"Yeah. I'm about one percent of the way through them," he tells me.

The thing with police work is it's hardly ever about speeding down a street somewhere to save a life, or pulling a gun on a suspect. It's about the mundane. Going over files. Taking and reading witness statements. It's about cross-referencing and making connections.

"That's a lot of files," I tell him.

"You want to be a cop again, right? This is part of the job. This is the life you've been desperate to get back."

Two other detectives walk into the room, each of them with coffee in their hands, making me crave some even though I fuelled up earlier. The four of us sit down and start going through them. We start making piles. We don't talk much. We just knuckle down and get the work done. The details are the same in many of them. Violent men with violent histories. Drug charges, rape charges, armed robbery charges, sprinkle in some murder too. No wonder the people of New Zealand want to be heard on their views of capital punishment.

"We need those damn lawyer files," I say.

"If the law firm could bill us for the time they'd be more helpful," Schroder says.

The piles we're forming are two possibilities. People it could be, people it certainly wouldn't be, but the problem is any of the men in these folders could kill if required. Nothing stands out. After an hour we're only a third of the way through and my pile of possibilities is the same as when I started.

"There's been another development," a detective says, stepping into the room, and it's Detective Watts, the man who had his face superglued to his desk by Landry. "We got a missing doctor," he tells us, directing most of the dialogue at Schroder. "A psychiatrist. Nicholas Stanton. Nanny showed up this morning and found signs of a struggle. Officers went down there and have just confirmed it looks like Stanton was attacked."

Schroder is no longer looking at Watts. He's looking at me, and we're both thinking the same thing. Then, to spell it out for us anyway, Watts carries on. "Two dead lawyers, an accountant, and a school teacher. Now a missing doctor. Could be related, right?"

Schroder keeps looking at me. Everybody in the room does. It's as if they're all waiting for my opinion before they react, but they're not. They're forming their own ideas on what this could mean.

"Nanny means children," I say. "How many?"

"Three," Watts tells us. "Stanton is separated from his wife, but he has full custody of the three children. The older two haven't shown up to school today. Daughters, aged eleven and eight. The one-year-old is normally looked after by the nanny."

"Let's go," Schroder says, standing up, and I follow.

CHAPTER TWENTY-FOUR

Caleb jerks awake in the car outside the slaughterhouse listening to the radio. Shit. He was only planning on closing his eyes for a few seconds, maybe five minutes at the most, but a quick look at his watch tells him he's been asleep in the driver's seat for three hours. The warmth from the sun combined with his exhaustion has knocked him out. He straightens up in the seat, his neck is sore from the angle he's slept on it. The midday news is on. There are many reports, except the reports don't have much detail. It seems the reporters don't know anything but that isn't stopping them from reporting it. He tries using the cell phone but the signal is too weak for the Internet to connect.

He steps out of the car and leans against it. The sun is still surrounded by blue sky, but it looks overcast toward town. The ground is still wet, but only in the shade. There are birds hanging about. He bends down and picks up a stone and starts throwing it up and catching it, not high, just to about the top of his head, over and over. The first time he came out here was fifteen years ago with James Whitby. People died that day. First there was the policeman. He didn't mean for that to happen. He knows that's why the cops told the inmates Caleb had raped and murdered his own daughter. It set him up for years of torture, and that made the cops happy and, in a way, he can't blame them for doing it.

Fifteen years ago. Christ, he can't believe it's really been that long. It's almost one-third of his life. His daughter has been dead for more years than she was alive. Can it really be that way?

Fifteen years. Crazy. There was still crime scene tape out here when he came that day. It was easy to find which room his daughter had died in. Just look for the blood. The entire place was so fucking cold he thought he'd lose his toes on the walk from the car to the doorway. He had a head start on the police but he was sure they would know who had taken Whitby, where he was going, just as he's sure that they'll come out here again once they realize who they're dealing with. It's all about symmetry. But he had to back then—there were rumors that Whitby was going to get away with what he had done because the confession had been beaten out of him—he couldn't allow that to happen. It was hard not to blame the police for that mistake, even though the police had beaten the confession out of Whitby in the hopes of finding Jessica alive. So Caleb had done their job for them.

James Whitby was unconscious in the backseat when he came here last. When Caleb closes his eyes he can still feel the moment, can remember the day. He can remember the long sleepless night earlier, holding his wife, the tears and the anger burning right through to a morning that didn't feel any better. The day started with rain washing at the snow. There had been no blue sky, no sun. He said goodbye to his wife and when he saw her again he had killed two men.

When he got to the slaughterhouse with Whitby, he didn't even turn off the engine. He was sure he only had a few minutes at the most before the police arrived, and he didn't want to waste them. It turned out he had longer. It turned out the police didn't figure it out until after they'd arrested him at home.

He dragged Whitby through the mushy snow into the building. He got him into the same room and laid him down in his daughter's blood and started slapping him until he woke up. Caleb tried to stay calm, he tried to ask why Whitby had hurt his little girl, but he did none of that. He couldn't control himself.

The cutting started right away. It didn't bring his daughter back, but it did stop other young girls from being killed. For that Caleb would spend fifteen years in jail. His wife would kill herself, she would kill their unborn baby, and for that James Whitby could no longer be punished.

He throws the stone toward the slaughterhouse, aiming for one of the few windows that has defied the odds by not being broken over the years, but misses—it hits the wall a few feet beneath it and bounces into the weeds.

It won't be dark for another five or six hours, and he doesn't want to risk carrying on his work until then. He'll go and see Ariel Chancellor. That's what he was going to do when he came out here earlier. He still doesn't know what he's going to say to her. Or do. First he'll go and see another psychic. Why not—he has all day to kill.

And speaking of killing—there is still the judge, there is still Mrs. Whitby, and then it's time to come back here. That's when the blood is really going to hit the floor.

Tonight at the slaughterhouse it's all going to come to an end.

CHAPTER TWENTY-FIVE

Town rushes past in a blur. Schroder's car has flashing lights built into the front and a siren that wails all the way to the doctor's house. Most people try getting out of the way for us, others get confused and come to a complete stop, blocking our path.

"What do you think?" he asks.

"What do psychiatrists and lawyers have in common?" I ask him.

"Other than overcharging?" he says, swerving at the wheel to avoid a car backing out of a driveway. "They can both end up dealing with very sick people."

"Exactly. What if our killer was a client, he blames his lawyer, he blames his shrink."

"Blames them for what?"

"I don't know. The same thing he blames his teacher, his accountant, and his divorce lawyer for. The same thing that put him in jail. His life has fallen apart and he feels these people are the reason why."

Stanton lives in a nice neighborhood, where friendly neighbors are all craning their necks to get a good look at the action. There are patrol cars blocking off the street and media vans clogging the traffic. There's a media helicopter circling and if we're lucky it might start raining reporters and cameramen. The house is a two-storey affair with a lush front lawn and manicured garden. There's a series of garden gnomes along the base of the house among the shrubs, some of them giving me a wink while others go about their work, one pushing a wheelbarrow, another holding a potted plant, another laying on his back with his eyes closed and a book on his stomach—probably the foreman.

The front door is wide open and there's a flurry of people moving around it. The fridge and pantry have been raided, tins and sachets of food have been knocked over and dropped on the floor. The doctor's car is gone. It's possible he's grabbed his children and gone on the run, but not likely because his wallet is still here. People don't go on the run without their wallets. There's a stroller in the corner of the living room. Why didn't he take it? There are drops of blood on the floor and plastic ties that have been done up and then cut. They all have evidence markers next to them, and a photographer is going from one to the next, taking shots. The girls' beds are unmade and their pajamas are dumped on the floor.

My phone rings and the caller ID displays the number I called earlier. It's Dr. Forster. I put the phone back into my pocket without answering it. This isn't a great time.

"Whoever did this took the doctor's car," I say, "which means maybe we're looking for two people, one to take the doctor's car, one to take the car they came in."

Schroder shakes his head. "There are other possibilities. Maybe our suspect took the girls with him and forced the doctor to follow in his own car, or maybe he walked here, or caught a taxi, or parked around the block. I'll get some officers to canvass the street. Knock on doors to see if there are any parked cars that don't belong," Schroder says.

"There has to be a name in his patient files common between these people."

"Stanton has an office in town. I'll get somebody working on
a warrant. Even if Stanton works alone we'll still need one. We
go breaking down doors and looking through patient files and
this is all a big misunderstanding, then the force will get sued
and you and me will lose our jobs. Even if it's not a misunderstanding, we're looking at the same result. Jesus, this could be
harder than getting a warrant for the law offices. These kind
of things . . . fuck, medical records for psychiatrists are always
a nightmare to get."

He makes a call and puts the nightmare into motion and
then we go through the study, hoping there may be patient
notes but there aren't. Stanton doesn't bring his work home
with him. There are photos of his family on the walls, but none
of them include the wife.

"You notice that?" I ask Schroder, pointing at the pictures.

"Yeah, can't have been a happy separation. If the nanny
doesn't know the details, some of the neighbors probably do.
Looks like the kind of street where people seem to know a lot.
Kent's talking to the nanny now."

The pictures of kids keep drawing my attention. Three girls
who right at this moment may be dead, or at the very least
scared half to death, only I'm only seeing pictures of two of the
girls. The younger one in the pictures has a big grin on her face
as if she's the happiest girl in the world. She must be around
six or seven in the photo. It must be Katy. I can feel the anger
building up inside of me. I want to find the man that took these
children and make him pay.

"You notice there are no photographs of the baby?" I ask
Schroder.

"Yep. Why do you think that is?"

I shrug. "Maybe he just hasn't gotten around to it," I say.

I check the message on my cell phone from Dr. Forster. He's
saying that he's returning my call and that he's with patients

for the rest of the afternoon, and at five o'clock he's going to go and visit my wife. I look at my watch. That gives me over four hours. He says he's spoken to Nurse Hamilton and they both understand my excitement, but tells me not to get my hopes up. He tells me that he hopes to see me there.

We keep looking around the house, but I can't focus, not fully, not when I keep thinking things may be changing with Bridget even though nobody else seems to think so. Forty minutes later Schroder gets the call. The warrant is ready.

Just when he hangs up Detective Kent approaches us. She smiles at us both, nods once, and says "I got some info. Nanny was pretty talkative. Erin Stanton walked out on her family six months ago. Just up and left. Apparently she was having problems with the baby. Was much worse than some of the usual postpartum stuff we hear about. Stanton tried prescribing her medication but she wouldn't take it. He tried getting her to talk to somebody else but she wasn't on board with the idea. She managed to find her own solution. It involved meeting some guy ten years her junior online and leaving this life behind. Stanton is still bitter about it. Nanny says she's never seen Stanton show one iota of warmth toward the little girl. She says he loves the other two kids, he'd do anything for them, but she says he looks at the baby the same way somebody would look at a pizza they weren't so sure they wanted. Nanny has been working here six months," Kent says. "She got hired a week after the wife walked out. She said the house was a mess. Says without a nanny this place would fall apart. Don't know if you've noticed, but there are no photographs of Octavia anywhere."

"Has anybody gotten hold of the wife or the boyfriend?" Schroder asks.

"Thought you'd want to do that," she says, and hands him her notepad. He jots down the number of the wife.

"And the boyfriend?"

"Nanny knows nothing about him, just that he's younger

and how they met. I'll speak to some friends and family and see what else I can learn."

"Okay, good job," he says, and Detective Kent smiles again at us both before heading back outside.

"What do you think?" he asks.

"I think you're a married man," I tell him, as we both watch her go.

"Huh. Good one, Theo. That's not what I meant and you know it."

I turn back toward him. "It's starting to look possible Stanton fled his house for a reason that doesn't extend to the other victims. No doubt he didn't leave on his own accord, but it may have something to do with the wife or the boyfriend."

"That's my thinking."

An officer comes inside, looks around and spots us, and comes over. He has a healing split lip and a fading black eye, which I guess he got from arresting somebody last week, or getting amorous with his wife when she wasn't in the mood. Or maybe when she was.

"We've found a car," he says. "Just down there," he adds, and nods toward the cordon where the media are growing in numbers. "Right in their midst."

"Doesn't belong to any of them?"

"According to the owner of the house it's parked outside, it's been there since he woke up this morning. He doesn't know who it belongs to. We've checked the neighboring houses. Nobody has seen it before. Plus, you look at this neighborhood, then you look at that car, and it doesn't line up. So we ran the plates—belongs to a guy named Donald Shrugs. He doesn't have a record and the car hasn't been reported stolen."

Donald Shrugs. Is that who we're looking for? A sense of excitement builds quickly as Schroder turns his attention to me.

"Look, Tate, could be nothing, could be that Donald Shrugs parked it there and is sitting inside another house on the block, or it's been stolen and he doesn't know, or Donald Shrugs is the man who took Stanton. Go check it out, then get it transported back to the department garage and get forensics onto it. Talk to the owner, but don't go alone. If Shrugs is our guy, then he has three missing little girls out there. I'll head to the doctor's office and get my hands on his files." He looks at his watch. "It's one o'clock now," he says, "should only take me ten minutes to get there. Stay in touch."

Schroder leaves the scene and I walk with the officer toward the abandoned car. He keeps glancing over at me with a weird look on his face. Either he knows my backstory or he wants to hold hands. He keeps licking at his split lip. Even though the city has clouded over, the temperature is still getting warmer. Ariel's prediction of rain tonight is looking way off. Somebody in the street or maybe in the next block over is cooking something on a barbecue, the smell of sizzling steaks and fried onions making my stomach rumble. The officer uses his radio and calls in for a truck. We're told it'll be here within thirty minutes. We have to pass through the media and they ask questions of us and we ignore them. Jonas Jones walks next to us for a few seconds, fishing for information before falling back into the crowd. We reach the car and I slow down. My heart starts to race a little.

"I've seen this car before," I tell the officer.

"It was parked here when you drove past earlier."

"No, no, it's not that," I say, shaking my head. "I didn't even notice it before, there were too many people in the way." I walk around it. It's a beaten-up Toyota older than my own. It looks exactly like the one I jump-started last night. I put on a pair of latex gloves and try the driver's door and it's unlocked. The keys are still hanging in the ignition. I turn them and the engine doesn't make a sound.

"Flat battery," the officer says.

"And whoever left it here doesn't need the keys anymore, including his house key," I say.

"If he has the keys, it's unlikely he stole it."

The man last night in the cemetery, is this who we're looking for? Was that Donald Shrugs? The beatings he took, are they why he is pissed off at the world? A couple of the journalists realize the car is of importance, and that realization spreads like a virus among them. Within seconds there are dozens of cameras in our faces.

"Get back, get back," the officer says, putting his hands in the air and showing them all his palm. "Get the hell back."

Other officers come down and start helping push the media back. A new perimeter is formed and it gives us room to take a better look at the vehicle. There's nothing on the dash or behind the seats, and the glove compartment has a map in it and nothing else. I check the ashtray and it's empty. There are dried blood spots on the passenger seat and plenty of them. They could have come from a weapon resting on it. Something like a knife. I look under the seats and find nothing.

The truck must have been in the area because it arrives within five minutes. A big burly guy in gray overalls steps out and walks around the car, taking a good look at it while he tugs at his handlebar moustache. He doesn't seem the kind of guy keen to make a lot of conversation. The flatbed is angled downward, turning into a ramp, and he winches the car onto it. Then the bed is flattened out and the car secured down with hooks and ratchet straps.

I call another of the officers over, a guy around my age who I've seen working most of the scenes so far. "Go with him," I tell him, and point toward the driver of the tow truck. "Make sure you keep an eye on that car."

"Yes sir," he says, and jumps into the cab of the truck.

"You got Shrugs's address?" I ask the first officer.

"Yep."

"Good," I tell him, "then let's go for a drive."

CHAPTER TWENTY-SIX

At one thirty me and Officer Split-Lip meet an armed response unit two blocks from the target. If Donald Shrugs kidnapped the doctor and his family, then he's a dangerous man. That's what the armed backup is for. It's to stop anybody from getting shot who doesn't deserve to be shot. They're just about to go in when Schroder calls.

"Got an update on Erin Stanton," he says. "She left her husband for a guy by the name of Brian West. He's a musician with a wife and a couple of kids that he walked out on roughly the same time. They moved to Australia two months ago so he could play in a band with a bunch of guys he used to know. They're there now and it's unlikely they're involved in any of this. No reason for them to be. They're flying in later today. Call me back once the team has gone in," he says, and hangs up.

The man leading the team is dressed in black and is wearing a bulletproof vest and seems a lot calmer than I would be if I were about to do his job. I hang back by the cars while the team moves forward. It only takes one minute for them to go through the house and give it an initial all-clear, then two more minutes to go through it again to make sure. I walk down to the house. It's a brick home around forty years old with a low iron roof and large windows. The driveway is lined with cracks that have weeds pushing through, except where oil stains have killed them. I walk through the house. Nothing out of the ordinary. It's a family home with ugly carpet but nice furniture. Some of the doors stick a little. There are toys on the floor and memos on the fridge. There are photographs on the walls and none of them contain the man from the cemetery.

I head into the lounge. There's a cordless phone lying on the armrest of the couch. It has a digital display on it. I scroll down the menu. One of them says *Mary's work,* and another says *Don's work.* I dial Don's work. It's picked up after four rings.

"Jeff speaking."

"Yeah, hi, Jeff, is Donald around?"

"Should be, hang on a second. . . ." He puts the phone down and I can hear footsteps, people talking, the noise of a photocopier nearby. A minute later Jeff comes back. The phone drags across the desk and is picked up. "Err, actually he's just left. Some kind of emergency."

"He's been there all day?"

"Yeah, why? Who is this?"

I figure the emergency Donald left for is this. I figure one of his neighbors called him at work and told him his house has been stormed into. "Detective Inspector Theodore Tate," I tell him. "I need you to give me Don's cell phone number."

"Oh, shit, has something happened? Is his family okay?"

"They're fine," I tell him, "but I need that number."

He gives me the number and I write it down, then realize it was probably in the phone's memory anyway. I hang up on Jeff while he's mid-sentence, dial the number, and a man answers on the second ring.

"Hello?"

"Donald Shrugs?"

"Is this the police?"

"It's Detective Theo—"

"Are you at my house?"

"Yes."

"What are you doing there? You broke in? Who the hell gave you the right to break in?"

"Calm down, sir."

"Calm down? You calm the fuck down. I'm on my way there right now and I've already called my lawyer. You are in so much fucking trouble, man."

"Listen, sir, you need to calm down or you're going to make things worse."

"Fuck you," he says, and he hangs up.

I head outside. I stand by the patrol cars and wait. Five minutes later a car comes speeding down the street. It stops at the cars and the door flies open and at least six officers point their guns at him and his body seems to make six different sounds, among them a high-pitched whine that comes from this throat. The anger drops out of him and he takes a step back.

"Down on the ground now," one of the men yells at him, and that's exactly what he does. Another man handcuffs him, then they drag him up. Somebody reaches into his back pocket and pulls out a wallet. He flicks it open and pulls out the driver's license and hands it to me.

"I told you to calm down, Donald," I say, looking from the license up to Donald and Donald isn't who I helped last night. Instead Donald is an overweight guy in his late forties with a shaved head and a diamond earring in his right ear and a nose that is one size too small to fit his features.

"What are you doing in my house?"

"You own a Toyota Corolla?" I ask him.

"You have no right!" he yells, the anger coming back now that the guns have been lowered.

"The car, Donald."

"What? No, no, I . . ." then he stops. He's figuring something out.

"What?"

"Shit," he says. "Listen, it's not me," he says. "Whatever you think I did, I didn't do. I sold that car three days ago. It was an old backup car and we didn't need it anymore. I put an ad in the paper and some guy came around and bought it. The paperwork is still being filed, man, but I don't own that car anymore. I promise you."

"You get a name from him? Any ID?"

"Just a name. James somebody. I can't remember exactly. But I filed the papers. It'll be on record."

"What did James look like?"

"What? Jesus, I don't know. Scary looking, I guess."

"Scary how?"

Suddenly he becomes animated again. He's eager to help, eager to get out of the handcuffs. "Oh, shit, real scary. He looked like he'd been beaten up really badly, and lots too. I didn't even want to get into the car with him for the test drive."

"How'd he pay?"

"Cash. It was only five hundred bucks," he says, talking quickly.

"Uncuff him," I say, turning toward one of the officers. "Don't suppose you still have any of the money?"

"Why?"

"So we can fingerprint it."

"No. It's all gone. Five hundred bucks doesn't last long."

He's got that right.

An officer uncuffs him and he starts rubbing at his wrists. "What did this guy do anyway?" he asks. "Kill somebody?"

"Thanks for your time, Donald," I say to him, and leave him leaning against his car. I can hear him complaining to anybody who's listening, which doesn't seem to be anybody, so he just talks louder. I find the officer I got a lift with and convince him to let me use his car, telling him he can get a lift back to the station with somebody else. He doesn't seem that happy about it but doesn't put up an argument.

I call Schroder. I tuck the phone between my shoulder and ear and drive carefully around the blockade that's slowly being disassembled. Media vans are approaching for what for them is going to be a nonevent.

"There are hundreds of files here," Schroder says, "any one of them could be relevant."

"Shrugs said he sold the car to a man named James. Apparently James hasn't filed his ownership papers," I say. Both buyer and seller must complete ownership forms whenever a car is sold privately. "Shrugs filed his. That'll give us a last name, assuming he used his real name, which is doubtful."

"I'll make the call."

"No files with the name James?"

"I'll check, but it's probably not even the guy's real name. The car has arrived back at the station. Apparently it's been wiped clean. No prints anywhere on it."

"Shit. There must be."

"Well, there aren't."

"Wait, wait, hang on a second. Check under the hood."

"What?"

I tell him about helping the driver jump-start his car. "There might be prints around the battery, or at least there should be something around the latch."

"I'll get it done. Where are you heading?"

"Back to the station," I tell him, "but first I'm going to go and get our suspect's real name."

CHAPTER TWENTY-SEVEN

Over the last year I feel like I've spent more time at the cemetery than I have anywhere else. There's always something here pulling me back, it happens so often they should reserve a parking space for me. The second of the four men I've killed died out here by accident. I buried him and nobody knows about it except him, me, and the God both him and me stopped believing in. The third guy I killed was out here too, only that wasn't so much an accident. Both men were killers. My priest was haunted by one of those men in real life, then murdered by the other. My priest so far is the only man to have died out here that I didn't kill, though the police for a while blamed me for it. The pope ought to give me a medal.

There are no cars in the parking lot. No signs of any life. The gardens have a little less color than yesterday, the trees holding onto a few less leaves; many of those that have fallen are lying on the stone stairs to the church, many of them bunched up in the doorway. A few of them follow me inside. Father Jacob is practicing a sermon. He acknowledges me with a nod, but keeps practicing anyway. I guess it's like being a stand-up comic—it's all in the delivery. I walk down to the front and it's not until I reach him that he stops.

"Theo," he says, and he steps down from behind the podium and offers his hand. It's cold. He smells faintly of cigarette smoke. "What can I help you with? You here to lighten the load?"

"Load?"

"When was your last confession?" he asks, his eyes flicking to the confessional booths off to the side.

"I have nothing to confess," I tell him, which is a complete lie, and one that I'm not going to confess about.

"Everybody has something to confess."

"Even you, Father?"

He smiles. "Shall we sit down?" he asks, sweeping his hand toward the front pew.

"I'm sorry, but I'm in a hurry."

"Too much of a hurry to sit down, huh? Well, then tell me, what can I do for you?"

"I'm looking for a man. I saw him here last night, and he may come other nights too. I think he can help with our investigation."

"Lots of men come here," he says, his smile disappearing, being replaced by a frown, "and anything they tell me is confidential, you as much as anybody must know that, Theo."

"Don't worry, I'm not heading down that path. I just want you to tell me if you know him."

"Hmm, I don't know. It sounds like we're on the border of priest-parishioner confidentiality."

"Like I said, I'm not asking if he confessed anything. But it's important. Three small girls were abducted last night and we believe he's the man who took them."

"Oh, oh, that is bad," he says, which is as good a summation as any. "What's his name?"

"I'm not sure. James, maybe."

"Is that it?"

"He was here late last night."

"I was asleep late last night," Father Jacob tells me.

"He's about six foot, weights around a hundred ninety points, around fifty years old . . ."

"It's not helping," Jacob says.

"He has scars on his face. Old scars, like he's been beaten up severely."

Father Jacob exhales loudly, then pinches the bridge of his nose with his fingers. He brings his elbow to his stomach while holding the pose and looks down. When he talks, he's talking toward the palm of his hand. "I'm not technically breaking my word to him or God by telling you this," he says, "but yes, there is a man who comes here some nights who fits that description." He looks back up at me and removes his hand. "I had to help him find his wife what, five or six weeks ago," he says. "She died fifteen years ago and he said he'd never been to see her grave. It was strange. Very . . . strange."

"Fifteen years ago?"

"Yes."

"Not nineteen?"

He shrugs. "I guess it could have been. My memory isn't as sharp as it used to be, but I think he said fifteen. There was a child too. His daughter. He didn't mention her, but I saw the grave."

"Jesus," I say, then, "sorry—that just slipped out."

Jacob nods. "The dates were a few days apart. The daughter died, then the wife. I remember that, but can't remember the dates. Maybe they were a week apart."

"Can you remember the names?"

His face scrunches up as he fights to remember. "I wish I could, but no. I'm very sorry."

"But you helped him find his wife. You saw their graves. You can take me there?"

"Yes, that I can certainly do."

I follow him out the rear entrance of the church and into the cemetery. Other than the dead, the grounds are deserted. The trees more than yesterday resemble the bodies in the ground, skeletons without life. We walk through a pathway that twists between some big oak trees before hitting the first row of graves. We head deeper into them. I'm starting to build up a sweat. The last of the summer insects start biting at my arms, trying to store enough blood in their tiny bodies to get through the days ahead. The clouds are getting thinner, suggesting there may be some more sunlight today after all.

"I understand your daughter is out here too," Father Jacob says.

I'm not sure how to respond, so I keep walking.

"It's the hardest thing in the world to lose a child," he says.

"There's a man who's about to lose three if we don't hurry," I tell him, and we break into a jog, row after row of the dead beneath us, and two minutes later when we reach the graves I'm out of breath and the back of my shirt is damp. Jacob, who's at least twenty years older than me, is puffing nowhere near as much.

"This is them," Jacob says, stopping in front of two graves that look like any other. Only they're not like any other.

"Jesus," I say.

"Theo," the priest says, giving me a bad look.

There are no flowers in front of them and the grass needs to be clipped around the base of the headstones. I read the inscriptions on the graves. Next to them is an empty plot, probably reserved for the husband and father.

Reserved for Caleb Cole.

It all makes sense now.

All that blood from fifteen years ago . . .

I start running.

"Who are they?" Father Jacob calls out.

I don't answer him because he's already thirty feet behind me, with more distance gaining every second as I race back across the graveyard, my feet pounding over the ground, over the edges of other people's graves. I pull out my cell phone to call Schroder, but before I can dial it rings anyway, Schroder on the other end.

"I got something," he says, and he sounds excited.

"So do I," I tell him. "Caleb Cole," I tell him, and it's all rushing back to me in detail. I remember standing in the snow, my feet freezing cold, Schroder was there too, so was Landry, so was a small dead girl sprawled out and covered in blood on the concrete floor. It's all so clear that for a moment my blood runs the same temperature it felt back that day. There are good places to die and bad places to die, and the slaughterhouse was about as bad as it got. I remember the fear we were going to lose a conviction because the suspect had been beaten by a detective using a phone book.

"I know," Schroder says.

"What?"

"The nineteen stab wounds. I just got off the phone with the ME. She ran a check. I mean, shit, we should have thought of it, right? But none of us did. Except her. We were looking for a connection to the past, right? So she looks for other victims that have come through the morgue with nineteen stab wounds, thinking there may have been something current, but what she got instead were two names from fifteen years ago."

I have to slow down so I can talk. "Jessica Cole," I say. "Was she one of them?"

"Yes. And the other was James Whitby. I'm still at Stanton's office," Schroder says. "Wait a moment," he says, and the phone thuds in my ear as he puts it down on a solid surface. I can hear a large filing drawer being opened. He's flicking through folders, his fingers sliding over the names. I can hear him talking to himself, he's saying "come on, come on, where are you . . . ," then a "yes!"

"Got it," he says, coming back on the line.

"Let me guess—you just pulled a file for James Whitby?"

"Bingo," he says. "Whitby was a patient of Stanton's."

"And Cole blames him?"

"Hang on, give me a second," he says, and I picture him leaning over the file, reading it. "Shit," he says. "Stanton was the doctor at Whitby's trial two years before Jessica Cole was murdered," he says, and I remember it clearly. James Whitby had abducted a young girl by the name of Tabitha Jenkins. He kept her for two days until he was caught. He went to trial. He was found not guilty because he was insane. He was confined for two years to a mental institution.

"What was Stanton's role?"

"He testified that they could help Whitby, that it wasn't his fault, but a result of an abusive upbringing."

Other people have arrived since I showed up, and some stare at me as I jog past them. I have sweat dripping off my forehead, and they look behind me to see what is chasing me, but all that's back there are two graves that have unlocked the mystery as to what the fuck is going on.

"So Cole blames Stanton," I say, because within a week of Whitby being released, he killed Jessica Cole. "What about the others?"

"I don't know, but they must be involved in similar ways," Schroder says. "One of them might have been Whitby's lawyer. Just wait where you are. You might be closer than I am."

"Closer to what?"

"Just wait. I'll call you back."

He hangs up on me. I'm at the car now. I have the urge to speed somewhere but I don't know where. I tap my fingers against the roof. I've left Father Jacob somewhere far in the distance. I stare at my cell phone and wait for it to ring. I start talking to it, saying *come on* over and over.

For four minutes the mantra fails, but by the fifth one it works. I figure that's worth knowing for the future.

"Caleb Cole was released from prison six weeks ago," Schroder says. "I've just spoken to his probation officer. Cole's been keeping all the appointments. Even got a job at the big tire factory in Brighton. We placed a call there but . . ."

"Hang on, hang on," I say. "Six weeks ago?"

"Yeah. He didn't show up for work today. I've got his address. I want you to check it out. Armed officers will meet you there. Okay? I'm at least twenty minutes away," he says, and he gives me the address. I write it down.

"Okay. But if it was six weeks ago he was released, how come we didn't come up with his name when we were going through the prison records?"

"Jesus, Tate, I don't know, it's not important," he says, "just do your Goddamn job."

"Uh, yes sir," I tell him.

"I didn't mean—"

"It's fine," I tell him. "And it's going to take me ten minutes to get there."

"Make it five," he says. "You've got sirens, so go ahead and use them."

CHAPTER TWENTY-EIGHT

Psychic number five is the same as the other psychics, as if the first four had their personalities blended up and poured into this fifty-something-year-old Asian woman with a receding hairline and a chin home to four good-sized moles, each of which is home to at least one good-sized hair, the longest of which—the length of a baby's arm—she must be keeping for luck. She senses dead people and can tell your destiny, and her husband gives tarot card readings too for an extra forty dollars. She doesn't put on a show like some of the others. Instead they sit at her kitchen table while she sips Asian tea with Asian prints on the walls full of Asian symbols that mean nothing to him. The incense burning on the windowsills is making his nose itch. She looks at his palms and tells him that she isn't a palm reader, takes her hands in his, and, like dial-up modems before he went away, she makes strange noises as she makes a long-distance connection.

"You've lost somebody," she tells him, when she's logged into the afterlife and, unlike dial-up modems, she makes the connection on the first try. "Somebody you care about."

When it's over he feels betrayed again, another hack taking his money from him, and most of all he feels annoyed at himself for putting himself through it. For some reason he thought her being Asian would have made it more real, more spiritual, and it makes the disappointment harder. He's running out of chances to talk to his family.

He doesn't thank her for her time. He pushes himself away from the table when she tells him his wife forgives him. He throws the money down and declines her offer of the tarot card reading.

Caleb is passing the living room when he sees his car on the TV. He sees it, and has taken two more steps before it registers with him. He comes to a stop and moves back to the doorway. The husband is on the couch with two golf ball—sized crystal balls in his hand, using his fingers to circle them around each other. He looks up and nods at Caleb but doesn't say anything, and Caleb watches as the reporter tells them Dr. Stanton and his children have been reported missing. She tells them there have been signs of a struggle and blood found at the scene. A car found on the same street has drawn the interest of the police, and they show the car again, and then they show it being loaded onto the back of a truck.

He figured they would discover Stanton was missing today. He figured there was a chance they would find his car—he just didn't think it was likely. Not so soon anyway.

It changes everything.

The woman follows him to the door, trying to sell him the idea of another appointment, saying she can give him a discount if he comes back. He keeps his back to her and walks quickly to the doctor's car, and she stops following him at the end of the footpath. He's suddenly aware that soon, if not already, a description of the doctor's car will be all over the news, along with the license plate. Can the psychic see it? He turns back toward her, but she's already making her way back inside.

His own car, he wiped it down last night. If there's any trace of him the police will find it. Same goes for the house—he wiped down any of the surfaces he touched. DNA can take weeks, he isn't worried about that, but fingerprints are quick. If they find his prints they will have his name within hours.

They won't find them. He was careful.

Damn it, why couldn't he have focused more last night? If he had, he could have gotten it all done. The cops could have found all the fingerprints they wanted because it all would have been over by now.

If they do get a print, and he doubts they'll find one, and get his name, the first thing they'll do is talk to his probation officer and get his address. They'll see he has gone, they'll call in at his work, then they'll come to the slaughterhouse. With the doctor and kids missing, they'll probably try the slaughterhouse first. All because of a stupid car battery. Why the fuck couldn't the psychics have seen that one coming?

The car battery. Ah, damn it! Last night, he'd have put his hands all over the front of the car when he was jump-starting it. Would the police fingerprint that area? No, he doesn't see why they would. Surely they'd check only the steering wheel and doors, parts of the interior. Maybe the gas cap too.

He has to think worst-case scenario. He has to imagine the police will know soon who he is.

New plan.

It takes him twenty minutes to get back to the slaughterhouse. The first half of the journey he has to stick to the speed limit, but once he hits the open roads he puts his foot down. The doctor and two of the kids look scared. As well they should. Octavia has fallen asleep. First thing he does is put a piece of duct tape over Stanton's mouth to shut him up. There is no time to mess around. No time to be polite.

"Drink this while I tell you all a story," Caleb says, handing Melanie a glass of cola.

"I'm not thirsty."

"You might not get another chance for a while," he tells her.

"I don't want it."

"Do you want me to hurt one of your sisters instead?" he asks, and points at Katy. Katy, upon being pointed at, starts to sing her version of the alphabet again.

Melanie sips at the drink. "It tastes funny."

"Melanie, I'm not fucking around here," he says, desperate to get this done. "If you don't carry on drinking it, I swear I'm going to start hurting people."

Melanie holds in her tears and starts drinking.

"That's good," he tells her. "You're doing good. Now, this story," he carries on, "it's about a little girl named Tabitha. One day this bad man saw her and he thought she was so cute that he wanted to hurt her."

Katy stops singing. She's focusing on what he's saying, and slowly she shakes her head. "That doesn't make sense."

"No, it doesn't," Caleb agrees, looking over at Dr. Stanton, "but sometimes in life that's just the way it is. The bad man's name was James and he began to follow her. Every day after school Tabitha would walk home, and this bad man, this James, he would be there. He knew where she lived. He knew which direction she took."

The girls are staring at him with big eyes, holding back tears and faces full of concentration. And fear—there's a good amount of fear in their faces too. And confusion.

"He knew everything about her. He had even broken in to her mom and dad's house and spent time in her bedroom, going through all of her things, looking at the pictures on the wall she had drawn, looking at her clothes. He was so obsessed by her that he would steal her underwear and store it under his mattress."

"That's gross," Melanie says.

"Why would he do that?" Katy asks, and both girls are scared but engaged.

"Because James wasn't like other people," he says. "He stopped Tabitha on the way home from school one day. He was on the sidewalk by a park calling for his puppy, only there was no puppy, but Tabitha didn't know that. He called and called and then he saw her, and he asked her, "Have you seen my puppy?" She hadn't, but she wanted to help. So she went into the park with him, and he took her across the other side, through the trees, and out the other side where his van was waiting. He took her home, and for two days he hurt her over and over while the police and her family looked for her."

"What did he do to her?" Melanie asks.

"He hurt her," Caleb says.

"But how?" Katy asks.

"That part of the story you don't need to know," he says, "but when he was done, he didn't know what to do, and he didn't want her telling people about all the things he had done to her, so he took a knife," he says, then holds up his, "that looked just like this."

The doctor starts murmuring against the tape, and Caleb can see him squirming against his bindings. All eyes in the room are on the knife, except Octavia, who is snoring softly.

"He was getting ready to kill her," he says, carrying on, "when the police knocked on his door. Somebody had seen a van in the area. The police were doing a routine check on people with that model van. They came to talk to him expecting nothing, but had known straight away there was something wrong. They forced their way inside and found Tabitha. If they had come to his house a minute later she would have died."

Melanie has almost finished her drink. Both girls are crying.

"Here," he says, and he takes the glass from her. He fills it up and hands it to Katy. She slowly sips at it, finding it difficult because she can't stop crying. The doctor is still squirming on the floor, perhaps this story giving him an idea of where things are heading. He isn't covering any ground and his face is almost purple. Melanie is slowly becoming tired.

"Your daddy knew what the bad man had done," Caleb says, still staring at Stanton, "and yet not long after that they became friends. Your daddy said all these good things about James, how it wasn't James's fault, how he was sick, how he wasn't able to control himself. Your daddy spent one hour with him, he got to know him so well that he told the world that what James needed was help, not punishment, because what James had was a sickness, a sickness brought about by his own upbringing. Your daddy took all that blame from James and he put it all elsewhere. He told the lawyers and the judge and the jury that it was James's mother's fault, that it was the school system's fault, how it was everybody else's fault except James's. They all listened and agreed because your daddy was very convincing. What James had could be cured, your dad said, if he was given enough care and understanding. So, instead of putting him in jail, he went into a hospital called Grover Hills, where people who didn't think properly were looked after. He was in Grover Hills for two years, and then your daddy said that James was all better, that James could be a productive member of society."

Melanie's eyes are heavy. She's yawning and struggling to stay awake. Katy isn't far behind. How long does he have?

"So your dad let James go, and they got him a flat in town where he would live alone, under the condition that once a week he had to go and see your daddy.

"The thing is, girls, your daddy shouldn't have made friends with such a bad man, nobody ever should, because that man wasn't cured at all. Within a week of being released he did the same thing to my daughter that he did to Tabitha, only the police didn't know where to look because James brought her here," he tells them, and he spreads his arms in a gesture that shows *here* is this room, that *here* is this entire building. "He kept Jessica here—that's her name, by the way, he kept her here and hurt her and the police knew who they were looking for but they didn't know where to look, and when they did know it was too late. When he was finished with Jessica he took a knife like this one," he says, moving the knife so each of them can get a good look at it, "and he stabbed her nineteen times," he tells them, "and her life and all her blood and everything she ever would have become seeped out onto the very floor you're resting on."

Melanie is asleep. Katy's chin is dipping down to her chest. It's hard telling the story—it's making Caleb feel sick. For fifteen years he's visualized the moment his daughter died. He's visualized the six hours of hell before it, the abduction, the fear. Every topic leads his mind to his daughter somehow. Everything he sees or hears can be linked back to Jessica in only a few steps. It's like seven degrees of separation. At dinner he'll see a knife and think about his daughter. He'll see a child on TV or in the street. He'll see an ad in the newspaper for children's clothes. Eating steak makes him think about the slaughterhouse. The cold weather, policemen, TV shows, speeding cars, abusive old women—they're all just a step away from visualizing this nightmare. There is no off switch. His daughter lying naked and dead on the floor, even though he never saw it, is an image he can't shake. The last thing she ever saw—he can't shake that either.

"And your daddy," his voice lower now, "he could have stopped that from happening. He was the one who told everybody James could be cured. He's the reason my little girl was killed. It wasn't just my daughter who died. My wife was so sad at what happened that she died too, and so did our baby boy who was so tiny he was still inside her. Your daddy took my family away, and that's the reason," he says, looking over at the doctor, "I have to do the same thing to him that happened to me."

The glass falls out of Katy's hand and smashes on the ground. Stanton reacts to it, and Octavia wakes up. Melanie and Katy stay asleep. Octavia looks at her father, then at her sisters, smiles, then frowns, then cries.

"There's been a development," he says, looking over at the doctor. "The police know you're missing, and soon they're going to figure out it's me who has you. I wanted to finish things out here tonight, but there's no time for that now. So the plan has to change. Instead four of us are going to go for a ride."

The doctor is struggling against the plastic ties, his face still purple. Octavia's cries are getting louder. And more annoying. He looks at her and her face is scrunched into an evil little grimace, her eyes closed tightly and her mouth puckered open. She inhales deeply, then lets out an even louder cry.

"It's okay, your daughters are okay," Caleb tells Stanton, having to talk loudly over the baby. "Now I know I told you earlier I was going to kill your family, and that hasn't changed. I'm going to assume your addition is better than your diagnosis, so when I said the four of us are going for a ride you know that means somebody has to stay. We're going to cull the group a little. I'm the driver and the man looking for revenge, so I'm essential. You're essential too. The girls, well . . . Goddamn it," he says, Octavia, breaking his train of thought. "Shut up, will you just shut up?"

She gets louder. He unstraps her from her seat and checks her diaper. It's wet. She's probably hungry too. He bounces her up and down and her crying only gets louder.

"Sssush," he tells her, rocking her gently. "If you don't stop crying, I'm going to have to wrap duct tape all around your face," he says, knowing she doesn't understand him, and knowing he wouldn't need to use that much tape. "Come on, Octavia, shush now."

She hiccups then throws up on his shoulder, then starts wailing again. He puts her back into her seat and straps her in, then carries the seat outside. He rests her in the sun and walks back into the office. He uses a wipe to clean his shirt and carries on talking to Stanton.

"Only two of your daughters are essential, and to me each of your daughters holds the same value. The question is, what value are they to you? One can stay here, and two can come with us. It's your decision. Oh, and I should add, the one who stays behind—she has to die."

One of the girls gasps from behind him. He turns to look at them. They're both still sleeping. At least he thinks they are. Maybe one is having a bad dream. He crouches down and rocks them. Maybe one of them is faking.

"Are you awake?" he asks Katy, then he asks the same of Melanie. "If you're faking, now is the time to tell me. If I find out you're awake I'm going to hurt you."

Nothing. Well, if one of them is faking he'll know in a few minutes' time, that's for sure.

He turns back to Stanton.

"I promise you, the one who stays won't feel a thing. And the others won't even know who you picked. None of them have to know you were picking favorites.

"So, Doctor, who's staying and who's coming? I'm not an unfair man," he says, and he can still hear the baby screaming outside. "I'll give you two minutes to decide. You don't have an answer for me in two minutes, I start cutting off Katy's fingers until you do," he says, and Stanton's grunts get louder, the veins are standing out on his forehead as he struggles to break free. He sounds like he's choking on his tongue. "Somehow I don't think you'll let me get through all those fingers, because if I do then I start on Melanie. Then I go to work on their feet, and by the time you finally make a decision there won't be anything that I haven't cut off. It's going to happen, Stanton, it's going to happen no matter what," he says, his voice calm and steady, and for a moment the doctor stops struggling as all the color drains out of him, no doubt his mind filling with images of what's to come over the next few minutes. He looks up at Caleb, his eyes pleading for him to stop all of this. Caleb reaches down and grabs the duct tape, ready to pull it away. "I'm a runaway train you can't stop, Stanton—all you can do is push some of your family out of the way. Save your daughters some pain, save yourself from having to see what a pile of fingers and limbs looks like bleeding all over the floor because it's not going to be pretty. Don't waste time on thinking you can save them all because you can't. You really, really can't. You've got a big decision to make. Two minutes to decide which one of your daughters doesn't get to walk out of here alive, that's all you have, Doctor, because the train has already left the station."

CHAPTER TWENTY-NINE

The address the probation officer gave Schroder for Caleb Cole takes me into a part of town where the streets are full of potholes and cracked sidewalks. It's three-thirty and I have an hour and a half before meeting Dr. Forster. I swing the car around a dead dog and then another dead dog a block later; maybe they're throwing themselves into traffic like lemmings to escape. I'm the first one to arrive, and since I'm in a patrol car, I stop at the end of the block. I don't imagine Cole is home, but I hang back because sometimes your imagination can get you into trouble. A few minutes later Detective Kent arrives, and a minute after her comes the Armed Offenders Unit. It's the same unit as before. They probably made it back to the station earlier and got told to hang around because things were getting interesting. They start planning their entry. They choose one of the scenarios they've practiced time and time again, one that involves a complicated unknown—they're dealing with a man who may have three children and their father hostage in there. They seem disappointed they didn't get to shoot anybody earlier, and seem hopeful things will be different this time.

"What do you think?" Detective Kent asks. "You want to bet that he's not in there?"

I think of Cole's keys hanging in the car he bought. "We'd both be betting on the same thing."

Cole lives in a big house that's a good sixty years old, which has been divided into four homes. You couldn't throw a stone in this neighborhood and not hit somebody who's done time in prison. This is one of those areas where ex-cons are billeted upon their release, the kind of area you want to avoid unless you've got tactical training, a rap sheet, or a very big gun. The armed officers split up to take different entrances. By the time the media vans appear, which is only two minutes later, the scene has already been cleared.

People are walking out onto their front yards to take a look around. They're giving the unit grief, telling us all to fuck off and die. A few of them I recognize from prison, a few from my time back on the force. I head into Cole's home with Detective Kent. The door has been kicked in, the latch is hanging from the frame surrounded by toothpick-sized splinters. There isn't much inside. A kitchen table. A worn couch.

"This place is like screwing the ugliest hooker in town," the man commanding the unit tells me. "It only took a few minutes to get the job done and it's going to take an hour to scrub away the feeling of being inside."

"He's right," Kent says once he's walked off. "He wrapped it up in a lot of charm, but it does feel that way."

There are kitchen drawers but nothing else, except a pile of empty pizza boxes on the kitchen bench. No bedroom drawers. Not much in the way of cabinets.

"Hard to believe people live like this," Kent says.

"I've seen much worse than this."

"I've seen worse too," she says, "but it's still hard making sense of it."

I check the manhole in the ceiling while Kent checks the manhole in the floor. I finish first and find her crawling out from beneath the floor in the bedroom, her hands and knees caked in dirt. She wipes her hands on the sides of her jeans.

"Nothing?" I ask.

"Just a sore neck. You?"

"Sore shoulders," I tell her.

"Maybe we should hire a masseuse to follow us around," she says. "Listen, I was wondering, when this is over if you wanted to . . ." she starts, but then my cell phone rings.

I grab it out of my pocket and give her the chance to finish what she was saying, but instead she nods and says "You should get that."

It's Schroder, just as I knew it would be because Schroder is the only person who ever calls. I update him while Kent wanders into the kitchen. I watch her check the fridge and behind it. There's nothing here. Cole has gone and he's not coming back, and there's no reason for him to have hidden anything. I tell Schroder as much and ask him to put a couple of officers in the house on the off chance Cole does return. Because of the reception the neighbors gave us, I tell Schroder that the people he sends need to be armed.

"What were you saying a moment ago?" I ask Detective Kent when I get off the phone.

She smiles at me and slowly shakes her head. "Nothing important," she says. "We might as well head back."

When we get back Schroder has run off copies of James Whitby's criminal record, along with his psychiatric record. I sit in the conference room reading it while Schroder fiddles with the coffee machine, trying to get it to fill his cup. The reason the courts found Whitby lacked the mental capacity to know what he was doing to Tabitha Jenkins was because he did lack the mental capacity. As a boy, Whitby had suffered severe beatings at the hands of his mother—she hit him on the head with an iron the final time before he was taken from her custody, which put him in the hospital for three weeks. The blow was so severe he never fully recovered; in fact for the first few days the doctors didn't think he would survive, the impact having left a permanent dent in the side of his head. The mother was angry at James for not waking up. She kicked him without success. She thought he was faking. The iron was still hot at the time. She had the idea that placing the iron on his chest would wake him up. She was wrong. She gave it a good go, before moving it from his chest to his stomach to each of his thighs. It was an hour later she called an ambulance, and when the paramedics showed up she was drunk in front of the TV yelling abuse at one of the soaps. Then she yelled abuse at the paramedics for not being able to wake her son so he could finish cleaning the dishes.

It was one of those cases that fall into the "for" column in the argument that serial killers are made and not born. In the hospital they found the true extent of previous beatings—broken arms, broken fingers, arms covered in cigarette burns. Whitby did survive, and his mother was given counseling and anger-management classes, was forced to pay a series of fines, and did see the inside of a jail cell—she was sentenced to fifteen months but was released in eight. After the hospital James was sent into foster care where he set fire to his bedroom and killed the family cat and kept exposing himself to his new sister. He was sent into another home and ultimately into a government-run home for troubled kids. At school he required special-needs teaching. He was constantly in trouble for hiding in the girls' bathrooms to watch them urinate. At seventeen school was over and he moved from the government facility into a single-bedroom flat. Within a month he became obsessed with Tabitha Jenkins.

Schroder brings me a coffee. I pick up the doctor's file and start thumbing through it. There's lot of medical jargon in here, all of it suggesting Whitby was an extremely troubled kid who should never have been on the streets of Christchurch in that condition. Stanton was working closely with him—there are notes here relating to Whitby's childhood, what it was like for him growing up, his relationship with his mother. There are notes from Whitby's attack on Tabitha Jenkins. Whitby's thoughts come across as confused. He found it hard to explain what it was about Tabitha that made him attack her. He was at tracted to her because she was beautiful, is all he'd say. Stanton had written down that he believed the attack on James with the iron when he was fourteen locked parts of his personality into that age, which was why he found himself drawn toward girls of that age or younger. When pressed on whether he knew what he was doing was wrong, Whitby said he didn't see a problem with it, and was confused why people did.

"I still don't get how we missed it," I tell Schroder.

"What?"

"The prison records. I mean, we were going through them, right? If Cole was released six weeks ago, we should have seen that."

"Right," he says, then shrugs. "I don't know what to tell you."

"We should have made the connection earlier. We could have . . ."

"I get it," he says. "Okay? We should have figured it out sooner, but we didn't. But we've figured it out now and that's the main thing, right?"

"Right." I look across at Detective Kent who is watching me with a blank look on her face. She gives a small shrug that Schroder doesn't see, then goes back to the file she's looking at, which is a copy of the one I'm looking at. I look down at the coffee. The cup has those stains around the rim of it that no amount of cleaning will ever remove. "The coffee still taste the same as when I used to work here?" I ask, rubbing my finger over one of those stains.

"A little better," he says. "I think the fucking janitor used to spit in it."

I pick up the coffee and get it halfway to my mouth then change my mind. "It's time I gave up anyway," I tell him. "Any luck connecting our victims?"

"We're getting close," he says, sipping at his own drink. "We'll have court records within the hour. You read much of that?" he asks, nodding toward the file.

"Yeah. Poor bastard never had a chance in life."

"So you read the mom's file too?"

I nod.

"She really is a piece of work. You ever see her?"

"No."

"I did. I picked her up a few years ago on a shoplifting charge. She got off on a technicality. She was in the supermarket drinking all the beer, so technically she never left the premises, so technically she hadn't stolen anything, and she only left when we escorted her, which means she wasn't choosing to leave. Thing I remember the most about her was her breath—I swear there was no way she'd been near a toothbrush in years. She was . . . was a creepy woman," he says.

"She put all of this into motion," I tell him.

He starts to shake his head, but ends up nodding. "I guess you can see it like that," he says. "So we have Stanton as being the doctor who got up on the stand and said Whitby could be saved, and we have another connection too."

"The other victims?"

He nods. "Want to have a guess at who defended Whitby?"

"It has to be one of our dead lawyers."

"Victoria Brown," he says.

"And the other lawyer?"

"We can't link Herbert Poole or Albert McFarlane to the case," he says. "I can remember parts of what happened," he adds, and so can I. He fills it in for me anyway. "I think Whitby was out after two years, and I think it wasn't long after that he killed Cole's daughter."

"You got Cole's record here?"

He hands me a folder and I open the cover. First thing to see is a photograph of Caleb Cole. It's fifteen years old and he doesn't really look much like the man I saw last night in the cemetery, but he looks exactly like a man I saw earlier this morning.

"Shit," I say, staring at the photograph.

"What?"

"Is there a photo of Cole's daughter anywhere?"

"Why?"

I stand up quickly, the chair pushing backward and nearly tipping over. "This morning in Ariel Chancellor's house, there were pictures on the wall," I say, talking quickly now. "Caleb was in one of them. This Caleb," I tell him, tapping the mug shot and showing it to him. "The one before all this started."

"The evidence is in the storage warehouse and it's being pulled right now for Jessica Cole's murder," Schroder says, sounding just as excited as I am. "There'll be photos in there. But I remember the news coverage was pretty comprehensive, so there might be some images online."

"Where's the nearest computer?"

We head into Schroder's office. He moves the mouse and his computer comes to life. He sits down behind his desk and I stand behind him, watching him use the keyboard and mouse, and it only takes him a minute to find the articles we want.

There's a photograph of Jessica Cole, the same little girl that was also in the photo I saw this morning of Ariel and Caleb. We start reading the articles and the rest of it comes back to us now, all the details.

James Whitby hadn't become obsessed with Jessica Cole. He had become obsessed by her best friend, Ariel Chancellor. The two girls met when they were five years old at school, they had been placed next to each other in class by alphabetical order and had become best friends. On the day Whitby planned to take her, the two girls were walking home side by side. He approached them with the same story he had given Tabitha Jenkins two years earlier, and they both fell for it in the same way, desperate to help the man find his lost puppy. When they realized it was a trick, they both ran. Whitby went after Ariel, but she was able to fit between a gap in a corrugated iron fence and she kept running. That same gap had sharp edges and caught Jessica's winter jacket and she didn't get the chance to free herself before Whitby snapped her up as, what he would say in his confession, *second prize*. Ariel got home and her parents called the police. The police figured out quickly who they were looking for. After all, a convicted and released mental patient who had raped and tried to kill a girl two years earlier lived only a block away from where Jessica was abducted. He didn't return home, and the police arrested him late that night after he went to see his mother. She stood on the doorsteps screaming at her son, calling him a *rape baby*, screaming that the best part of him ran off her thigh and stained the bedsheets. Her abuse is all there in black-and-white, printed by the reporters for the world to read.

Once at the station, it took twenty-four hours for Whitby to give up the location, and I remember a detective beating it out of Whitby. It was a pretty big deal. I remember we all knew the confession may not stand, that Whitby's lawyer was going to rip our case to shreds in court. I remember the despair around the station knowing that. I remember the guilt of the detective who had gotten the information out of Whitby, his actions understandable when he was trying to save the life of a small girl, but unforgivable when that girl was found dead and the killer was looking at going free. I remember one of the detectives tipping off Caleb Cole what had happened with, I imagine, no idea of what Cole would do next. Cole never said who had told him Whitby was going to be released.

None of that was in the papers. It probably would have made it, if people had found out, but because the case never made it to trial, Whitby never had the chance to tell what had happened. He had told his lawyer, who this time wasn't Victoria

Brown, but the lawyer never went public with it after Whitby's death. That lawyer had children. He knew we were all better off with his client in the ground. Instead he came into the station and said that unless the man who had beaten Whitby lost his job, the media was going to get a hell of a story. So the detective jumped before he was pushed and the lawyer went home satisfied.

I never saw Caleb Cole. I wasn't there when he was taken to the morgue to identify his daughter. I wasn't there when he stood in the station foyer shouting for vengeance. And I wasn't there a day later when Whitby, on his way to court from the holding cells in police custody, was hit by a furniture-moving truck Caleb Cole had borrowed from his brother-in-law. The collision between truck and transport van killed the police officer driving and the second officer in the car broke both arms and permanently lost his sight in one eye. Whitby survived the crash but not what followed. Caleb dragged him out of the wreckage and to his car, which had been parked nearby. He drove him to the slaughterhouse.

Caleb Cole tore James Whitby apart.

He used a kitchen knife. Every time he put the knife into him, he dragged it up or down, creating cuts that almost tore Whitby apart. I never saw the scene. I wasn't one of the officers who got the call to go there and help and I was thankful for it. I know there were pieces of Whitby all over the floor, things that had been sliced so badly they fell out of him. I know parts of him were scooped into a bucket. I know it was so bad the medical examiner had no idea whether Whitby had been hurt in the car collision because there just wasn't enough left of him in once piece to tell.

And I know, thanks to the medical examiner, that if you count those wounds up it came to nineteen.

Caleb Cole drove home after Whitby was dead. He was covered in blood. His wife didn't recognize him. She screamed when he walked in the door and their neighbors called the police. She said he looked like he'd bathed in it. She said he looked like he had stepped out of a horror movie. Cole didn't say anything to her, he went and showered and when he came out she was sitting on the couch with the knowledge of what he had done. They held each other until the police arrived a few minutes later. He didn't resist arrest. He pleaded guilty to everything. Four days later his wife killed herself. She had lost her daughter on a Monday, and by the weekend she had lost everything else. She didn't leave a note. Fifteen years Cole got. He tried to kill himself twice within the first week. Then he was on suicide watch for three months, and the moment he was off it he tried to kill himself again. He didn't try anymore after that, though others tried for him.

"Victim number two was a teacher, is it possible he taught Whitby?" I ask.

"We'll know soon," Schroder says. "Along with victim number one."

"Victim number three, Hayward. It must be a safe bet the connection is with Ariel Chancellor. He simply picked the wrong moment to pick up a prostitute. Also I'm thinking, if Cole blamed Whitby's lawyer, maybe he blamed the judge too. That makes the judge a potential target, and also might be a chance of catching Cole."

"Good thinking," Schroder says. "We'll get the judge out of there and put some armed officers inside the house. Maybe we'll catch a break and nail Cole breaking his way in."

"Mrs. Whitby too," I say, looking down at her mug shot, taken while her son fought for his life in a hospital room. In it her hair is sticking up at the back from where she spent a few hours slouched in the couch watching TV. Her eyes are half-closed, she's drunk and tired, and looks like she just doesn't give a damn about anything. "Like I said before, she set the ball rolling on all of this."

"You should go back and talk to Ariel Chancellor," he says. "Take Kent with you. There's a whole lot of different questions you can ask her now that you couldn't this morning. Maybe they've stayed in touch. Maybe Chancellor will be able to tell us something that can help track him down."

"Sure," I tell him. I head for the door.

He reaches into his pocket and grabs out the packet of Wake-E.

"You remember when we found her?" he asks.

I stop at the door and turn back. "I remember."

"Landry was there too," he says. "How the hell have fifteen years gone by?" he asks.

"I don't know."

"I'm thinking, since Cole took Whitby out to the slaughterhouse," Schroder says, "that means there's some symmetry there. What do you think? You think he might go there again?"

I think of the snow, the blood, I think about how the slaughterhouse must look now, and I imagine Caleb Cole holed up there with the doctor and his family. If not there, then where else?

"It's a good idea," I tell him.

"I'll check it out."

"Want me to tag along?"

"I can handle it," Schroder says, and he tosses a tablet into his mouth and I head out the door.

CHAPTER THIRTY

"Tick tock," Caleb says.

"Please . . ."

"Tick. And . . ." Caleb says, then looks down at his watch, counts off a few beats in his head, ". . . tock. Time's up. It's been two minutes."

"No, no," Stanton says.

"Which one?"

"I can't."

"I was hoping it wouldn't come to this," Caleb says, and it's true. "So be it."

He picks up his knife. He walks over to Katy. He has to get it done. If he holds back, if he lets the doubts creep in, then he may not do what needs to be done. He has no room left for humanity, all he has room for is the plan, and if he pulls back now it's not going to happen. He has to focus on that. He looks at Katy. He can't think of her as Katy Kitten. He has to look at her as a tool. But God how she reminds him of his own daughter, the same way they . . .

Stop it! Shit like that is only going to make it harder!

He moves toward Melanie instead.

Munchkin Mel. The same thing, really. . . .

"Please, please don't," Stanton says. "I'm sorry, I'm so sorry, I am, I really am."

"It doesn't help."

"Don't do this! Fuck, fuck, don't do this. You don't have to do this!"

He crouches down over Melanie. "Choose somebody, Doctor, make it as painless as possible."

"I can't," Stanton screams. "Don't you see that? If it were you, if you'd had three children and had to decide, you couldn't have done it either," he says, and his words are quick and hopeful, as if there is enough logic in the idea to make Caleb stop doing this.

And it is a good point. But Caleb isn't here to debate good points. He's here to make Stanton suffer.

"Choose," he says.

"It's impossible."

"I agree. It's impossible, but you still have to choose. One dies now, or all three die now. Focus on that and it becomes less impossible."

"You're insane."

"Maybe. It still doesn't change the fact that if you don't give me a name in the next five seconds you're going to start seeing a lot of blood."

"I—"

"One," Caleb says.

"Wait—"

"Two," he says, and he remembers giving his daughter similar countdowns, only he'd give her till the count of three to tidy up whatever mess she had just made or he'd put her in time-out. He's giving Stanton two extra seconds. He's being generous.

"Octavia. I choose Octavia."

Caleb feels his stomach drop and his throat tighten. He straightens up and stares at Stanton and slowly shakes his head. "I don't know whether to be impressed or disgusted, but I'm certainly surprised."

"Fuck you."

"Why don't you like her?"

"I didn't say that," Stanton says, looking down.

"Yes you did. You wouldn't have decided so quickly." Caleb lifts his hands into the air, the knife catching the light coming through the dirty windows and sending a white spot across the wall like a shooting star. "You still had three seconds left. See, I think you knew all along who you were going to choose. Why is the decision so easy for you to make?"

"Are you so fucked in the head that you think this is easy for me? That it could be easy for anybody?"

Caleb scratches at his face. He ignores the jab and thinks about Octavia. He waggles the knife at Stanton and the shooting star races back and forth. Then he shakes his head. "It doesn't make sense," he says. "I mean, how you chose somebody so quickly. Less sense is how you chose the baby."

"None of it makes sense. How about you choose, huh? How about you go and have a family and I make you choose who dies first."

"Explain it to me," Caleb says. "I used to be a math teacher. I understand about statistics. You must have weighed up values of life or something. Tell me. Or is it really that simple? Did you just choose the one you like the least?"

"I've done what you wanted," Stanton says, looking up and looking defiant. "Are you happy? That's what you wanted, isn't it?" he asks. "You sick, twisted fuck."

"Happy? I'm not doing this to be happy," Caleb says. "Look at you, you should be ripping your own arms off to try and get to me."

"Is that what you want?"

"I thought it'd have been harder than this for you."

"You've made your point, Caleb. You really have. Anything you do to my kids is just you getting off on hurting people."

"Why don't you like her? Is that why she doesn't have her own nickname?"

"What?"

"You want something to match the others, right? How about Obsolete Octavia?"

"You're wrong. I love her the same as the others."

"Obsolete Octavia. I like it. And it does seem you have no use for her. However in this case you're going to have to choose somebody else. When I said before I was going to start cutting off fingers, did I mention Octavia's name?"

"Yes," the doctor says, not looking so sure.

"Actually no. I would never cut the fingers off a baby. What is wrong with you?"

"With me? How can you—"

"Choose somebody else."

"What?"

"You have to choose between the other two girls."

The doctor stares at him, his eyes wide open—he's hearing what Caleb is saying, Caleb is sure of it, he's just not understanding it. Then he blinks quickly a few times as if trying to wake from a really bad dream. "You can't do that," he says, sounding like a kid in a playground defending himself to a teacher. "That isn't what you said before, you can't just change your mind like that. I made my decision! It's not fair!"

"It's an unfair world, Doctor, I've said it before and I'll say it again. Now, I'm not going to cover old ground with you, but you need to make another decision. I say you've got about ten seconds. I think that's probably a better time than two minutes. It makes it more instinctual."

"No, no, you can't make me decide something like that."

"You decided two minutes ago that it should be Obsolete Octavia."

"No, no, you can't do this."

Caleb crouches back down. He grabs Melanie's hand and spreads her fingers, then puts the knife against the top of her index finger. He looks over at Stanton, who is not only crying now, but who has gone bright red. He inhales loudly, snorts, then strings of bloody snot explode from his nose, hanging down over his lips and sticking to his chin. His hands are bound behind him. He keeps trying to wipe at his face with his shoulder. Veins are sticking out in his neck.

"Choose, Stanton."

"Okay, okay damn it. Give me a minute."

"You have five more seconds. Tick tock, Doctor."

"Okay, okay. Fuck," he says, crying harder now. "Choose me," he says.

Caleb nods. He had expected that answer. Only it was the answer he expected first.

"Okay."

"What? Oh, Jesus, Jesus, no," and the words are barely out of his mouth before he manages, just like Octavia, to wet himself. "Please don't kill me."

"You're pathetic," Caleb says.

"Please—"

"Tell you what, Stanton, if you really mean it I'll kill you right now and let your children go. Is that what you want?"

"I . . . I don't want to die."

"Don't worry, I'm just kidding."

"You're kidding? You're not going to hurt anybody?"

"Oh, no, I'm not kidding about your daughters, just about you. So save your breath begging for your life. That would be too easy. You have to go through what I went through fifteen years ago." He has to experience it all. He has to understand loss.

Right through to the end.

That's the point of all of this.

Stanton looks confused, and bolstered by the fact Caleb doesn't want to kill him he becomes more insistent. "Yes," he says. "Yes, it's that easy, just kill me and let my children go. You don't want to hurt them."

"You're such a slimy bastard," Cole says.

"They've done . . ." Stanton says, and then hiccups loudly as the words get jammed in his throat and die. He makes a high-pitched squealing sound as he panics to replace them, and then they come again. "They've done nothing to you. Nothing."

"Just like my family did nothing to you."

"I didn't kill your family! James Whitby killed your family!" he cries, using his playground voice again.

Caleb can hear Octavia crying louder outside. She's probably distressed at the sounds she's hearing from in here. Distressed at being obsolete. He's going to have to feed her soon. "James Whitby was a loaded gun," he says, "one you fired into a crowd."

"It's not like that. You don't understand, I was only doing . . ."

"Come on, Stanton, stop trying to defend it. You're a coward. You proved that by choosing to kill a baby before you'd take your own life."

"I'm choosing to die now."

"I'm going to cut Melanie's fingers off now," Caleb says. "Maybe then you'll see I'm not fucking around."

The next words out of Stanton's mouth are muffled as he squirms across the floor, fighting with the bindings, his face pressing into the concrete as he talks, the side of his cheek getting grazed. He inches his way closer. Caleb admires the determination. "Stop," he tells him, and when the doctor doesn't stop, he tells him again, this time more forcefully. "Stop!"

The doctor stops. He looks up at Caleb, and he keeps the knife over Melanie's fingers.

"Caleb, listen to me, listen to me. You're becoming the thing you hate. You'll become the man who killed your daughter."

"Not just my daughter," Caleb says, "my entire family. And it's too late—I've already become him. Pat yourself on the back, Doctor, you're the reason why."

"No, no, you're worse than him. And, in this world of yours, if your son was still alive, would that mean somebody who loved me would be allowed to kill him for what you're doing?"

"What do you mean?" Caleb asks.

"I think you know. When all this is over, are you okay with somebody who loved me or my children coming along and hurting others you love?"

"There is nobody left that I love."

"That's not the point!"

"No, the point is you helped to take away everybody I loved."

Stanton is shaking his head. "It wasn't like that. And you're still avoiding what I told you, and that's because you see it. If you hurt me, it will never end—at least that's the way it would be in your world. Somebody I love will kill somebody you love, and it will go on forever."

"Like I said, there is nobody I love."

"Goddamn it! Why don't you get it?"

But Caleb does get it, it's just that it doesn't change anything. It can't. It's not about the future, it's about the past; it's not about hypotheticals, it's about payback, about an eye for an eye. It's about being old-school biblical. He holds Melanie's index finger apart from the others, puts the tip of the knife into the floor and slowly lowers the edge of the blade so it touches the skin.

"Wait!" Stanton screams, his voice sounding raw. "Just wait. Please, please, wait—"

"You took too long to decide," Caleb says. "Somehow I knew you would. I sympathize with your situation, Doctor, I really do, but you're not acting like a man who believes what I've been telling him. There'll be some resistance, probably a hard crunch, but it'll happen. I hope I can get right through in one cut. I don't want to keep hacking at the same fingers over and over. Let's hope she doesn't wake up."

Stanton, hysterical now, thrashes up and down, he looks like some 1980s meth addict trying to break dance. "Wait, for the love of God, let me think!"

"No," he says, curious as to why there is much more anger from Stanton now that he has to choose one of the other girls. However he's running out of time to be too curious. He needs to get this done.

"I'll fucking kill you if you touch her, I swear, I swear I'll kill you."

"We'll see," Caleb says, "but by then your daughters are going to be dead."

He pushes down a little further. The blade starts to indent her finger, but there is still no blood. Just a fraction more and a bit of a forward and back movement too, then the bleeding will begin. He doesn't want to do it, but what choice does he have? A puddle of snot and tears are pooling beneath Stanton's face, dirt covering his skin, speckles of blood from his grazed cheek. And still he thrashes up and down, perhaps only a few more seconds from having a heart attack.

"I . . . I can't. I fucking can't."

"You can, you've proven that already. Let's see how many fingers we have to get through before you remember that. You're condemning them both, Stanton, when all you have to do is give me a name."

"Wait!"

"Simple arithmetic. It's all about the greater good."

"Don't."

"Now, Stanton, now," he shouts. "Who dies? Who the fuck—"

"Wait—"

"—dies because I'm going to—"

"Please, please, just wait—"

"—start cutting, I swear I'm going to fucking cut them all into—"

"Don't!"

"—little pieces, I'll cut them all day long until—"

"No, no."

"—there's nothing of them left. Let's start right now!"

"Melanie," the doctor says, crying, blubbering like a baby. "Please, please, God forgive me, God forgive me for what I've done," he says.

Caleb takes the pressure off the knife. "Good choice," he says, and he steps away from the girl and tucks the knife into the side of his pants. "A very good choice. I'd have made the same one. Get rid of the one with the smart mouth."

Stanton doesn't answer. Caleb reaches him and swings a foot into his stomach. The doctor grunts, then Caleb rolls him onto his back. "This will help," he says, and he jams a funnel into the doctor's mouth and pokes five sleeping pills down it. They hit the back of the doctor's throat, then Caleb follows it with water and another punch to the stomach. The doctor swallows them. Caleb takes away the funnel.

The doctor coughs and struggles to compose himself, and when he does he sounds short of breath. "You're . . . you're worse than Whitby," he says. "Whitby was, was sick," he says, puffing. "He had genuine mental problems, what you've . . . you've got inside you is, is evil. Whitby couldn't help himself, but you, you're making decisions to delib . . . deliberately hurt people. Whitby didn't think about that, he didn't think anybody would mind what he was doing. He just didn't get the world. They should never have let you out."

"Maybe," Caleb says, "but they did, the same way they let everybody out at some point. You're the one fighting to let the nutcases out earlier than anybody else."

He picks Katy up and carries her out to the car, past the crying baby. He lays her across the backseat and throws a blanket over her. When he comes back in he can see the doctor is struggling so hard against the plastic ties that each of his wrists are bleeding. He's also struggling hard to stay awake.

"Please don't do this," Stanton says, his voice sounding raw.

"No more debate," Caleb says, and he shows Stanton the

knife. "It's not the same knife I used on the others," he says. "Your daughter, she gets her own. She won't be contaminated by the blood of those monsters who let Jessica die. She won't feel anything, I promise you."

"No, no," Stanton says, shaking his head, crying harder than Caleb has ever seen another person cry, and he's trying to squirm toward him, kicking dust up off the floor, the rage and fear fighting off the sleeping pills. "Anything . . . I'll do anything, anything you ask . . . it doesn't matter what just anything, anything . . . please, oh God, please don't . . . no don't hurt her . . . just give me a chance to . . ."

"Jessica, she felt everything," Caleb says, and he unzips Melanie's jacket and opens it. "He stabbed her over and over, but your daughter, I'll only cut once. I promise, she won't feel it," he says, and he lines the knife up.

He pushes it quickly into Melanie's chest.

For a second there is nothing. No noise. No blood. Nothing. The girl doesn't even move.

Then the second turns into a second second, and before it can reach a third Stanton begins to choke on his own vomit.

The base of the handle is flush against the girl's chest. Caleb keeps his hands on it, holding it down, pressing firmly. Her face doesn't twitch.

Cold blood pools out from around the knife.

It soaks slowly into her T-shirt and onto his hand.

He pulls away the knife and rests it next to her, then wipes his hand across the floor. He looks over at the doctor. He's stopped squirming. His mouth and neck are covered in blood and vomit, and he's struggling to breathe through it all. Caleb gets up and closes the distance. He reaches down and drags the doctor to his feet, but the doctor's legs just buckle beneath him. He's still sobbing. Loud sobs that Caleb doesn't have the time for. He smells of piss and shit. The sleeping pills have been thrown up, the edges of them slightly dissolved, two of them hanging from Stanton's chin. He drags Stanton out of the room, and still he keeps crying, so he strikes him in the side of the head, once, twice, and the doctor goes quiet, the blows more efficient than the sleeping pills. He gets him out to the car and fits him into the trunk, and each time he lifts the man now it's harder than the last. He wipes the rest of the blood off his hand onto the doctor's pajama top.

He goes back and looks over Melanie. The police will be here soon to take care of her. He lays her more comfortably on the blanket. He rolls up the corner of it and props it under her head as a pillow. He places her hands across her chest in the blood and interlocks her fingers, then drapes another blanket across her. He tucks her in. He strokes her hair from the side of her face, trapping it behind her ears and brushing her fringe back. He has shown her a grace his own daughter never received.

He uses the marker on her before stepping away. Her young skin is smooth and easy to write on.

When he leaves the slaughterhouse with Octavia and Katy in the backseat, Stanton in the trunk, he knows it's for the last time. The plan is changing, but the end result will still be the same. He'll go and see Ariel Chancellor. He's still unsure exactly what he wants to say to her, or do with her, but he has time to figure it out on the way.

CHAPTER THIRTY-ONE

The day is moving quicker than it should, partly because of the unfolding events, partly because of daylight savings, mostly because that's what happens in a murder investigation when things start to fall in place. The day is still light, but with the sun heading toward the horizon a little quicker every day it's only a matter of weeks until it's dark by five o'clock. I've been given the use of an unmarked patrol car that doesn't struggle to start and has a heater and window wipers that work.

While Schroder takes a team out to the slaughterhouse, I drive to Ariel Chancellor's house and park out front. It's taken me a little longer than I'd have hoped, the first of the boy-racers that Schroder warned us about are already warming up the streets for later on tonight. I don't have Detective Kent with me because I don't need help asking a bunch of questions, and I need to get through it quickly so I can see my wife. I have twenty minutes before my five o'clock appointment with Dr. Forster, and from here it's a twenty-minute drive, longer if the boy-racers decide to circle the nursing home. I figure I can be ten minutes late, maybe even twenty. It'll take Forster half an hour or so to look over my wife. So that gives me ten minutes to talk to Chancellor.

I knock but nobody answers. If I were still a private investigator, then right now I'd consider breaking in. I weigh that up against my responsibilities as a policeman, then I weigh those up against my responsibilities as a human being who's trying to save the lives of three young girls and their father. All that weighing pulls me around the side of the house where my feet sink halfway into the boggy lawn. There are patches of mold growing around the edges of the back door. I use a lock-pick set that has come in handy over the years and will continue to do so in the future, even in my role as a policeman.

I call out a *hello* before making my way inside. The air temperature drops a few degrees. Any damper and I'd need swimming trunks. I step into the living room. To the right is a kitchen with rinsed dishes forming a pile next to the sink. There's mouse shit along the floor near the oven, and beside a rubbish bin is a dead mouse broken in half in a spring trap. On the dining room table are a couple of fantasy paperbacks that possibly help Ariel escape her past and present. Next to them is a small plastic bag with half a dozen white tablets in it, all on display for somebody to steal—or in this case eat, because there are holes in the base of the first bag and some of the tablets are scratched up and there's a dead mouse on the table that got high really quickly and OD'd before he could share the find with his friends.

I take a look at the photographs I saw here earlier today. The edges have curled over the years, the colors have faded from the memories. I pick up one that has Caleb Cole in it, along with Jessica and Ariel. It can't have been taken long before James Whitby destroyed all their lives. Ariel looks happy. There is life in her eyes that has since been extinguished. Back then she was a ten-year-old girl who dreamed of ponies and rainbows and watched cartoons on TV. Back then she had a best friend and the world was bright and happy and she was a princess. Then a crazy man made that world dark.

Even at ten Ariel would have understood what happened. At eleven she would have understood it more. By high school it was probably ruining her life. The guilt, the shame, the knowledge she got away and her best friend didn't. In this photo is a girl that never knew what lay ahead, would never need to know a world of drugs and prostitution, would never need to live in a run-down home with mouse shit on the floor and holes in the ceiling. James Whitby may not have killed her, but he took away her life.

I move through to the bedroom. My cell phone rings. It's Schroder.

"Got an update for you," he says.

"You're at the slaughterhouse?"

"About five minutes away. You spoke to Ariel?"

"Just pulling onto her street now. So what's the news?"

"It's pretty moot now," he says, "but fingerprints found under the hood came back as a match to Caleb Cole. And the court records have arrived. Want to have a guess at who was the jury foreman?"

"Albert McFarlane?"

"Try again."

"Herbert Poole."

"Bingo. Victoria Brown said Whitby had the mental age of a ten-year-old and wasn't responsible for himself. Dr. Stanton was a critical piece of her defense. And, get this, she also had some character witnesses."

"McFarlane?"

"Exactly. He used to be Whitby's teacher. He spoke about how much Whitby had changed since the attack that hospitalized him. He told the jury that Whitby was basically a good kid, and everything he did was a result of the abuse."

"Brad Hayward?"

"No mention of him. Has to be what you said earlier—he

was just a random guy Ariel Chancellor worked last night, which must have upset Cole. Listen, we've got people sitting on the other jury members making sure they're safe, along with everybody else listed in the case. We got Cole's mug shot out to the media—everybody by the end of the day is going to know who Caleb Cole is. We'll find him soon. Look, I gotta go—we're pulling up at the slaughterhouse."

"Good luck," I tell him, and he hangs up.

I tuck the phone into my pocket and Schroder is right about finding Caleb Cole soon, because when I turn around he's standing right in front of me. Before I can react, he swings a fist and punches me in the face.

CHAPTER THIRTY-TWO

His fist gets me in the side of the jaw and the first thing that happens is one of my headaches explodes into existence. It feels much worse than earlier this year when the glass jar was smashed against my skull. The second thing that happens is I stumble backward. Another fists gets me in the forehead and it's like somebody has set off a flashbulb inside my head, one of those old press ones that would flash white, then have smoke puff out from around it as it went dark. For two seconds I can't see a damn thing, but I can hear him coming at me. I lift up my arms but he manages to hit me again. I fall onto the bed and then his face starts to appear from behind the dark clouds and he looks as surprised as I feel. He jumps on top of me.

"Who are you?" he shouts.

The room is spinning. My back is sinking into the mattress.

"Huh? You fucked her as well?" he yells.

He puts his hands around my throat and squeezes. I grab his hands but can't push them away. Something inside my skull is trying to break free, it's stomping around and banging at the walls.

"Shaleb . . ." I say, and it takes a lot of strength just to say his name, but it sounds different in my head and feels different on my tongue.

He lets go. I grab my throat and rub it. He climbs off me and steps away. "What did you just say?"

I get up onto my elbows. I start to cough, each cough vibrating through my skull. "Shisshen," I say, my throat ticking, my mind woozy, "Shesh me shelp you."

He comes in and takes another swing at me, I block it, but he buries his left fist into my stomach. The air rushes out of me. He turns and heads for the door and I get to my feet, half doubled over. My right arm hangs by my side, not working, it flaps around as I race out of the bedroom. By the time I reach the hall he's already in the kitchen.

"Shate!"

He doesn't wait. I reach the door and he's already scaling the back fence. I manage two paces before everything changes angles—the trees, the fence, the house, everything shifting varying degrees and I throw up, first falling to the ground on all fours.

The headache fades a little. Feeling returns to my arm. I press at the sides of my head and get my eyes open and Caleb's face is staring at me from the other side of the fence as he lowers himself down. Then he's gone. I get to my feet. My legs take me three steps sideways and one step forward, then two sideways and two forward, and then more forward than sideways until I reach the fence. I hang on to it, suck in some air, and climb. I drop down into the neighbor's backyard, where the lawn comes up past my ankles. Cole is almost at the opposite fence. The thing inside my head is still banging to be heard, but at least it's no longer stomping around and setting off distress flares. It's going to let me get through this and wait for the next opportunity.

I grab my phone and call Schroder. I reach the fence and he hasn't answered. I drop the phone into my pocket and climb into the next neighbor's backyard. When I hit the ground Cole is running down the side of the house. I pick my phone back up and it's gone through to Schroder's voice mail. I hang up and call the station. I try asking for backup but the words don't come out. They ask me to repeat myself and I do, but it's still no good. I reach the road and Caleb has gone right. I follow, but he's still gaining ground. He turns down an alleyway. I suck in a deep breath and tell the dispatch officer who I am, and that I'm in pursuit of Caleb Cole, and none of the words come out how I want them to. The dispatch officer doesn't hang up.

"Do you need medical attention?" she asks.

I try asking for backup.

"Are you intoxicated?"

I reach the alleyway and Caleb is already at the end of it. I can barely breathe. Four months in jail followed by two months of eating all the wrong food have me in the worst shape of my life. And getting smacked in the head hasn't helped. I swing my arms harder and try to pump by legs faster but it's not working. Caleb goes right. I'm at least ten seconds behind and the distance is increasing with every step. He looks over his shoulder and doesn't look as convinced as I am that I'm losing the race, so he pushes himself harder. I push myself harder too but there's nothing there. The legs won't respond. Then he starts to slow down. He's been in jail for fifteen years and had to eat that same shit much longer than I had to.

I close the distance. I shave a second off, then another, I close in on him and then I can't run anymore. I start to pull up, my lungs burning, my energy levels drained. My throat is sore, my head is pulsing, my face feels like it's going to explode from the heat. I think of the three girls and I keep going. Caleb sees I've closed in on him. He turns into the closest house and runs down the side of it. He pushes through a gate into the backyard of a house with run-down cars parked in the driveway. People are staring out the window as I follow him. They're getting up and coming to the door, already yelling. Caleb scales the fence. The back door of the house opens and a dog races out after me, somebody yelling at it to "rip those fuckers apart." I reach the fence and the dog grabs my leg and digs its teeth into my calf. I scream out, hug the top of the fence, and kick out with my other foot, connecting with the dog's head. It doesn't let go. I kick it again for the same result. I pull myself up higher, the dog coming with me, and Caleb is standing right below me on the other side. He grabs my shirt and pulls me down. I'm the rope in a tug-of-war between man and beast. The dog comes halfway up the fence and comes free when it starts to lever over the top. I hit the ground hard. Caleb kicks me in the stomach, steps back, then comes forward and kicks me again.

"You. You're the guy from last night," he says, puffing and leaning forward with his hands on his knees. "You've been following me?"

I try to talk. The words don't form the way they should, but I grab hold of them, I force them out and they're a little clearer now. The headache is leaving.

"Caleb," I say, "I can shelp."

"Let me do what I have to do," he says, having to yell to be heard over the dog as it barks and bangs its paws against the other side of the fence, the taste of blood not enough for it. My cell phone must have hung up in the fall because it starts ringing.

"You can't, can't . . ." I say, and have to spend a few seconds sucking in air. "The girls, shoe can't shurt them."

"What kind of monster do you think I am?"

He kicks me again, then takes off toward the house, runs down the side of it, and is gone. I get to my knees but can't get any further. I roll onto my back and grab my phone. Before I can answer it the people from next door put their heads over the fence.

"You kicked my dog, you fucker," one of them says, and he

starts to come over. He's joined by his buddy who says "you're going to fucking pay." Both of them have shaved heads with similar scars running across them that look like badges of honor. Maybe they got that way playing with knives.

I pull out my badge and show it to them. They look at each other, passing a look as if unsure of what to do next, unsure whether kicking a police officer to death is going to be worth the years in jail they'll have to spend for it. I can already see their lawyers going to work, showing pictures of their dog and saying how it was my fault it bit me, how as humanitarians these two men had to defend its honor, that only coldhearted individuals wouldn't have kicked the shit out of me.

"Just go back inside," I tell them, the words feeling right now. "Backup is here," I say, knowing how bad things are going to get if they don't believe me. "Go back inside and don't do anything stupid."

"Pig," one of them says, and the other one spits on me and the guy who spoke seems to hate the idea he didn't spit on me first, so makes up for it by spitting on me twice. Then they climb down off the fence, yell at the dog, and take it inside.

My phone has stopped ringing. I wipe the spit off of me onto the lawn. I follow the path Cole took out onto the street, taking as much weight off my left leg as I can. Nobody comes out of the house. My pants are damaged, and when I roll them up there's a row of puncture holes, all of them leaking blood. The phone starts ringing again. There is no sign of Cole. No sign of any of the patrol cars.

I sit down on the curb and put the phone to my ear. "Yeah?"

"We're at the slaughterhouse," Schroder says, and I have to press my finger into my other ear to drown out the dog, but instead all I can hear is my heart beating. "Cole was here. So was Dr. Stanton. Tate, one of the girls, Cole has left one of the girls for us to find. She's fine, Tate, a little scared, but other than frightening her, Cole hasn't hurt her at all."

CHAPTER THIRTY-THREE

Caleb's hands hurt. Wrapping them around that man's throat, Jesus, his fingers are so sore he could swear the pain would be easier to deal with if he just chopped them off. And the running—another dozen steps and he'd have dropped dead. His right hip feels like it's swiveling on glass, both legs feel like metal spikes have been driven through the balls of his feet into his shins. He has to control the pain, otherwise he's going to have a hard time killing the judge.

He has no idea who the man is. If he's been followed, then . . . but no, he wasn't followed, the man was at Ariel's house first. So he has to be a cop, and if so, then the police have made the connection. But what about the cemetery last night? A coincidence?

The man referred to him by name.

He reaches the doctor's car. The day is getting darker. Katy is asleep in the back, and Octavia is in the front in the car seat with a blanket pulled tightly from the headrest to the floor, acting like a tent over her seat. Last thing he needed was somebody seeing her and calling the police. He puts a small piece of duct tape over the little girl's mouth to keep her quiet. Katy is also covered by a blanket, but the pills he ground up into her drink are keeping her from complaining. More cops will be on the way. He starts the car and pulls calmly from the curb, careful not to draw attention to himself even though every instinct is telling him to put his foot down and get the hell out of here. He switches on the lights. Where are the cops? He doesn't see them and he keeps turning corners so he won't have to, putting distance between him and the house. He leaves the suburb and heads toward town, having to stop and wait at three green lights where intersections are jammed to a halt with brightly colored Japanese cars, all of them being driven by young men listening to loud music.

Still no cops.

He's not a monster, and when this is over, people will see that. He's a man trying to bring balance to the world. What about the next child rapist to be treated and released by Dr. Stanton? What of the next baby killer to be defended by Victoria Brown to be released on the world, their punishment no greater than a slap on the wrist? No, he's not the monster, they are—they are monsters of this world for defending those people, and they must learn there are consequences for their actions.

The judge signed off on the entire thing, the judge was happy to sentence James Whitby to no more than two years in a mental hospital and never follow it up. The judge was happy to wash his hands clean of the entire affair, damn the consequences, and move on to the next case. So right now those consequences are going to come back and damn him.

If the police know him by name, is it possible they know who the rest of his targets are? He is two blocks from the judge's house when he decides it isn't just possible, but extremely likely.

He needs a different car, but he has no idea how to get one.

He would hear stories in jail about how to steal one. It sounded difficult. Some would say you had to touch certain wires. Others said you just jam a flathead screwdriver as far as you can into the ignition until you break the lock, turning the screwdriver into a key. Even if he could figure that shit out he doesn't think his fingers would be nimble enough to do the work. He could always pull a knife on somebody, carjack them, but he can't see that scenario going well. He sees police chases and people getting hurt needlessly. Like the cop back at Ariel's house—he could have choked him, or left him to that dog, but he wasn't to blame for any of this. Cops were the ones that had tried to help him fifteen years ago. Cops were the ones who tried to put James Whitby away two years before that.

It's five fifteen and the streetlights come on. He drives around the block and parks one street over outside the same number house as the judge. He sits in the car and watches the evening getting darker. He switches on his phone. Over the weeks since being out of jail, he's eaten pizza at least every second night. It was his favorite food before being sent away, and he's been making up for not having a slice in fifteen years. He calls the number from memory and he orders three pizzas along with garlic bread and fries, and says he'll pay by cash. The person repeats the order back to him, and then he gives the judge's address. The person tells him it'll be there within thirty minutes, otherwise his next order will be free. In some movies he's seen on TV over the last few weeks the police can track a cell phone signal in a matter of a minute; other times they have to use different cell towers in the area to try and triangulate it. Caleb doesn't know how difficult it really is, but Caleb switches the phone off, not wanting to take the risk, unsure of how the police would have his number anyway. He keeps the blankets over the girls, neither of them show any sign of waking. When Jessica was small and couldn't sleep, he'd put her in the car and drive around the block over and over until she drifted off, then he'd drive around the block once more for good measure, then slowly pull back into the driveway and sneak her into her room. He would have done that a hundred times over a few years, but they all merge into one memory, one that he smiles at as he climbs out of the car fifteen minutes after making the call.

It's a nice neighborhood. Dr. Stanton's car doesn't stand out here. Nice homes, nice gardens, probably nice people who would give you the time of day if you asked. It means he has to be more careful. There are still other cars occasionally going by, people coming home from work. Nice people tend to phone the police if they see strange men hanging around their nice neighbors' nice homes. He looks at every window in view to make sure nobody is watching him, and when there are no other cars in sight, he runs onto the front yard of a two-storey house with large windows with curtains pulled across each of them. There are lights on inside, but there are lights on in all the homes and he has no choice but to try.

He reaches over the side gate and is able to unlatch it. It opens quietly. He listens for any signs or life, especially a dog, but there is nothing. The backyard has some light on it near the windows, but nothing near the fence line, and that's where he heads, sticking near the bushes and making his way to the tree in the corner. He steps behind it. Something a few feet away moves through the leaves and he pauses, and even though it's only a hedgehog or a cat, there is a moment, a brief moment, when he thinks a flashlight is going to light him up before a police baton knocks him down.

The hedgehog scurries off. Caleb scales the fence. He can see down the side of the neighbor's yard and out into the street and the judge's house is one house down on the opposite side of the road. Not a bad guess. He stays on the fence and waits. It's dark outside and the temperature has dropped. He balances himself so he can rub his hands. Two minutes later a car slows down outside. It comes to a stop. Caleb stops rubbing and fixes his attention on the driver as the interior light comes on.

The driver spends five seconds checking something, probably the address, before getting out. He carries the pizzas and only makes it halfway to the door before two people jump out of a nearby car, and at the same time somebody races out from the front door of the house. They close in on the pizza delivery boy, who drops the pizzas.

Caleb doesn't hang around to watch anymore. The judge isn't there, and even if he was, there would be no way to get to him. Whitby's mother will be the same.

He walks back to the car, slowly shaking his head. He switches on the radio and listens to the news as he drives. The police have been to the slaughterhouse. They've found Melanie Stanton alive and well.

He punches the steering wheel. Octavia wakes up. He can hear her moaning through the duct tape. Caleb drives with no idea where to go next.

CHAPTER THIRTY-FOUR

My headache has gone and there are flecks of vomit on my shirt that I've tried to wipe off with my hands. It's five-thirty before I see the first of the patrol cars that Schroder sent out to the neighborhood, which means I've been leaning against my car for thirty minutes. I flag it down. The guy behind the wheel looks pissed off and ready to arrest me until I show him and his partner my ID, at which point he then just looks pissed off. I'm pissed off too and ask what the hell took them so long, and he explains it in two words—boy-racers.

We drive around the neighborhood with him doing all the driving and me doing all the bleeding and his partner stretching his head in every direction as he points a spotlight out the window lighting up the shadows. None of us are talking. Emotions are running high. There is no sign of Cole. During that time five other vehicles help in the search. The streets are quiet. Cole has moved on. I had it within my power to stop him. I was close, so close to getting Stanton and his other two daughters back.

In the end I'm in enough pain and there's enough blood in the backseat that we head for the hospital. Dog bites are not something I want to mess around with. It's almost six o'clock when we hit the edge of town, and another half an hour to drive the final few miles thanks to the boy-racers and their cars and their desire to be accepted as part of what soon must be called a gang, or a cult, but for the moment is simply known to the rest of Christchurch as a fucking huge headache. I'm angry at missing the appointment with Forster and Bridget. We pull up outside the emergency room entrance and neither of the cops walks me inside. The good thing about the bite is it's keeping me awake. The bad thing is my shoe is full of blood. The waiting room is full of people who have messed up at some point during the day, they've hit themselves with hammers and tripped on power cords, school kids with broken arms from soccer, housewives who have walked into doors when dinner wasn't ready on time. I show my badge. That and the holes in my leg give me priority to the annoyance of everybody in the room. I'm taken through the doors into a cubicle and told to take my pants off. A few minutes later a doctor comes in. He prods the wound with his finger and not a lot of sympathy.

"Looks bad," the doctor says, and he looks bad too, with his comb-over and bloodshot eyes, his breath smelling of coffee. "You'll have to stay off it for a few days, and you're going to need some shots. I'll get a nurse to come along and clean it up, then I'll come back and stitch it. My advice is to stay away from dogs."

The nurse is a heavyset woman with kind eyes and an even kinder smile. She tells me that I look like I've been through the wars. She tells me the wound is going to be okay, that the last dog bite victim she had to help had his nose, cheek, and ear removed. She tells me how sad that was, and still she keeps smiling as if she's telling me how sweet her grandchildren are. She gives me two shots in my arm and both of them hurt. She finishes cleaning me up and I'm alone for ten minutes with a throbbing arm and throbbing leg before the doctor returns, other doctors and nurses passing in the hall, some looking fresh, others like they've been on their feet all day. He takes a look at the wound and nods. He injects it and waits a minute before poking a needle at it.

"You feel that?"

"No."

"Good."

Some of the holes are deeper than the others, some wider, all of them look about as mean as each other.

"I've been getting headaches," I tell him.

He doesn't look up from his work, just keeps on stitching. "What kind?"

"Bad ones," I say, and I tell him about the attack that started them with the glass jar, and about what happened today.

"You need to see somebody," he tells me.

"I'm seeing you."

He shakes his head. "You know what I mean. Why haven't you been to see anybody already?"

"I just figured they'd disappear."

Finally he looks up in mid-stitch. "And how's that been working out for you?"

"Not well," I admit.

"You taking painkillers?"

"No."

"Why not?"

"I have an addictive personality. I didn't want to risk it."

"Okay. So your plan was to never do anything about it, just a wait-and-see attitude, and now you mention it just because you happen to be here. Is that the same logic you put into your job, Detective?"

"No," I say, breaking eye contact with him. I wish I'd never bought it up.

"No. Exactly. Just headaches?" he asks, putting down the

thread and the hook-shaped needle. He reaches into his top pocket and pulls out a flashlight.

"Sometimes I get dizzy too. And earlier I couldn't talk."

"You were punched, right?"

"Yes."

He shines the light into my eyes. "Both pupils are dilating normally," he says. "What else?"

"Nothing."

"Loss of time? Have you collapsed? Are you forgetting things? Loss of motor skills?"

"My arm wouldn't work earlier after the attack, but only for a minute."

"Okay," he says, and he puts the flashlight back into his pocket.

"Okay?"

"Here's what we're going to do. I'm going to finish stitching you up, and then I'm going to have you admitted."

"I don't have time for that."

"What do you have time for? For dying? Because that's what might happen if we don't take a better look at you. You've had trauma today to a preexisting trauma from an attack where a glass jar was broken against the side of your head. You obviously have some intracranial injury. When you were slugged in the head today that could have killed you. You hit your head against a wall tomorrow and that could kill you. You could just as easily die tonight lying down in bed."

"Thanks for sugarcoating it for me. Listen, I'll be careful, I promise, and when this case is over I'll be right back. Can't you just write me a script?"

He sighs, then slowly nods. "Fine," he says. He pulls out a prescription pad. He scrawls across it and hands me the top sheet. He's written "Walking out of here might kill you." He's underlined it. I fold it up and slip it into my pocket.

It takes over thirty stitches and twenty minutes to close all of the wounds. When he's done the nurse comes back and ban-

dages me up. Then she insists on taking me into another room
in a wheelchair. It's a smooth ride. The office she wheels me
into has pictures of brains on the wall, illustrated cross sections
of it, and a model brain on the desk.

"Wait here," she says.

"Honestly, I feel fine now," I tell her.

"Good. Then what I'm saying should make sense to you."

It does make sense. She steps out of the room and I sit in the
silence listening to my body, and it's telling me that for now
it's okay. It's telling me there are more important things to be
doing. It makes a convincing argument, so convincing in fact
that I climb out of the wheelchair and step into the corridor. I
take the opposite direction from the way I came, loop around
the halls until I find an exit, then leave. I do all of that with
perfect balance. There are taxis parked outside and I climb into
the one at the front and take a ride to the police station.

The boy-racers must be blocking the other side of town or
have gone home to jerk off to *The Fast and the Furious*. The car
I used before has been driven back for me. My leg hurts when I
walk, and hurts when I don't walk, though not as much. I call
Dr. Forster on the way into the police building and have to
leave another message.

I start to feel a bit dizzy walking into the police station, and
I feel sick when the elevator takes me up to the fourth floor—it
feels like the world is dropping out from under me—but for the
most part I feel pretty good. I lean against the wall to keep the
weight off my leg. If my next assignment involves infiltrating
a line-dancing ring I'm going to lose my job. The doors open
and reveal every detective in a state of information gathering,
they're on phones and on computers and reading files. Schroder comes over from the coffee machine and takes a look at me.

"They don't have to cut it off?" he asks.

"You look like shit," I tell him.

"Funny, I was going to tell you the same thing."

"Where's the girl?"

"In my office," he says. "We need to interview her, but first we have to clear something up. We're looking for Ariel Chancellor. So far there's no word on her whereabouts, but to be clear you got there and found her door already open, saw drugs on the table, and that gave you reason to enter. That how it played out?" he asks me, but he's not really asking, he's telling me the scenario.

"Exactly."

"That's what I thought. Run through it for me."

We walk to his office, the dizziness from the elevator gone. I run though it for him, changing the details from breaking in to walking in an open door and calling out *hello*.

"Well, nobody in the area saw a thing," he says, "but we did get a complaint from one of the neighbors. They said you kicked their dog in the head."

I tighten my jaw and hold onto a sudden burst of anger. "They let it loose on me. They were telling the damn thing to attack!"

"Well, they're making a complaint. They're going to push it, no doubt to see if they can get a settlement. They're saying you trespassed and abused them and assaulted their pet."

My hand curls into a fist and I look at the wall wanting to punch it, and there are already other fist-shaped holes in it. Most of those holes have been signed and dated, a wall of fame of sorts, smiley faces drawn next to some. I relax my fist. "Are you shitting me?"

He shrugs. "I wish I was. I got a sketch artist coming upstairs to talk with you—just to get a more current description of Cole."

"Unbelievable," I say.

"Let it go, Tate, we've got more important things to worry about."

"Like interviewing the girl."

"About that," he says. "You remember Benson Barlow?" he asks.

Barlow is a psychiatrist I met six weeks ago out at Grover Hills, the now abandoned mental institution where an ex—mental patient was holed up with a collection of dead bodies and an even bigger collection of really bad ideas.

"What about him?"

"He's on his way to talk to the girl. I figure it can't hurt. She's pretty traumatized. She's not talking much, but she's shaking and crying a hell of a lot. We've got a female officer in there with her now trying to comfort her, but it's not going great. Poor kid was initially found covered in fake blood. Probably came from the same shop the fake knife came from."

"Fake knife?"

"Yeah, one of those types where the blade goes into the handle."

"So he pretended to kill her?"

"Looks that way," Schroder says. "Plus the only thing she's really said is the same thing a few times, which is she was the one chosen."

"Chosen?"

Schroder shrugs. "Hopefully Barlow can find out for sure, but I'm guessing she was the one chosen to be killed. Or fake killed, as it turned out."

"For the doctor's benefit?"

"What other reason is there?" he asks. "Like I said, that's all she's said because she's so damn scared. My guess is he sedated her first. I mean, not much point in pretending to have stabbed her if she's lying on the floor moving around okay."

"He asked me what kind of monster I thought he was," I say, picturing him standing over me after he'd kicked me in the stomach. Caleb Cole with his scarred face and clenched fists. "I don't think he's capable of killing children, but he must want Stanton to think otherwise."

"Well, he's still a monster, and he still has the two younger ones. As for Melanie, he left her out there with a bag of food, drink, and a bunch of blankets. She could have lived out there for a few days as long as she didn't wander off looking for help and dying in those woods. Anything could have happened to her out there."

"Maybe he was planning on phoning in her location."

"Maybe. We'll ask when we drag him in here," Schroder says.

The elevator doors open and we can see Barlow from across the floor. It must be comb-over Tuesday, because Barlow comes in with the same haircut my doctor had and looking just as tired. He looks to his right first, then left, but doesn't spot us.

"He pulled me over the fence," I tell Schroder.

"What?"

"The dog. It had a good hold of me and was pulling me back down. I'm telling you, that stupid thing was going to rip me apart, and those bastards in that house, they were going to let it. Cole, he reached up and pulled me free. He saved my ass."

Schroder gives me a cold stare. "Look, Tate, do we have a problem here?"

"What? What kind of problem?"

"With you and Cole. Are we in danger here of you sympathizing with him?"

"No, of course not."

"Are you sure? I know you and him both went through similar things when you lost your daughters, and I know part of you probably doesn't hate Cole for killing those he thinks is responsible, but he's a bad guy and he's hurting innocent people."

I throw my hands up in the air. "Jesus, Carl, I know that, okay?"

He sticks with the cold stare. "Are you sure?"

"Of course I'm sure," I say.

"Good," he says, and gives a slow nod of acceptance. "I just had to be sure, because it would be a major fuckup, Tate, to be on his side." He gives it a second to sink in, then carries on. "The evidence and case files have arrived from both Whitby cases," Schroder says, "from where he hurt both girls." Barlow sees us and his forehead raises up and he says or mouths the word *ah* to nobody in particular and heads in our direction. "They're in the conference room," Schroder says. "I haven't had a chance to go through anything yet. And, just quickly, we have another problem."

"We do?"

"At least you do. What the hell happened to you?"

"What do you mean?"

"I heard a recording of your call for help. You sounded like you had a tennis ball jammed in your mouth."

"Caleb hit me pretty good."

"He must have. Are you sure you're okay? You look a little unsteady."

"I'm fine."

"Okay. Well, next time I tell you to take somebody with you, how about you listen to me?"

Barlow reaches us. We swap *how's it goings* with each other as we shake hands with him. He's wearing a turtlenecked sweater and plaid pants. He's looking exactly how you'd imagine a psychiatrist who's about to head out for eighteen holes to look.

"I've read Whitby's psychiatric file," he says, and he puts on his grave face as his voice drops an octave, "and I can assure you that a man like that would never have been let out of my custody. He was a ticking time bomb," he says, with all the accuracy that comes with hindsight and confirming my belief that psychology is a science that has evolved from many, many mistakes. "Now, tell me, how was Melanie Stanton found?"

Schroder spells it out. Melanie was found wrapped in a blanket and her clothes were covered in fake blood. She had been drugged. She woke up saying she was the one who'd been chosen. Across her forehead Caleb Cole had written *I'm sorry.* She was taken to the hospital and checked over, cleaned up, and put into a fresh change of clothes, where she woke up. Then she was brought to the station. So far she has been unresponsive to any questions.

"You don't have a healthier environment?" Barlow asks.

"Like what?"

"Well, a room with pictures and crayons and toys would be a great start. Somewhere children can feel more comfortable."

"This is a police station," Schroder says.

"But you must interview children here, right?"

"We had a room like that," he says, "but we had to extend the conference room. Look, the office is the best we can do," Schroder says, and I can tell he's trying not to sound pissed off, "and we don't have time to mess around."

"Detective, we're going to need to make time. I can't just . . ."

"I know," Schroder says, "but there are other lives on the line here, Doctor. That's why I've called you. I have faith that you'll do the best you can in the time we have."

Barlow nods. "Well said, Detective," he says, smiling. "So, what about her mother? What's the situation there?"

"She's on her way. She was out of the country with her boy-friend. Mother and father separated six months ago. She left him," he says, and explains the situation.

"We should wait for her," he says. "It may help."

Schroder shakes his head while I do the talking. "We waited for you," I say, "and we're all out of waiting."

"If time is what you're worried about, then I need to go in alone," Barlow says, "and when her mother arrives, don't send her in—let me finish first. If she walked out on her family, then her showing up now may only make Melanie more prone to shutting down."

"I need to go with you," Schroder says.

"No, absolutely not," he says, shaking his head. "Two grown men both trying to talk to an eleven-year-old girl? It will only frighten and stress her even more, especially when one of those men is desperate for answers. She isn't a suspect here, she's a witness, but more than a witness she's a young girl who's scared and who doesn't know where her family is. Trust me, if I go in alone there's a chance I can bring her out of her shell, and if you come in with me, she might not talk for a week. If at all. And I know what you want me to ask, Detective. You want to know what the man who took her said. You want to know what he did to them, and you want to know if she heard where he's going next. He left her alive, Detectives, so I very much doubt he did that with the risk she can be of any help."

"Or maybe whatever he has planned will be over before anything she says can be of any help," I offer.

Barlow nods. "Good point," he says. "Now, gentlemen, you called me because you know I can help. How about you let me go ahead and do my job?"

CHAPTER THIRTY-FIVE

Barlow heads into Schroder's office, and I head into the conference room for what I'm hoping is going to be nap time, but the knife betrays any hope of that. It's one of those joke-shop knives, where the blade slides back into the handle. It's sealed up in a plastic bag and sits right in the middle of the table. When I was a kid one of my friends at school used to keep stabbing himself with one of those knifes as a joke. It wasn't funny back then, even less funny now. Dr. Stanton is out there somewhere believing his older daughter is dead, seemingly murdered by a toy that's designed to give people a bit of a laugh.

The case files have been stacked on the desks. Two other detectives are going through them. We're careful to keep the Whitby and the Cole case files separate. I sit down and feel like resting my head on the desk and switching off for a few hours, but the doctor's warning is weighing heavily on my mind and I'm worried if my head touches anything other than a pillow it might be lights out permanently. I find a photograph of Jessica Cole taken not long before she died, this beautiful little girl that reminds me of my own daughter. Jessica died out of an act of intent; my own daughter, Emily, died out of an act of stupidity. One man was evil, one man was drunk, the result was the same. However maybe things aren't that black and white. One man was sick, one man was an addict, neither man was fully in control of himself. Does that make it any easier to deal with? No. If anything it makes it harder. It means other people could have stepped in and never did. Doctors, shrinks, family, or friends—where the hell were these people to get Whitby the medical attention he needed, or to stop Quentin James, the man who killed my daughter, from buying another drink?

Schroder is partly right. I can feel a connection with Cole. I can understand his need for revenge—but he's targeting the wrong people. He took care of James Whitby fifteen years ago and it should have ended there. I took care of Quentin James and it stopped with Quentin James. I blame society for letting him get behind the wheel of a car, I blame the courts for not putting him behind bars for the numerous other drunk-driving convictions he'd had, but not enough to kill the lawyer who defended him, the judge who failed to put him away, the bartender who sold him his last drink. If Cole had stuck to killing only James Whitby I wouldn't have given him a medal, but I would certainly have understood his pain.

I put the photo of Jessica down. Inside the cardboard box of evidence is the murder weapon. It's heavy and the blood on it is maroon and crusty. It's over the entire blade and handle. I remember that Whitby left it inside Jessica when he was done.

The sketch artist comes into the room. He's a tall guy with big forearms, the kind of forearms you get maybe from drawing with heavy pencils. We move off to the side and he sits opposite me, and sets his pad up and looks at me as if I'm the subject and he's trying to figure out what would make a good backdrop. He has a photograph of Cole next to him, and he uses that as his base, and what I give him isn't much of an update. Scars are added, a twisted nose is added, fifteen years are added. Cole is young in one picture, worn down in life in the new one, his face is a map of his time spent in jail.

We're just wrapping up when Schroder's phone rings. He answers it and I hear his half of the conversation. Something about pizza. My stomach rumbles and I like the idea of Schroder ordering some, but the sketch artist doesn't because he leaves to get the new image scanned and released to the media. Only it becomes apparent a moment later that Schroder isn't ordering us dinner.

"You rung the restaurant?" he asks. He listens to the response, his body completely motionless as he absorbs the information, except for his face, which is slowly tightening into a frown. He's staring at something out the window a mile away. "And the phone number?"

He keeps listening, then hangs up and turns toward me.

"Somebody used a prepay cell phone to call a pizza delivery," he says. "He had it delivered to Judge Latham five minutes ago."

"A test to see if we were watching?"

"Exactly. And the test worked—our guys busted the delivery boy as he was approaching. That means he's figured out that we know what he wants. Damn it," he says, snapping a pencil in half, "the officers on the scene, they should have known better. I should have known better and gone myself. Next time that's what I'll do. There's still the mother's house," he says.

I shake my head. "He's not going to try any of the other places now. He knows they're traps."

"We missed him," Schroder says. "We messed up."

I know. I stare out the window at the same spot he was looking at earlier.

"We saved the judge, though," he says, and he's right. We've saved a faceless judge I've never met and maybe one Schroder has never met either. We saved him from being killed in front of his family. It doesn't seem like a big deal. Of course it is—but right now our emotions are invested with those little girls. That's who we're focusing on. They are the truly innocent ones in all of this. Of course all the victims are innocent—but the others didn't help themselves. The girls—they shouldn't be part of this. So it's hard to be excited about the judge and easy to focus on the fact that twice today we could have caught Cole and failed.

"We should take that as a win," Schroder says. "Put up a tick for the good guys," he says, but he's wrong—we shouldn't take it as a win—we should just take it as scoring a point.

We're hoping for answers from the files. From Melanie. Cops all over the city are looking for Ariel Chancellor and Dr. Stanton's car. They're visiting everybody on a long list that Schroder and a few other detectives came up with earlier, people involved with the cases from years ago. I keep thinking about the pizza Cole ordered and what happened to it. I start obsessing about it. More importantly my stomach starts obsessing about it. My run in with Caleb Cole made me want to eat better and start exercising, but both my stomach and brain agree that can wait until tomorrow.

"How long do you think it's going to take Barlow?" I ask, nodding toward the office, wondering if there's some time to order some takeout.

Schroder shrugs. "I wish I knew. Jesus, we have a name, we know what he wants, but going through this," he says, looking at the table of evidence, "feels like we're treading water."

We keep treading because there are no other options. We come up with more names, other people involved in the case, less likely targets but targets all the same. The police who arrested Whitby. The detectives who testified. No logical reason Cole would go after any of these people because they were on his side, but just as equally he might. We know he's looking for Ariel Chancellor, but how does he see her? As a daughter figure, or does he blame her, thinking she left her best friend to die? I keep checking my phone, hoping Dr. Forster will call. I phone the nursing home but Nurse Hamilton has gone home for the day.

There are other evidence boxes here. Things from the car crash where the policeman, Officer Jeffrey Dale, was killed. He was a couple of years older than I was back then. He was the first cop to die in the line of duty after I joined the force and wouldn't be the last. I remember seeing his wife on the news, their children, a family torn apart. A man had gone looking for justice and had killed an innocent man by accident to get it. The entire thing was tragic. You understood it, you sympathized with the dead cop and his family, and you sympathized with the man who accidently killed him. The whole thing was hard to accept.

I use the vending machine in the hall. I dump a bunch of change into it and come up with four chocolate bars, the calories totaling more than I can count. Erin Stanton, the doctor's wife, arrives. She's in her early forties and her makeup has streaked and her long hair is a tangled mess. She's wearing a white dress with a leather jacket over it and carrying a motorbike helmet. I guess they went home from the airport and dumped their luggage, then came right here. She looks flustered. Her boyfriend is also holding a helmet, has a much thicker leather jacket, and looks nervous about being here. His black jeans have holes all around the knees and a few in the ass, not from fashion but from wear. His hair is just as long and just as tangled, and he's also wearing the same amount of eyeliner as Erin, only his isn't streaked.

Detective Kent meets them a few feet from the lift. She asks them to be patient and they don't want to be, Erin saying they have a right to see Melanie, and told they will as soon as the interview is over. They say that's not good enough. Then they're reminded why Melanie is being interviewed—in the hope the police can find her sisters and father.

"I just want my babies safe," she says.

"And your husband too," Kent says.

"He's a dick," the boyfriend says. "What kind of Mickey Mouse operation is this?" he adds, trying to assert some control but falling extremely short, "when you need to rely on an eleven-year-old girl to do your job for you?"

Detective Kent gives him a long hard stare until he looks away, then Erin tries to force her way past in a direction she's hoping Melanie is. She calls out, and Kent grabs her by the arm and starts to lead her away.

"I have a right to see my daughter," she says.

"Let her go," the boyfriend says, and pulls Kent's arm off her. Within five seconds two other detectives have him against the wall, while Detective Kent leads Erin back the way they came.

"I'm sorry, I know it's hard, but you have to trust us on this," she tells Erin. "Just give us a few more minutes, then you can spend all the time you want with her, I promise."

I head back to the conference room. I keep one chocolate bar and hand out the other three. The gesture is appreciated, especially by Detective Hutton, one of the detectives who looks like he's lived on nothing but candy for the last ten years. I feel like I'm one of the team. They ask how my leg is doing and I tell them. They tell me it's good to have me back on the force, and they seem to mean it. Hopefully my future is with these people. Together we are going to fight bad people and help good people and we're going to make a difference.

We're bonding and we're killing time as we eat our chocolate bars. We take ten minutes for ourselves and talk about families and the weather and nothing at all to do with the city or the crime rate. It's the best ten minutes I've had in a long time.

Right on nine thirty, over an hour after Benson Barlow stepped into Schroder's office, he steps back out of it and closes the door behind him. We rush over to him, hoping he's going to give us something to bring us one step closer to finding Dr. Stanton and his family alive.

CHAPTER THIRTY-SIX

Six years ago he saw a man die in prison. Others died while he was in there, most from natural causes, many from drug overdoses, a few from beatings. People would smuggle contraband into the cells all the time. There was a big market for drugs and needles, cigarettes, food, or a hip flask of vodka or gin. They'd smuggle in cell phones, they'd bring in magazines full of pictures of naked women, and on one occasion that he remembers a magazine about landscaping. On this occasion somebody smuggled in a roofing nail.

The roofing nail got handed off to one inmate and jammed all the way into another. Nobody knows how it came from the outside world to the inside world of this man's head, traveling through his ear canal on its way to a home run. The attack was quick and nobody saw it, but the dying lasted long enough for the guy to scream and to thrash his legs about on the floor as they all stood around watching. Nobody tried to help. Nobody showed much emotion. It was like watching a football match where you weren't invested in the outcome. The guards came over. By then the guy had stopped moving. They picked him up and rushed him to the infirmary and Caleb never saw him again after that and nobody really much spoke about it. He was just a guy nobody really knew and death didn't change that about him.

Looking at the blood on the floor, and the death jitters of a man fighting for life, that was the first time Caleb accepted he would feel nothing watching others die. When he killed James Whitby, he felt something. He felt anger and relief, he felt disgust and he felt euphoria, he felt pure hatred, he felt like he could murder the world.

Watching the man in jail, he felt nothing. It was a good thing. It was something he could use. He knew he would need it when he was released from jail, and it's come in handy.

But right now what he is feeling is anger. He's going to miss out on the judge and the bitch mother and the emotion is rushing back. He isn't sure where to go. Since seeing the pizza boy jumped on, he has spent one hour driving aimlessly, then another hour parked out near the beach where he used to live when he first met his wife. Since then he's been driving aimlessly again, listening to the news. The reporters have dropped the Gran Reaper handle and replaced it with his real name. They say to be on the lookout for Caleb Cole, that he's considered armed and dangerous and if you see him to call the police.

Obsolete Octavia is asleep, a small snot bubble growing and shrinking from her left nostril as she breathes. Katy Kitten is asleep too.

The lights ahead are red and he sits at them with his foot on the brake, listening to Octavia breathing and waiting for the bubble under her nose to pop when a purple car with neon lights and a dent in the passenger door pulls up next to him. The music is nothing more than thumping bass, and the two boys in front can't be much more than sixteen. They look over at him, the one closer raises his eyebrows and gives one sharp nod, his head going up first and then down, his eyes fixed on Caleb the entire time, then the driver guns the engine so loudly that Cole's car shudders and Octavia wakes up and screams. Then the driver guns it four more times before the light turns green and they take off, the passenger leaning out the window and screaming "asshole!"

"It's okay," he tells Octavia, only it isn't, because she's crying hard now and her face is turning red and she seems to be running out of air just as quickly as the country is running out of hope for its future. Katy is murmuring from the backseat, the drugs wearing off.

He drives through the intersection and pulls over. He knows the one thing that may help the situation. He opens another jar of baby food and shovels a spoon toward Octavia, who manages to get it into her mouth and swallow it all while still carrying on. Soon he's going to be dealing with a fat baby. At least it hasn't crapped itself today. He finishes off the bottle, then realizes he's left the plastic cup back at the slaughterhouse. He has nothing to give Octavia, and it takes her two seconds to realize the same thing and the crying gets louder. He looks in the backseat and sees nothing, then checks the glove compartment. There's a small bottle of water in there that's half empty. He unscrews the lid and takes a sniff—it smells okay, it could only be a few days old. Or it could be a year old. He tosses it back. Octavia is throwing her arms around, really starting to wind up.

He starts the car. Like with Jessica, the movement and engine noise calms her. He knows this area. There is a dairy a few blocks from here, he drives to it and pulls up outside. He locks the car and runs inside and buys a small box of orange juice and runs back out, telling the owner to keep the change. He punches the straw into it and hands it to Octavia who, in an instant, forgets all about crying as she stares at it, making a smacking noise with her lips before sucking on the straw.

"Good?" he asks.

She doesn't answer, but stares at him while drinking. Her eyelashes are clumped together and look like starfish appendages.

He starts the car. Katy is moving around a little more. The doctor will be waking soon too. He can't keep driving. He needs to make a decision and he has to find a location. Somewhere the police won't think to look, which means a location that has no relevance to him. Somewhere abandoned. Somewhere he can get some sleep and refuel on energy and where he can think about Mrs. Whitby and the judge and how he can get them. There have to be plenty of abandoned places in Christchurch. There are industrial buildings shut down because people have gone bankrupt. Empty houses in every neighborhood where people have packed their stuff together and gotten the hell out. He can't just pull over at a park somewhere and sleep in the car.

He passes a liquor store, one he used to come to on the way home from work sometimes when he'd pick up a bottle of wine to share with Lara over dinner. He slows down, trying to remember the last time he was here but he can't, not specifically, all he can remember are images of the years of different visits. Why would he remember? It's just a liquor store. He hasn't even thought about this place in fifteen years. There are four cars parked out front. He drives past, slows down, does a U-turn, and parks on the street. All the cars are empty, all the people inside the store. He takes the knife and steps out of the car and runs to the closest one, a purple one with neon lights and a dent in the passenger door. He crouches down and slides the knife into the back tire, and then crawls along and slides it into the front one. He doesn't move around to the other side, but he does start to carve the word *asshole* on the hood. It's more difficult than he would have thought—he can't form the curves in the s, not with his fucked-up hands, so it ends up looking like a backward z. He gives up halfway through the e when he sees people getting ready to exit the shop.

He carries on driving. It dawns on him that he isn't driving as randomly as he first thought. That's why he knew about the dairy. It's why he recognized the liquor store. He's been homing in on the house he lived in back when things were the way they were meant to be. The house was sold not long after he went into prison. None of the money went to him. The mortgage was big enough as it was, and what was left went into funeral costs and lawyers' fees. He came out of it with nothing. All the furniture was sold. His clothes, his possessions, everything he owned was sold or dumped and back then he didn't care. It was just stuff. His family was dead, and who really cared about your TV or favorite sofa finding a new home?

His house comes into view, only it's not his house anymore. Last time he saw it, it was, but last time was from the back of a police car. His hands were cuffed behind him and his hair was still damp from the shower and there was blood under his fingernails. He knew he would be going away but he also thought he'd be coming back—he didn't know then that the policeman he'd hurt was dead.

The policeman. For the first few years he used to think about him all the time. Sometimes he'd scream out at night, other times he'd wake up in a cold sweat, lean over, and throw up on the cell floor. When he had access to the Internet in jail, he used to sit in front of the computer with his fingers over the keys ready to type that cop's name into it, but he never did. He didn't want to know if he had a family, if he left behind children. It was too hard. Reason he stopped trying to kill himself was because of that cop—Caleb knew he himself deserved to be punished for what he did, like everybody else. Killing himself fifteen years ago—no, he owed the cop more than that. He owed it to him to suffer, but now he has suffered enough. Like Jessica and Lara and his unborn son, that cop died because Dr. Stanton stood up for the wrong man.

He has no idea whether the people in his house are the ones who bought it fifteen years ago. The fence is new, the roof has been painted, and the garden looks nothing like it did back then, a few of the established trees are still there but the other ninety percent has been ripped out and replaced. However the essence of the house is still the same. There are lights on inside. He wants to knock on the door and ask to take a look through. There are memories locked away within those walls, small moments from his life, insignificant days that will come back to him. For a moment, even if only for a second, the world would feel quite okay.

"Where are we?"

Katy's voice pulls him out of the thought. He turns around and watches as she wipes her eyes with the back of her knuckles the same way Jessica used to when she fell asleep in the car whenever the drive was longer than thirty minutes. She leans forward and entwines her other hand with her sister's, who is still asleep.

"Go back to sleep," he tells her, keeping his voice low.

"I'm not tired. Where's Melanie?"

"She not here."

"Where is she?"

"Melanie was a good girl so I let her go. She didn't keep talking, and she was quiet when I told her to be and she didn't keep asking questions."

"Where's Daddy?"

"You're off to a bad start, Katy," he says.

"What do you mean?"

"I mean you're not very good at being quiet."

"I'll be quiet once I know where Daddy is."

He rolls his eyes. Jessica used to be the same way. It was always quicker just to answer her questions. "He's in the trunk."

"Why?"

"Because I didn't want him back there with you."

"Why?"

"Because there wasn't enough room."

"He could have sat in the front seat and Octavia could have sat back here."

"I didn't want him in the front seat. I wanted him in the trunk, and that's where he went."

"He could have fit back here too."

"You're not listening to me," he says.

"Is that your house?"

Maybe it's not quicker this way. "Do you know what quiet means?"

She nods.

He nods too. Then he sighs. "Yes, I used to live here."

"With your wife?"

"Yes."

"And your daughter?"

"It was a long time ago."

"Until a bad man took them away." She bites her knuckle and sucks on it for a few seconds, then pulls it away but rests it on her lower lip. "Are you a bad man?"

"Yes," he says, but he's not a monster.

"Did you hurt Melanie?"

"No."

"Do you promise?"

"Yes."

"Are you going to hurt Octavia?"

"No."

"Are you going to hurt my dad?"

"Yes."

"Bu . . . bu . . . but you can't," she says.

He tries to feel something for this kid, some empathy. Is he that far gone that he feels nothing? He searches, he really searches, he wants there to be something, and there must be if she reminds him of Jessica.

Only he's not that man anymore.

Katy is starting to cry so hard that she has to cover her face. Stanton starts banging from the trunk of the car. The bastard is awake. Katy looks up, her eyes are red, and yes, he does feel bad for her. None of this is her fault. Her father brought this on her, but she is a tool, a tool that is a means to an end.

He would be best to remember that.

"Daddy," she cries out.

"Shut up," Caleb says, the words low and harsh. "If you say one more word, just one more, I'm going to hurt you. Okay?"

She goes quiet. The banging in the trunk gets louder. Last thing he needs is to be driving around and have somebody hear it. He looks at the knife with the flecks of purple paint on the end of it but leaves it on the seat. He gets out of the car and pops the trunk. Stanton is still bound, and he stops kicking against the wall when Caleb looks down at him.

"You keep doing that," he says, repeating the speech to Stanton that he just gave a few seconds earlier, "and I'm going to take it out on your remaining daughters. I'll do to Katy what was done to mine. I'll do *everything* to her that was done to mine. Then I'm going cut them into tiny pieces and jam them down your throat. You get my drift?"

The doctor mumbles something for a few seconds, and then nods. Caleb slams the trunk down. One of the neighbors is staring out the window at him. Derek Templeton, fifteen years older and fifteen years fatter than the last time he saw him. Once he helped Derek install a kitchen. They did most of the work but had to have the countertop made by professionals. They used plenty of power tools and hammered everything into place and the process was a mess but the end result was fantastic. Derek bought them pizza and beer and they sat outside on the deck with their wives and made a toast to good times. Right now Derek has a look on his face that suggests he can't quite believe who he's looking at. His waves are slow and jerky with no arm movement, all side to side from the wrist, the wave of a man confused by what he's seeing. Caleb finds himself waving back, the human instinct kicking in, both men reacting to it, each of them moving like marionettes.

Caleb lowers his arm. Derek stops waving. They stare at each other from across the street like gunslingers ready to draw down on each other. Then Derek disappears. Caleb gets back into the car.

He doesn't even know why he came here. Part of him, at least subconsciously, must have been aware of where he was driving. He supposes he was hoping the house would be as he left it, the furniture would have been returned, every surface covered in dust, the smells of his wife's perfumes and the scent of her body clinging to the air. The house would be empty but inviting him back to a part of his life long since gone. Whatever piece of him thought he could return home couldn't have been any more mistaken. The past is the past, you can't change it, and Caleb Cole knows that better than anybody.

CHAPTER THIRTY-SEVEN

Before we can say anything, Benson Barlow puts his hand up the same way a publicist will to a news crew before running off a statement about why their client was caught naked outside a restaurant in town. He moves toward us and we take a few steps back so Melanie's mother and her boyfriend can slip into the office behind him. We can hear Erin gushing over Melanie, while the boyfriend doesn't seem to know what to say. We can almost hear the mother's tight hugs being thrown around her. We don't hear anything coming from Melanie.

"She's struggling," Barlow tells us, "I've got her talking but, well, things for her are going to be tough moving forward."

"What—" I start, but he interrupts me.

"I believe I can give you the answers to your questions. You want to know what Cole said to the girls, and you want to know if they went anywhere else, or if she knew where else they were going."

"And?" Schroder asks.

"She says he told them a story about a little girl named

Tabitha. She says Caleb told them a bad man named James hurt her, and that her dad told the world James was okay and wouldn't hurt anybody else. Evidently, Caleb explained a great deal to her. She understands that Tabitha was attacked, and she understands the man who did that went free because of her father, though she isn't sure exactly how. She knows that man went on to kill Jessica Cole. She said Caleb made both her and Katy drink some cola and that it tasted funny, that he was really insistent they drink it, and then they fell asleep."

"Why leave Melanie behind?" I ask.

"This is where it gets tough," Barlow says, and his voice has a small waver to it. "You both have children," he says, then looks at me and shakes his head. "I'm sorry," he says, "I didn't think."

"It's okay," I tell him.

He pauses for a few seconds, what I'm thinking he thinks must be an appropriate time, then carries on. "Melanie said," he says, then pauses again, this time to compose himself. He smiles, one of those trying smiles people give when something is just too tough to mention. "Melanie said Cole told her father this morning that he was going to kill her and her sisters."

Barlow plays with the collar of his shirt and isn't looking either of us in the eye.

"She said it was going to happen tonight, out at the slaughterhouse. She said Caleb was keeping his voice down low so they couldn't hear him, but she still heard bits of it anyway. She said he was going out for the day, but then he came rushing back in the afternoon and he seemed panicked. That's when he gave them the drink."

"He drugged them," Schroder says.

Barlow nods. "Melanie could feel herself getting sleepy, so she knew she had been drugged, so she pretended to fall asleep. She heard part of the conversation Cole had with her dad before she actually did fall asleep. He told Stanton that they were going to leave one of the daughters behind, and the one left behind was going to have to die. It was up to Stanton to decide which one."

We all take a moment with that idea. All three of us put ourselves into that impossible situation of having to choose who lives and who dies. My stomach and chest suddenly feel very empty. The back of my neck breaks out in a cold sweat. What would you make the decision on? How could you make it? You couldn't—only it seems as though Caleb would have threatened violence or death to all of the children until Stanton made a decision. Even then an impossible decision. How do you choose?

You can't.

You just can't.

And yet somehow Stanton made it. He was strong enough to pick a name to save the others. Stronger than I could ever have been, perhaps stronger than anybody in this room. He chose a name to save the other two girls.

Nicholas Stanton is a man breaking down.

"Melanie cried out when she heard that, but continued to pretend to sleep. Cole said if one of them was pretending he would punish them, but she kept pretending anyway. She said she doesn't remember much after that, just that she was really scared, then next thing she knew she was waking up in a hospital."

"Poor bastard," Schroder says.

Barlow nods. "You're seeing it from his point of view, and of course you would since you're a father. But look at it from Melanie's point of view. She's connected all the dots. The fake blood. The drugging. She knows Cole faked her death. Which means she knows she was the one her father chose to be left behind. She survived, but her world has fallen apart. She's the one her father chose to die."

"Bloody hell," Schroder says. "Will she be okay?"

"Would you?"

"I guess not."

"You think Cole is going to hurt the other daughters?" I ask.

Barlow stares at me for a few seconds while thinking about it. His head bobs up and down from left to right and back again. "Unlikely. He wrote *I'm sorry* across Melanie's forehead. She said he was mean to her father, but kept trying to be friendly to her and her sisters, and he would only snap at them when he was really stressed. I think he genuinely feels bad for those children. But he'll use them to get what he wants."

"Which is?" I ask.

Barlow shrugs. "If it were just about killing Stanton, he'd have done it already. If it were just about making him think all three girls were dead, he'd have done that already too. He has an endgame, I don't doubt that—I just don't have any idea what it's going to be, other than making Stanton suffer for as much of it as he can. Maybe he wants Dr. Stanton to get a little taste of what he went through all those years ago when he lost his daughter."

"To what end?" Schroder asks.

Just then Melanie comes out of the office. She slams the door behind her and looks up at Barlow and Schroder and me. She's crying. "I want to go home," she says.

"You should—" Barlow says, then he's interrupted by Erin Stanton coming out of the office.

"Melanie—" Erin says.

"You're not my mother," Melanie says, looking back, then to us she repeats "I want to go home. Only I don't even know what home is anymore."

"Melanie," Erin says, lowering herself down to hug her daughter.

Melanie turns her back on her mother, and her mother sobs into her hands and stands back up. The boyfriend stands a few feet into Schroder's office watching uncomfortably. He's holding on to his helmet, probably thinking that this is all just too much for him.

"I want to go home."

"Soon," Barlow says, taking her hand. "I promise. But for now you need to wait with your mother."

"She walked out on us."

"I'm so sorry, baby," Erin says.

"I don't like her."

"Don't say that, baby," Erin says.

"I don't like my dad either," she says. "He wanted me dead."

"It wasn't like that, Melanie," Barlow says, trying to sound soothing.

"I know what it was like," she says. "He was trying to do the best he could. He didn't want any of us to die, but he did choose somebody and that somebody was me. I'm the one worth the least."

"Come home with me," Erin says.

"No," Melanie says. "You're even worse."

Erin tries to embrace her daughter, but Melanie pulls away. "Come with us, Melanie," she says.

"I don't think that's such a good idea," Barlow says. "Listen, why don't you go and wait back in the office," he says to Erin, "and I'll come in soon with Melanie and we'll talk about things. Okay?"

"We don't need some psychic telling us how to fix our kids," the boyfriend says.

"It's *psychiatrist*, you moron," Melanie says.

Even Erin rolls her eyes at her boyfriend's comments before disagreeing with Barlow. "She's my daughter," she says. "I think I know what's best for her. She needs to be around family."

"Right now she needs to be around somebody who hasn't abandoned her," Barlow says.

"Fuck you," she says.

"I didn't mean to upset you," Barlow says, "but the fact remains she's feeling vulnerable and abandoned and right now—"

"That's why she needs to come home with us."

"Give me some more time with her," Barlow says. "It's why I'm here. Let me help."

Erin gives an exaggerated sigh, but then she and the boy-friend disappear into the office, and Barlow hands Melanie a ten-dollar note. "Go and get us something from the vending machine," he tells her. "I'm starving."

"What do you want?"

"I'll have the same as what you're having."

She disappears. Barlow doesn't suggest we all hide before she comes back.

"Sweet reunion," Schroder says.

"I had tears in my eyes," I say. "You think you can help?"

"You mean do you think I can explain to an eleven-year-old girl what a bitch her mother is for walking out on them? At the same time I have to explain why her dad chose her over the others." He shakes his head. "All I'd be doing is justifying Melanie's feelings. Still, I'll see what I can do."

"She's opened up a lot since you've been here," Schroder says, nodding toward the vending machine. "Did she give any idea what panicked Cole into changing his plans?"

"Nothing. Just that this morning his plan was to kill them tonight in the slaughterhouse, and this afternoon he came rushing back and had changed his mind."

"When we found the car it was surrounded by reporters," I say. "It would have made the news. It's possible that did it."

"He's probably addicted to the news," Barlow says. "He'll be trying to learn what he can in an attempt to stay ahead. He must know it can only be a matter of time before he's caught."

"If he's addicted to the news, can we use that somehow?" I ask. "Can we leak some information, true or false, that might make him make a mistake or reveal himself?"

"I'm not sure," Barlow says. "Maybe. Let's think about how."

Detective Hutton comes over and interrupts us. "We just got a witness hit on Cole," he says, then looks down at his notepad. "Guy by the name of Derek Templeton. He was a neighbor of Caleb Cole's years ago. Says he just saw him hanging around outside his old house a few minutes ago. He thought he was talking to something in the trunk of his car before taking off again. Says Cole looks different, but it was definitely him."

"Get a patrol car out there to take a look around, then have them sit on the house," Schroder says.

"Also, since we released Cole's picture and details to the media, we've had a few psychics leaving messages."

"Jones?"

"Among others. They're all saying the same thing—that they have information."

"They say what that info is?"

"No. But they did say they wanted to talk to somebody higher up the food chain, and would want to be recognized for their help. A few of them said you wouldn't regret calling them back. You want to call them?"

"What do you think?"

Hutton nods and wanders off, digging into his pockets looking for something on the way, something edible I imagine.

"This is the house he used to own?" Barlow asks. "I assume he doesn't own it anymore?"

"It was sold when he went to jail," Schroder says.

"Unlikely the people inside it are posed any threat," Barlow says, "but it's interesting. Since his plans have changed, it's quite possible right now he has nowhere to go. He can't go back anywhere that we know he's been. He wants access to the people on the rest of his list," Barlow continues.

"So where do we look?" Schroder asks.

"Locations from his past, from his daughter's life. The crime scenes, somewhere to do with Whitby. The answer may be in your case files. He used to be a teacher? Then try his school. Try the cemetery where his family is. Try his childhood home. His childhood school. He play sport? Then try a park somewhere, or a clubhouse. Jessica was murdered in the slaughterhouse, but what about the place she was abducted from? Try there. And of course James Whitby's mother."

Barlow looks at both of us, giving us both the most serious look a man with a comb-over can muster before carrying on. "It's going to come down to how badly Cole wants to make these people pay," he says, then pauses, "and at what point he's ready to cut his losses and end things with Dr. Stanton. If I were a betting man, I would say he isn't going to be satisfied unless he can get to the mother. After all, behind any serial killer you'll usually find a domineering mother or mother figure, and you certainly had that in James Whitby's case. Look at what that woman did to her son, look at what she made him. This woman—this woman," he says, and doesn't seem to know how to finish.

"And Ariel Chancellor?" I ask.

"He's probably trying to reach out to her. If you find her, you might find him."

"We're not having any luck finding her. We've had patrol cars looking for her for the last three hours," Schroder says.

"You tried her parents?" Barlow asks.

Schroder looks at me, and I shrug. "Worth a shot," I say.

"It's worth more than that," Barlow says. "If Ariel and Jessica were best friends, then Ariel's parents would have known Jessica's parents too. Maybe they can offer some perspective. Maybe they'll have a location in mind."

"Let's go back a few steps," Schroder says. "It still doesn't add up. Even if Cole pretends to kill the other girls, he won't be doing what was done to him because Stanton will find out he's been lied to. It's not the same."

"He won't know," Barlow says, "because when Cole is done with the girls I have no doubt Nicholas Stanton is going to die. And I have no doubt that after going through what he believes to be happening, Nicholas will be begging for death. I mean, who wouldn't be after seeing that?"

"So why hasn't he done it already? If he knows we have everybody from fifteen years ago under guard, why not finish it now?" I ask.

Barlow shrugs. "Who's to say he hasn't already?"

It's a chilling thought.

"Which means if he hasn't done it already, he has something else in mind," I say.

Barlow nods. "And Caleb is the only one who knows what that is."

CHAPTER THIRTY-EIGHT

Caleb parks on a quiet street near town behind a car that is similar to the one he's driving right down to the color, and climbs out. He tightens his jacket around him and blows into his hands. Octavia is staring at him through the window, the juice box in her hand. Katy is watching too. There are wisps of fog, only just a few, up high around the bulbs of the streetlights. It takes him a minute to use the pocketknife he found in the glove compartment to unscrew each plate. He puts the old ones on the other car, hoping the owner won't immediately notice. He remembers from his old life that when you had to take something apart, or fix something, there would always be one screw that would be way too tight and the head of it would strip away, making it useless. Every two-minute job in his life that required the use of a tool became a thirty-minute ordeal.

But not this time. Even the two of the eight screws that are rusted come away without much effort. He'll take that as an omen. And why not? He's owed some good omens. The doctor stays quiet in the trunk.

He gets back into the car. This all should have been over by now. He fucked up last night. He should have paced himself, ignored that asshole from town who paid for Ariel, just gotten into his car and gone door-to-door like a salesman, selling the people responsible for all of this a death that was long overdue.

He wanted to finish it in the slaughterhouse, but the reality is he can finish it on the side of the road if he has to.

Judge Latham—if he had to choose to let one of the two slide, it would be him. The judge made a decision on the facts presented to him. He believed the defending lawyers and the doctor—he deserves to be punished, and maybe in another life that will happen.

The mother—there's no choice there. He has to get to her. And driving around with the doctor and two daughters in his car is only tempting fate. The doctor will only stay quiet for so long.

He needs somebody who can help him. He can't drive to Whitby's mother's house. He can't try the pizza trick again. His neighbor from way back when would have called the cops. There is nobody in this world he can turn to.

Katy is sitting up in the seat behind him. She still isn't saying anything. She tightens her mouth to prove just how quiet she's being.

"Put your seat belt on," he tells her.

He expects her to ask why. Instead she does as he asks.

"Are you cold?"

She nods. He turns on the heater and points the vents toward the back of the car.

It may not be true that there is nobody in the world who will help him. There is one other woman. He wanted to go and visit her. He wanted to see if she was doing okay, but he never did. He felt if he visited her, all he would be doing was picking at the scabs of her life and reopening old wounds.

She is his only chance.

He uses his phone to look up her address.

CHAPTER THIRTY-NINE

There's a media circus outside the department and I have to drive through it on my way to see Ariel Chancellor's parents. I'm using my own car again because all the others are in use. I drive out the gates and through the barrage of questions and bright lights, fighting the temptation to find out how well reporters work as speed bumps. It's after ten o'clock, town is lit up from streetlights and nightclubs, the alcohol in the city starting to flow. More boy-racers will fill the streets as the hours tick by, teenagers with nowhere better to be or nothing better to do, all of them slaves to the current fashion of drinking as much as they can as quickly as they can. A few of them are already throwing bottles from their cars, arcing them out over the street into the path of pedestrians or oncoming cars. I have to slow down a few times to avoid hitting clusters of drunk people staggering out into the road.

I head home and spend five minutes cleaning up a little from my run in with the dog. I ball up my pants and throw them into the trash. I put on a fresh pair and am about to head out the door when my cell rings. It's Dr. Forster.

"You missed the appointment," he says with his smooth-talking voice. Forster is the kind of guy who makes you feel like you're his friend when he's talking to you. He has the kind of voice that would probably make cute woodland creatures follow him around if he sang.

"I know."

"I've seen you on the news. You're working again?"

"Trying to."

"You're working on this Caleb Cole thing?"

"Yeah."

"It's awful," he says. "How can a man do all of that?" I'm not so sure he's really after an answer so I don't give him one, and he carries on. "I saw your wife," he tells me.

"And?"

"And I looked her over. I spent an hour with her. Physically, she's in great health. The nurses are doing a great job of exercising her. They're taking care of her."

"I know," I say. "But did you notice anything?"

"I've made an appointment for her to be brought into the hospital," he says. "I can see her in three weeks."

"You've noticed something, haven't you," I say, trying to keep the excitement from taking over.

"She's responsive to flashing light," he says. "Nurse Hamilton said last night she stood at the window and stared at the police lights. She said nurses through the night kept finding her there until they ended up sedating her."

I didn't know she had kept going back to the window. My heart is starting to race. "And?" I say, knowing there's more. Or at least hoping.

"And this morning, at the pond, I think it's likely she was looking at the sun reflecting off the ripples caused by the breeze. More flickering light. So I ran a penlight past her eyes.

She was unresponsive. But when I tried the test a few minutes later her eyes followed the light."

"She's never done that before."

"No."

I sit down. "So that's good, right?"

"I don't know," he says. "With brain injuries, there's always a lot going on. Or a lot that's not going on. You can't just get in there and take a look. Sometimes the brain rewires itself, other times it just atrophies. In three weeks hopefully we'll know more."

The word *hopefully* is as unappealing as the time frame. "Three weeks? Why not tomorrow?"

"Because Bridget isn't my only patient, Theodore. If there are any changes, Nurse Hamilton will let me know. It's very important you don't read anything more into this than what happened—her optic nerves had an automatic response and her eyes followed the light. I repeated the test five more times while I was there over the hour, and failed to get the same result."

"But the tests—"

"The tests will happen in three weeks. And then we'll know more."

"So there's a chance that—"

"Theo, there's always a chance. Miracles happen every day. But that's what they are—miracles. I'll send you the details of her appointment."

When he hangs up I head outside, knowing the next three weeks are going to go slower than the four months I spent in jail.

It's a ten-minute drive to the Chancellors' house and the streets are mostly empty, a few people are out for walks holding hands, they're bundled up in jackets, sometimes a dog or two on a leash with them. It's only a matter of time now before the decreasing temperatures mean thicker jackets and shorter walks. I like the way dogs look at everything as if they're seeing it for the first time, the excitement at a tree, a lamppost, at a stick being thrown.

"We haven't seen our daughter in two years," Harvey Chancellor says, looking at my badge. "I'm almost too scared to ask what Ariel's done."

"Nothing," I tell him. It's getting cold on the doorstep and he doesn't invite me in. It's a single-storey house with a bird feeder in the middle of the front lawn. There are three cats sitting beneath it and no birds. "But she may be able to help us find somebody."

"Who? Caleb Cole? He's the man everybody is looking for, and if you're here then you must know we used to know him. But not anymore. We can't help you."

"Can I come in? There may be something you can tell us that might help find Ariel or Caleb."

He slowly nods. He has thick gray hair that bounces when he does, something that other men his age must be jealous of. "Okay."

The house is warm and there's lots of modern lighting and showroom colors, and when I sit down in the living room all I want to do is put my feet up and take a nap, just a quick one, maybe only six or seven hours. Mr. Chancellor sits opposite me, and his wife comes and joins him. Both Chancellors are in their late fifties and are dressed ten years beyond their age, with Mrs. Chancellor wearing a dressing gown that covers every inch of skin from the neck down and looks like it would make a great job of cleaning the car. Her hair is brown with a few streaks of gray running through it, and she has a hair clip in the side of it that looks heavy enough to damage her neck. She offers to get me a coffee and I tell her it would be great. Giving up coffee almost lasted half a day. I figure that's pretty good. There are pictures of Ariel on the walls, but none of them are the same woman I saw this morning. These are pictures of another Ariel, a daughter from a different life. The living room is hot, there's a heat pump blasting warm air. There's a crime show on

TV. The forensics leads are well-rounded people, finding hairs in one scene with microscopes, then kicking down doors in another. The TV is on mute so for the time being they have to arrest their suspect in silence.

"Ariel works the streets," Harvey says, "has done for a long time. We tried to stop her and we tried to get her help, of course. I mean, what parents wouldn't? I say that because it's important to us you understand that, that you don't think we abandoned our daughter. The more we tried the worse it got. She used to run away a lot. Not right after the thing with Jessica, but about a year later. Within months she was a different girl. Losing Jessica that way, it changed her. It wasn't until she was around thirteen that she really started blaming herself. I think that was when she finally understood what had happened. She hated James Whitby and she hated herself." He looks around for his wife, then smiles at me when he seems to remember she isn't there. "Coffee won't be too long," he says.

I nod and don't say anything, wanting him to continue. One of the forensics leads on TV has just shot somebody. That's the thing about TV—the bad guys often end up dying. I wonder if that's how it will end for Caleb.

"We got her counseling and it didn't help. She was prescribed antidepressants and the day she got them she took them all. We got her to the hospital just in time. The doctors said another few minutes and she wouldn't have made it. They said that as it was, it was a miracle she did."

I think about the word *miracle* again, and part of me is afraid that the miracles in this world are limited and that Ariel Chancellor has used one up that could have gone to my wife. It's a stupid selfish thought, but there it is, unmasked and real.

"After that she would sneak out at night and come home drunk. She started fooling around with the boys in her school. She was expelled from high school at fifteen when she was caught having sex with two students at the same time for a handful of change in one of the science labs. We got her into another school and the same thing happened two weeks later. She ran away more and more, and each time we found her she was higher than the last. When she turned seventeen we hardly ever saw her again."

He gives me the speech and is candid about it in the way a man can be when he's given the speech so many times there is no more shame in it, not that there is shame at what his daughter did—she was a victim of a crime—but perhaps shame in the fact they couldn't help her. He doesn't sound disappointed, doesn't sound upset—just accepting that this is the way life turned out.

"He used to write to her," he says. "Caleb, from jail."

"Write about what?"

"About how much he loved her and how much he hated her. About prison life, about his daughter, about the son he never had, about his wife."

"You still have the letters?"

He nods. "We wanted to throw them out, but we always thought one day we might need them."

His wife comes back into the room carrying a tray with three cups on them, catching up on the conversation. "I'll go and get them, shall I?"

"I think they're in the closet," he says, "up on the top shelf behind the jigsaw puzzles."

"They're in the spare bedroom," she says, "under the bed in a box." She puts the tray down on the coffee table and walks back out.

Harvey gives me the eye roll and half shrug. "This is why it's so important to be married at this age," he says.

I nod. I will also be married at his age, and before today I thought Bridget would never be able to tell me where I left my favorite T-shirt—but maybe that isn't going to be the case.

"I see you know what I mean," he says, giving a small laugh.

"Sorry?"

"You were smiling," he says.

"Tell me about the letters."

"In the beginning they were okay," he says. "In them Caleb says how sorry he is Ariel went through what she went through, and how he was thankful both girls hadn't died. Then they became angry. So angry I was amazed he was allowed to send them. I made a complaint and the prison said there was nothing they could do because he was getting the letters out without them being screened. They said it happens all the time, inmates handing the mail to other inmates who are being visited by family, and they said it was a violation of his rights to take away his ability to write. Can you believe that? A guy is writing to my daughter about how he wishes she had been raped and murdered instead of his own girl and the prison authorities say he's the one with the rights?"

I wince at hearing those words. "That's what he was saying?"

"And worse, let me tell you," he says, a slight nod while he talks, and the slight nod is just enough to make the words spill out faster. "The letters would change in tone. One would arrive and say he didn't blame Ariel in the least, another would arrive and call her a slut, that it was her fault his daughter had died, that if she had been any kind of friend she wouldn't have run away and left her there. And the worst thing—well, the worst thing is we kept reading them. Honestly, I couldn't tell you why."

"I'm guessing Ariel never saw the letters?"

"No," he says.

Mrs. Chancellor brings in the letters and hands them over. They form a fat stack, held together by a rubber band, the corners and edges discolored and twisted. The coffee is still too hot to pick up. I pull out the top letter. Cole's handwriting is barely legible.

"It's because of his broken fingers," Chancellor says, nodding toward the letters.

Caleb had winced when I shook his hand at the cemetery after I jump-started his car. Those same hands found the strength the following day to wrap themselves around my throat.

"Before all of this happened, how well did you know him?"

He gives a slight shrug. Harvey Chancellor is all about slight gestures. The small nod, the small shrug, the small laugh. I hope for his wife's sake he makes up for it in other ways.

"We knew him and his wife. We met them because the kids were best friends. You know how it is, when children grow up together you get to know their parents. Caleb was a good guy. I liked him. I didn't know him that well, but we'd see him at birthday parties and school events, and of course every weekend or so one of us dropped one of the kids off at the other's house for playdates. He loved his family, no doubt there. They had plans—they were having another baby, I remember that. His wife, God, she was lovely."

"Really lovely," Mrs. Chancellor says, and she's sitting on the armrest next to Harvey on the couch. "And stunning too. A real beauty. She never had a mean thing to say about any of the other parents or students, and she certainly had plenty of opportunity to. Some kids are real shits, excuse my French," she says, "but it's true. Have you ever met a couple that is so happy, so deeply in love, that you get the feeling they've never fought a day in their lives? Marriages always take work," she says, "as I'm sure you know," she adds, looking down at my hand and seeing my wedding ring, with no idea exactly how much work my marriage is taking, "but their marriage didn't seem to take any. It's a rare thing, and you tell people that and they tell you you're wrong, that no marriage can be like that, but I swear theirs was. The Caleb we knew over those years, he died back then just as his wife and daughter did. The man who wrote those letters, he isn't anybody we ever met. He's a stranger and a monster and we pray for him, Detective, we both pray for him."

"These people he's killed," Harvey says, "why them? Who are they?"

I run off the names for him.

"I don't recognize any of them," he says.

"Should we?" his wife asks.

"One was Whitby's lawyer," I say. "One was the foreman of the jury. Another was a character witness for the defense. The other one we believe is somebody your daughter was acquainted with on a professional level. And Dr. Stanton is the man who said James Whitby could be cured."

Harvey goes pale.

"Those poor girls," Mrs. Chancellor says. "They must be scared out of their wits. The news said one of them was found okay, is that true?"

"It is," I say, answering her, but I'm looking at Harvey. Harvey looks physically ill, like all the bones in his body have become poisonous.

He notices me, makes a slight swallowing gesture, then says "I don't know where Ariel is, or have any idea where Caleb may be."

"Caleb is looking for her," I tell them. "If we find Ariel, we may find Caleb."

"You probably think we've given up on her," Mrs. Chancellor says, "the way we let her work the streets, but that's not true. We love her, and if we could bring her home we would."

"She'll die on those streets," Harvey says, and his voice breaks a little as he says it, for the first time showing some real emotion toward his daughter. Part of him must still see her as the little girl in the pictures on the walls. "I don't . . ." he says, and he chokes up, and in the tradition of Harvey Chancellor, he only chokes up a little, "I don't doubt it."

His wife gives him a look, one that says a whole lot of things—it tells him she loves him, that she feels bad for him, that she wishes he wouldn't think that way even though both of them do.

"When you find her, tell her to come home, will you?" Mrs. Chancellor says, still looking at her husband.

"I'll do my best."

"I'll see you out," Harvey says, and we all stand.

When I step outside, he follows me and closes the door behind him. I turn toward him. "One of those names didn't sit well with you, Harvey. Why don't you tell me what you couldn't say in front of your wife?"

"Listen," he says, and then he says nothing, giving me nothing to listen to but the night, a car passing by one street over, somewhere there is water running, and somewhere somebody slams a door. I let him fight with what he has to say, knowing that if he doesn't get there I'm going to shake it out of him.

"I'm listening," I tell him, after a long ten seconds have passed.

"The thing is, I've seen you in the news over the last few years," he says, and I wonder where this is going, whether I'm going to have to defend myself. "Two serial killers have died and you've been with each of them when it happened. The man who killed your daughter disappeared."

"He fled the country," I tell him.

"I'm not trying to accuse you of anything," he says, "but my point is I get the idea you're the kind of man who does the right thing and not necessarily the legal thing. Am I right in thinking that?"

"What are you getting at?"

"Just answer the question, son," he says.

I realize I'm holding my breath. I let it out loudly. "Mr. Chancellor, Harvey, if you have something to—"

"Just answer the question, son, and this can go a whole lot quicker."

"The right thing."

"Always?"

"I've answered. Now what is it you want to say?"

"There's another letter."

"What?"

Chancellor is nodding as he talks, only now the gesture is much bigger. "Caleb wrote my daughter another letter."

"What kind of letter?"

"It would be six, maybe seven years ago. My wife, she doesn't know about it. Nobody does. There's something in it that I should have taken to the police back then, but I didn't want to see anybody else hurt."

"Who?"

"If I show you the letter, do I have your word you're only going to use it to try and find Caleb, and nothing else?"

"I can't promise anything like that without seeing it," I say.

"Then forget I said anything," he says. He reaches back for the door, but he doesn't turn away. "And before you threaten me, I don't have the letter. I threw it out and can't really remember what it said, and by the time you fuck around with trying to find it it'll all be too late to help anyway."

"There are two girls' lives on the line here," I remind him. "One of them is eight years old, the other one only one."

"I know. And another girl's future. I don't say this lightly, Detective. You have no idea how much I've gone through this in my mind over the years, always settling on an answer, then asking the question again just when I thought I was comfortable with it. Just hurry up and give me your word and then you can go and save them."

I don't know what is in the letter, but I know I'm not leaving here without it. "Okay, I promise, it stays between you and me."

He stares at me and says nothing.

"I mean it," I tell him. "I promise it'll stay between you and me."

"Wait here."

He disappears. I stand on the doorstep getting colder. A few minutes go by. No doubt he thinks the letter is in one place when it's in another. I pace the path up and down from the street to his door. My hands and feet are cold. I'd sit in my car and wait if it'd be any warmer than outside. Instead I sit on the front step and look at the letters he gave me. They're hard to read because I can't focus on them correctly. The letters seem a little blurred until I hold them further away from my face the way my dad used to do before he got glasses.

The letters are like Harvey said, the first one is dated three months after Cole was sentenced to jail. In it Cole tells Ariel he thinks she's a brave little girl for dealing with what she went through, and he's proud of her for running home and getting her mother to call the police. The second is almost a repeat of the first, only in it he wishes Ariel had run faster, or gone into the first house she saw rather than waiting to get home.

His third one describes what it's like in jail. He had a very different experience from what I had. We were kept in different parts of the prison: I was in a high-risk ward with pedophiles and other prisoners with targets on their backs; he was in a high-violence ward because he was a cop killer. It's not until the fourth one that the tone changes. He asks Ariel what she had been wearing on the day, who she had been flirting with, why she had brought the attack on herself and then deflected it by running away and leaving Jessica behind. There is a lot of hate and anger in the words, and Mr. and Mrs. Chancellor had every right to complain to the prison. The next letter he forgives her, only to change his mind in the following one. Prison gave him lots of time to think. It was making him crazy.

He calls her an angel. A slut. A princess. A whore.

Harvey Chancellor finally opens the door behind me. I stand up and he hands the letter to me along with a reminder of what I promised.

"What's in here?" I ask.

"Victoria Brown," he says. "We've heard her name on TV today, but it didn't mean anything. But her job, that does. She's not mentioned by name, but she's in there," he says, nodding toward the letter. "It was written after her assault."

"And you didn't tell the police?"

"No, I didn't go to the police, Detective Inspector," he says, sounding pissed off at me, "because the person who did it, she was innocent too. She didn't ask for any of this. And you believe in payback, don't you? That's why I'm telling you, and that's why you're going to keep your promise."

"Because?" I ask, looking down at the envelope.

"Because the person who put Victoria Brown into a coma," he says, "is the little girl all of this started with. It was Tabitha Jenkins."

CHAPTER FORTY

The door swings open and Tabitha Jenkins gives Caleb a smile. It's been seven years since the first and only time he saw her.

She has dyed her hair. She used to be blond, now it's dark brown, the style still the same, and it looks good on her. It hangs over the side of her face and he can't tell if she still has the scar Whitby gave her. She's tanned too, from summer days spent in the sun, maybe working in the garden since the yard is full of well-groomed plants. She's wearing worn jeans and a tight T-shirt and this little girl from all those years ago who visited him in jail is all grown up.

On her part, at least at first, there is no recognition. He can tell she thinks she's looking at a complete stranger. The smile on her face when opening the door is still there, and it widens when she looks down at Katy, and widens even more when she looks at Octavia, who is asleep again, resting on his chest with her head on his shoulder and his arm beneath her. He has a bag slung over his shoulder with diapers and wipes in it. Then her smile falters as she takes another look at Caleb.

"Can I help . . ." she starts, her words turning to fog in the air, but then it comes to her, Caleb can see it happening as her eyes grow wider. A woman like this having gone through what she went through, he's surprised she even opened the door.

"Hello, Tabitha."

"Caleb?"

He nods. "I need your help."

"My help?" Her face goes through a myriad display of emotions before setting on confusion. "When did you get out of prison?"

"A while back. I just need to talk to you," he says.

"I'm hungry," Katy says. "And cold. Can we come inside?"

Tabitha crouches down in front of Katy and composes a smile. Octavia murmurs something into his neck and he can feel a line of drool touching his skin but she doesn't wake up.

"My name is Tabitha," she says, "what's your name?"

"Katy with a y," Katy says.

"Wow, does the y go at the start?"

"No, silly, it goes at the end!"

"Pleased to meet you, Katy with a y at the end," she says, and offers her hand. Katy with the y takes it.

"I'm scared," Katy says.

"Scared? Of me? You have no reason to be scared of me."

"Scared of him," Katy says, and points at Caleb, and Tabitha's smile disappears. "I don't know where Melanie is and my dad is locked in the car and . . . and I need to pee," Katy says, crossing her legs and bouncing up and down. "Badly."

Tabitha stands back up. "Caleb, what is she talking about?"

"You haven't seen the news?" he asks.

She shakes her head. "I make a point of never watching the news. Ever. Why? Who are these girls?"

"He kidnapped us," Katy says, "and I really, really need to pee."

"The bathroom is through there, sweetie," she says, and steps aside and Katy disappears into the hall. They both watch her disappear, then Tabitha turns quickly toward Caleb. "What in the hell is she talking about?"

"Can we come in?"

"No. Did you kidnap these girls?"

"I haven't hurt them."

"Caleb—"

"They're Dr. Stanton's kids."

"What?"

"Dr. Stanton—"

"I know who Dr. Stanton is," she says. "Where is he?"

"In the trunk."

"Oh my God," she says. "What are you doing?"

"I'm punishing those who hurt us."

"Us?"

"The people who didn't defend you," he says. "The people that let Jessica die."

"What are you talking about?"

So he tells her about the lawyer, the teacher, the jury foreman. He tells her about Victoria Brown. Tabitha starts shaking. He tells her about taking the children to the slaughterhouse and leaving one of them behind.

"Oh my God," she says, when he's finished.

"These people killed Jessica," he says.

"No, Caleb, they didn't. James Whitby killed your daughter. Those people, these girls—"

"Please, Tabitha, let us come inside. Let me explain it to you."

"No, no, you can't be here."

"Please."

"Let me think," she says, putting her hand up to her face. After a few seconds she starts nodding. "I'll hear you out," she says, "but only if you leave the girls with me."

"Okay," he says, knowing it won't be the last time he lies today.

She leads him through to the living room. It's a nice place.

Nice furniture too. Not expensive, but cozy. There are lots of pictures on the walls, way more than Ariel has and these are framed, lots of family photos, lots of pictures with friends, smiles in all of them. None of them with her and a man looking intimate but there are many with her and another woman. In some they are embracing, in others they're holding hands and smiling at the camera. In all of them her face is tilted away from the camera slightly as she tries to hide away the scar.

He doesn't understand it. How can she be so normal?

How can she have been so happy over the years?

He lays Octavia down on the maroon-colored couch. Her eyes are still closed.

"Let me get her a blanket," she says. She leans down behind the couch and grabs hold of a woollen blanket and is about to cover the girl up.

"First, can you change her diaper?" he asks, putting the bag down on the floor.

"What?"

"Her diaper. It's wet."

"Why don't you do it?"

"I'm not very good at it."

"What makes you think I am?"

"Because—"

"Because what? Because I'm a woman?"

"Yeah."

"Fine," she says, and she unpacks the bag. She lays the blanket down on the floor and undoes the nappy.

"You seem so normal," he says. "You've moved on?"

"Yes," she says.

"How can you forget what happened to you?"

"I haven't forgotten," she says, for the first time elevating her voice. "It's part of who I am now." She reaches up and traces the line of her scar, brushing back her hair in the process. James Whitby had given her that with a single slice of his knife. It runs from the side of her left ear around her jaw and under her chin. She seems to catch herself touching it, and quickly lowers her hand. "I help others," she says. "Other women and children who have been through similar things. I'm a rape crisis counselor. I know what women have been through. I can relate to them and I can help them."

"You surround yourself with other people's pain?"

"Do you remember what you told me in jail?" she asks, tossing the used diaper into a plastic bag. She wipes the baby dry and throws the wipe in with the diaper before tying the bag closed. She repositions the replacement. "Well?"

He nods. He remembers all of it. She was the first visitor he'd had in a while, and the last one he ever had. His parents had visited regularly and then less regularly and then death made things permanent. His friends had visited regularly in the beginning too until it became just too awkward. Seven years ago one of the guards came and got him. Told him somebody was there to see him. He figured it would be a reporter, maybe somebody writing a book. Or a lawyer coming to tell him something he didn't want to hear. It would kill a few minutes, and there were worse ways in jail to kill a few minutes.

"You told me I owed it to Jessica to live for both of us," she says, "that I had to experience twice as much, to do all the things she would never be able to. You told me I had to be good to people. To help people."

"And do you remember why you came to see me?" he asks.

"Of course I do."

"Then tell me."

"Why? What's the point?"

"Because I want to hear you say it. I want you to remember that we're on the same side."

She shakes her head. The nappy is done up and she adjusts it, then lays Octavia on the couch. She puts the blanket over her, tucking it beneath her chin.

"I want you to remember that you were about to throw your life away for some accident that—"

"It wasn't an accident," she says.

In jail she told him she didn't remember much of what had happened when Whitby took her, that the doctors told her she had repressed it and that one day it would come back. He told her that doctors don't really know what they're talking about, and if they did Jessica would still be alive. She agreed. He was glad she agreed. He liked her. Then she told him a week earlier she had been out shopping at the mall with her friend. She had gone to the bathroom. Standing in front of the mirror fixing her makeup had been Victoria Brown. Nobody else was in the room. She didn't even think, she just acted, and she moved in behind Victoria Brown and shoved her head forward into the sink as hard as she could. Caleb liked her even more then. She felt bad at what she had done. She never intended to put the woman into a coma. She never intended anything. She never even knew where the rage had come from. They agreed then that the doctors had been right—that the pain of what had happened to her had all come back in that moment.

He told her not to feel bad. She told him she did. She was going to go to the police. He told her turning herself in wasn't going to help Victoria. He told her she had done a good thing by stopping somebody making money from defending child rapists, that her incarceration wasn't going to make Victoria wake up from her coma. He told her she would be throwing away her life, and she said it didn't matter. He believed her, but he also knew from experience that she didn't really understand what throwing away her life really meant.

"Back then . . ." he says, and for the moment he is back in jail with its cold walls. She had sat opposite him and said nothing and he had matched her word for word. The silence wasn't weird. She smiled and her face changed, it was a sad smile but in the movement of flesh and skin her scar disappeared and she was beautiful, there was no doubt she was beautiful, then she said something that made him, for the first time, feel less alone.

"You thanked me for what I had done," he says. "You thanked me for killing James Whitby. If he were still alive, would you want me to kill him?"

"No."

"I don't believe you."

"My parents were strong. They looked after me and got me the help I needed. Now I return that help to others. I wish you'd been strong for your family."

"I was strong. I did what nobody else was prepared to do. And that strength helped you and your family move on."

"That wasn't strength. Look at where it got you. You could have moved on with your family."

"Moved on? My daughter was murdered. People don't move on from that."

"That's not how I meant it," she says. "But some deal with it. Some better than others. You don't forget what happened, but after time you can still have a normal life."

"A normal life," he says, and it's all he ever wanted. Normal changes when you get the call that your daughter has gone missing.

"A, b, d, b, d, f, c," Katy says, staring at them from the hallway, half of her face poking around the edge of the doorway. When she sees them notice her, she steps into the room. "This is a nice house," she says, "but smaller than mine. Do you have any cookies?"

"We have some," Tabitha says.

"Chocolate ones?"

"Yes."

"I like chocolate ones, but Daddy doesn't let us eat them much."

"Your daddy's a wise man," Tabitha says.

"Not that wise," Caleb says.

Tabitha throws him another angry glance and he realizes unless she paces herself she's going to run out of them. She picks up the plastic bag with the diaper, then takes Katy's hand and leads her into the kitchen. She tosses the bag into the trash, washes her hands, then takes a packet of cookies from the pantry and tears it open. She offers one to Katy, then one to Caleb. He waves them away.

"Are there any toys here?" Katy asks.

"There are some stuffed toys in my bedroom. Why don't you go in there and play with them?"

Katy disappears, and Caleb and Tabitha move into the dining room. He leans against the wall and she leans against the table.

"You have a girlfriend?" he asks, looking at one of the photos next to him.

"What's that got to do with anything?"

"Is she here?"

"No, but she'll be back soon. What are you planning on doing to the girls?"

"Nothing."

"Are you going to kill their father?"

"No."

"No?" she says, her forehead forming a row of half a dozen creases. He doesn't think he has heard anybody ever sound as disbelieving.

"I've killed four people in the last two days," he says, and she flinches. "I have no reason to lie."

"Four?"

"There was another one last night."

"Who?"

"Nobody important."

"I'm sure they were important to somebody."

"Not to me," he says.

"They must have been important enough for you to kill."

She has a point.

"If you're not going to kill the doctor, why do you need him?"

He shrugs. "I want Stanton to walk in my shoes for a little while. I want him to know how it feels to lose a daughter."

"So you are going to hurt his children."

"No."

"I don't understand."

"He's only going to think I've hurt them."

"So the girl you left at the slaughterhouse, he thinks you hurt her?"

"Yes."

Her frown gets deeper. "He thinks she's dead?"

"Yes."

"Oh my God, Caleb! That's awful. Is that part of walking in your shoes?"

"Yes," he says, "and it's sure as hell better than what happened to Jessica."

"And you need Katy and Octavia because you want to keep making your point, but you're planning on letting them go, and you're planning on letting him go too?"

"Yes."

She sits down at the dining table. "This is insane, you know that, right?"

"It's what needed to be done."

"You've killed four people."

"They were bad people."

"They were good people doing what they thought was right," she says. "We need people like that to bring balance to this world."

"If you believed that you never would have put Victoria Brown into a coma."

She hangs her head and directs her words at the table. "I've changed since then."

He moves toward her, puts his palms on the opposite side of the table, and leans forward. "You help people now, that's admirable. Now it's time for you to help me."

"With what?"

"You can start by remembering some of that hatred toward Mrs. Whitby. I want you to help me get to her," he says, knowing she'll never agree, but that isn't why he's come here. He's come here because he needs somewhere to stay. But right now he just wants her to be on his side. And one thing he's learned in life is that sometimes if you ask for something more than what you want, you may just get what it is you're after.

"You what?"

"She's being watched by the police. I can't go anywhere near her. But you can."

"You want me to attack Mrs. Whitby? To try and kill her? Is that what you want?"

"Yes," he says, fully aware of how that sounds.

"And for that I'll spend ten or twenty years in jail."

"No you won't. I'll make sure of it."

"And how are you going to do that?"

"Because you'll tell them I made you do it."

"And how are you going to make me do it?"

"Easy. You just tell them I was threatening the children."

She stares at him so hard that he takes his hands off the table and straightens up. "Are you . . . are you threatening these children?"

"No, of course not."

"I'm not going to help you, Caleb," she says.

He nods. "Then I want you to let us all stay here. It might take a day or two, but the investigation will slow down and the police will lower their guard, and when they do I'll be able to get to her. But tonight and tomorrow I'll have no chance, and I don't have anywhere else to go. Please, Tabitha, I'm desperate."

"You can't stay here. Anyway, Wendy will be home soon and what am I going to tell her?"

"Tell her the truth. Tell her it's something you need to do, that you owe me for not telling the police it was you who put Victoria Brown into a coma."

"I should have told them myself."

"But you didn't. It would be awful if they found out."

She looks at him, getting the implied threat, and suddenly

he feels bad for saying it. He holds up his hand. "I didn't mean I'm going to tell them," he says.

"As long as I help you."

"No, no matter what happens, I'll never tell them. You're the only other person who stood up for what was right."

"You can't stay here, Caleb," she says. "And I should have gone to the police back then."

"Then this life," he says, spreading his arms, "wouldn't be yours. Your girlfriend would be with somebody else, standing in photos hanging on some other woman's wall. The people who come to you for help, they would go elsewhere and maybe they wouldn't have somebody care about them the same way you do. The people you're helping, are you really going to turn your back on them? Is that what you want?"

"What I want is for you to leave, and for you to leave alone." She gets up from the table and moves toward him. "The others can stay."

"No."

"Please, Caleb," she says, and she reaches out and puts a hand on his arm and it takes him back to that day in jail when she cried after he told her she had to live for Jessica too. He had put a hand on her shoulder and a guard had come over and physically separated them. Caleb had shoved him. The guard fell over and that gave Caleb five seconds to hug Tabitha. She returned the hug. It felt amazing. She promised she would always remember Jessica and honor that memory. Then two guards separated them. They forced him back to his cell. They beat him when they got there. They broke one of his ribs.

He was thankful for her visit.

She never came back.

Her touch now relaxes him. He doesn't feel so alone. "You can't carry on like this. It will kill you."

"That's the plan."

"What?"

"Nothing."

She pulls away her hand and puts it to her mouth. "Oh my God, you don't want to live through this, do you?"

He can hear Octavia snoring softly from the living room. Katy is in the hallway staring at them, the cookie in her hand. There's a bite mark out of it but she isn't chewing—she's motionless, listening. He wonders how much of the conversation she has heard. He can't let her talk to her father.

"The only thing I have to live for is justice. When I have that, there is nothing left."

"You're going to kill yourself?"

"No. Of course not."

"Then what?"

"It doesn't matter."

"It matters to me."

"I can't go back to jail."

"There are circumstances behind what you did, you can plead temporary insanity, you can—"

"No," he says. "There were circumstances last time too."

"Caleb—"

"I'm not going to kill myself," he says.

"What then?"

"Can we stay here or not?"

"No. But you're not leaving with those children."

He shakes his head. "They're coming with me."

She blocks his view of Katy. "I mean it," she says. "I promise I won't call the police, not straightaway. I'll give you thirty minutes. That gives you plenty of time to go anywhere in the city. It gives you time to think about what you want to do next."

"I need them."

"You only need their father, and you'll still have him. Part of me hates him too. I know what he did to you, I do, and right now I'm offering to help you, Caleb. I'm going to compromise for the safety of these girls. I'm going to let you drive away with their father as long as you leave the girls here. Even if you don't intend them any harm, it can still come to them. What if the police try to stop you and you crash your car? Or there are shots fired and one of them is hit? What if Katy gets so scared she gets hurt trying to run away?"

"They're going to be okay," he says.

"But you can't know that! What happens here is permanent. You're scaring these children, Caleb, you really are."

"How about this," he says. "You call Wendy and tell her…"

She leans in and at first he thinks she's going to slap him, or beat his chest with her fists, and he stands solid, allowing her to do it, only instead she leans in and hugs him. He can smell her hair, her skin, and he likes it. It makes him think of his wife, makes him realize how long it's been since he's held on to a woman. He can feel the anger draining away from him.

"I'm not going to help you hurt anybody," she says, her voice soft and soothing and warm against his skin, and he imagines it's the same voice she uses on those she helps. "Please, Caleb, for my sake, and for Jessica's, let's make sure no more children are hurt."

He nods. Hurt children are the last thing he wants. "When is Wendy due home?" he asks.

"Soon."

"How soon?"

"Any minute now."

He pulls back from her and holds her by the shoulders. "You're lying," he says. "Please, just tell me the truth."

"She's visiting her parents. She's in Auckland. I'll be picking her up from the airport tomorrow night."

"In that case I have another plan," he says, and he grabs her by the arm and leads her into the bedroom.

CHAPTER FORTY-ONE

Schroder calls me as I walk down the path to my car. He tells me they still don't have Caleb Cole in custody. I wasn't really expecting that he would. He says there is still no sign of Ariel Chancellor. That doesn't surprise me either. He doesn't tell me anything that I didn't know before leaving the station earlier.

"Just the same bullshit psychics calling us wanting their fifteen minutes. Have you learned anything new?" he asks. He sounds desperate, but not desperate enough to have given those psychics a call back. A day ago I was just a guy giving a drunk detective a lift to a crime scene. Today he's hoping I have some answers.

"I've learned dog bites hurt like a bitch," I tell him, then update him on the letters. "Hopefully they'll give up something. I'll be back soon," I tell him, and climb into my car.

I don't bother going through the letters I didn't get to when I sat on Chancellor's doorstep earlier. I put them all down, except for the one Harvey gave me in the end. I open the envelope and slide it out, hoping there'll be something in it that will help end this madness.

> Dear Ariel,
>
> I know it's been a while since I last wrote to you, and I know what you must think of me. I just want to start out by saying I'm sorry. I've written you some pretty nasty letters over the years, but I'm okay now. I've dealt with things and can see none of it was your fault. It never was, and I genuinely feel sick at ever blaming you when the blame is with others. I wish you all the best in your future. I ask that you remember Jessica and honor her memory by being the best person you can be. I see you as a daughter, maybe as a replacement daughter, I don't know, but I do love you and do want all the best for you.
>
> Jail is tough. I hate it here. Does it make me regret what I did? No, of course not. I still have seven years to go in here, but there are girls out there now who are sixteen or seventeen or eighteen years old who would have been dead if I hadn't taken care of James Whitby. It's possible you are one of those girls. Whitby was obsessed with you, and who knows what he would have done? Two more years in a hospital with Dr. Stanton and he would have been "cured" and fit for life, free to carry on with his obsessions—that's if he had even been sentenced. If he had been placed in your neighborhood again, then what? I do have some regrets I suppose. I could have waited and killed him when he was released and hidden his body, I could have tried to have gotten away with it, but that's in the past, and anyway, the prisons and hospitals don't exactly let the public know when inmates are being released, or where they are being placed. I will be counting on that too, when it's my time to be free.
>
> Today a girl came to see me. She used to be just like you. Young, beautiful, smart, compassionate. Two years before James Whitby killed Jessica, he tried doing the same thing

to her. She was the one he was supposed to go to jail for but never did. James Whitby hurt her, but so did many others by letting her down.

I know you're angry about what happened to Jessica, so I know you'll keep this a secret too—but the girl, she hurt that woman who defended Whitby. She has the same anger as us. That anger, that's what is going to get me through the next seven years, and when I come out I promise I will hurt those who hurt Jessica and this girl and, to an extent, have hurt you too. I know you feel guilty at what happened (how can you not?) and I'm sorry that my shitty letters to you over the years only made you feel worse. I don't hate you, I don't blame you.

Having this girl coming to see me is like a sign. Revenge is all I have. I'm changing in here, I have what another inmate in here calls "the darkness" growing inside of me. He thinks by the time I'm released I'll be capable of anything, that the darkness will have grown an appetite and will need to be fed.

I would like to see you when I come out of jail. I would like to see the person you have become. You were my daughter's best friend and for that friendship you gave her I am truly grateful. I hope you write back to me. I would like you to come and see me one day, but understand if you won't. I am not a monster. I would never hurt you. I'm a father, I'm hurting—I loved Jessica so much, I loved my wife, and these people took that away from me. They will hurt others too, and they must be held accountable.

I wish you all the best, and I wish you the best of lives,

Caleb

If Harvey Chancellor had handed this letter into the police, these deaths all could have been avoided. Or if Cole had started killing, we'd have made the connection immediately.

Tabitha Jenkins would have been arrested and she would have gone to jail—that was the price. One woman's imprisonment would have saved four lives, and perhaps more.

My own car isn't equipped with the technology of patrol cars, so I can't look up Tabitha's address on a built-in computer, but for the last few years I've been in the habit of carrying a phone book in the car. I look up Tabitha's address, and on the way there I call Harvey Chancellor.

"You could have saved a lot of lives with this," I tell him, swerving to avoid a car speeding out of a driveway.

"I know."

"Don't you feel bad?"

"Hang on a second," he says, and he goes quiet and I imagine he's walking away from his wife, wanting to be able to talk without her listening. "I feel bad for the doctor's kids, sure, but for the others? No. Fuck them," he says, sounding like a different Harvey Chancellor than the one who sat opposite me in the living room sipping coffee. "Those people, they ruined her, Detective. And don't forget your promise. I don't want to read in the news tomorrow you've arrested Tabitha. You gave me your word."

"She won't be arrested," I tell him. "But you should have come to us seven years ago. We could have made a deal."

"You'd have put her in prison."

"She put somebody in a coma!"

"And Victoria Brown helped put Jessica Cole into the ground."

He hangs up on me. A car pulls up next to me at an intersection, the side window is wound down and the passenger leans out and vomits down the outside of the door, sees me, and gives me the finger and yells at me to fuck off before laughing hysterically. I reach Tabitha Jenkins's house. It's a small home in a quiet street where everybody has tidy gardens. I tuck the letter into my pocket and walk up to the door. I knock and wait and then knock and wait again. The lights are on but she isn't answering. There's no car in the driveway. I head over to the garage and look through the window. There's a car parked inside. Just no signs of life. Houses come with a feeling—when I was a cop I could always tell the difference between there being nobody home and nobody answering. This house doesn't feel empty.

I move to the living room window. I angle myself until I can see through a gap in the curtains. There are no signs of a struggle. I tap against the glass. Nothing. I move around to the back door. There are a few options aside from the wait-and-see option. I can call Schroder for backup, which takes time. I could kick down the door, but then I'm in trouble for breaking and entering. So I get out my lock pick. No harm, no foul. If I'm wrong, I lock up after me and walk away. If I'm right, then time is of the essence.

I crouch in front of the lock. It takes me a few minutes because I can't see much. Then there's a click and the door relaxes a little and I turn the handle. I step inside.

"Hello?"

I wish I had a gun. I have nothing. I head into the kitchen. There is blood all over the floor. Only it doesn't quite look like blood. There's an empty tin of tomato sauce sitting on the kitchen bench, next to a can opener. I can imagine Tabitha opening it, then getting a fright and dropping it. I move past it. There's a knife with sauce on it in the sink. I reach for a clean one, then hesitate. If Tabitha is in the shower because she got sauce all over herself, then she's going to scream when she sees me and I'm going to lose my job. I pick one up anyway. I keep it down by my side.

"Hello? Tabitha?"

I can't hear a shower running. Tabitha wouldn't sleep through the noise I'm making. Near the front door is a side table, on it a set of keys, a handbag, a cell phone.

"Tabitha?"

The sense you get as a cop when you're about to find a dead

body is kicking in. It's the same bad feeling I got when me and Carl were the first to arrive at the slaughterhouse to find Jessica Cole. You hope one thing and get the complete opposite. Being a cop is all about that. Yet right now it's just a feeling. Nothing here to suggest anything bad has happened. Only a set of keys and a cell phone and a handbag by the door.

There's an open packet of cookies on the kitchen table. I have an instant flash-forward of my future, of me sitting at the table cramming cookies into my mouth as Tabitha Jenkins walks in, a pile of crumbs forming around me.

She could be asleep. Or next door. Maybe she's gone running.

I check the living room. I check the first bedroom, which looks like a guest bedroom. The second bedroom has been turned into an office. The computer is going. There's a spreadsheet open on the monitor. It looks like Tabitha was doing her taxes. Probably figuring like the rest of us the balance between giving the tax department its due and surviving.

Toilet. Closet. Bathroom. Nothing. I head to the master bedroom. The door is closed. I put my hand against the handle and my head against the door. I can't hear anything. I suck in a deep breath. I have a real bad feeling about what's going to be on the other side.

CHAPTER FORTY-TWO

He has to find somewhere to go. He can't go to a hotel. People are looking for him. He's too sore to sleep in his car. He needs a bed. Somewhere comfortable. He thought Tabitha would help. He's disappointed in her. He thought about staying there but decided it was too risky. Anybody could come by.

Fifteen years ago when he needed help, he could have asked any of his friends. Any one of them would have helped him kill James Whitby—at least in that moment of asking. When it came down to it, he knew none of them would be able to go through with it. What he did do was go and see his brother-in-law. He asked Adam if he could borrow his truck. Adam didn't ask why he wanted it. He just handed over the keys and wished Caleb the best of luck. A week later Lara was dead and Adam has never spoken to him again. Now he uses his cell phone to call him. Katy stares at him from the passenger seat, her face wet with tears, but at least she's sobbing quietly and for that he's thankful. Out of the three girls, she really does remind him of Jessica the most.

"Hello?"

"Adam?"

"Yeah? Who is this?"

"It's Caleb."

There is silence on the other end. Caleb waits it out, waiting for his brother-in-law to hang up, hoping he won't—and he doesn't. Instead he comes back with "Hang on, give me a minute."

Caleb hears a door closing and then footsteps, and thirty seconds later Adam is back on the line. "Jesus, Caleb, how have you been?"

"I've had better days," Caleb says.

"I'll say. You're all over the news. You've been doing some bad shit. You hurt those girls?"

"I would never do that."

"That's what I've been telling Marie," he says, and Caleb wonders what his sister-in-law looks like these days, wonders how much money she is spending on still chasing the Barbie-doll looks she was chasing when he last saw her. "I kept saying as fucked up as Caleb must be, he'd never hurt any kids. So what do you want, Caleb?"

He stares out the windshield. The street is empty of people but he can count at least a dozen cats wandering about, some of them staring at each other, two of them looking as though they either want to fuck or fight. He's aware that Katy is listening to every word he is saying. He will have to drug her again soon.

"I need some help."

He imagines Adam the same way he was fifteen years ago. The current Adam may be bald, he may have put on a few extra pounds, but the look on his face right now will be the same, a look of pained confusion.

"Geez, Caleb, I can't do that. Last time I helped you . . . fuck, you remember."

"I didn't know that was going to happen. Any of it."

"No, because you were only thinking of yourself, and you're

doing the same thing again. I have my own family, Caleb. I can't get into trouble for you. They've spoken to me by the way, the police. They want me to call if I hear from you."

"Will you?"

"I should. I should hang up and call them right now."

"But?"

"But it depends on what you have to say."

The two cats are still stalking each other. They've decided on a fight. The other cats are all watching the show. They're forming the kind of circle where money would start exchanging hands. Or paws.

"On?"

"On what you're doing with the girls?"

"I'm not hurting them," he says, staring at Katy who won't look back at him. She's also watching the cats, her hands on the window forming a seal between the glass and her face as she tries to get a closer look.

"Then what are you doing?"

"I've just let one of them go," he says. "She's safe and sound and the police will find her tomorrow. And I promise I'm not going to hurt the other one."

Katy flinches at the remark but keeps looking out the window. She is starting to hum her cute little song, and he hopes the vocals don't kick in.

"What about the doctor?"

"He's going to pay for what he did." One of the cats runs forward and the second one turns and runs. The first one chases it across a front lawn and up over the fence. The other cats look as though they don't know what to do now. "Are you still in the furniture-moving business?"

"Yeah. Unfortunately. Though I don't do the lifting anymore, my back is shot from too many years of it. But I'm not lending you the truck again. Everything else that happened was bad enough, but the final insult was the insurance company wouldn't cover the damage. It was a write-off, Caleb. I lost my niece, my sister, then I nearly lost my job. It took me years to pay off that loss."

"I don't want your truck, Adam."

"No? What then?"

"You still rent furniture to real estate agents to put in empty houses going on the market?"

There's a few more seconds of silence. Some of the cats are wandering off and Caleb starts looking at the houses, looking for signs of life. He should be safe. Nobody called the police when his daughter was being abducted—why would they call the police for seeing a man sitting in a car?

"Adam?"

"Why?"

"I need somewhere to stay. I can't go to a hotel. I need somewhere I can hole up for the night, maybe even two. Somewhere empty you've filled with furniture would be perfect."

"Geez, Caleb, I don't know."

"I'm desperate."

"I know, I know, but you're also hurting people. I can't be part of that."

"I'm only hurting the same people that took away Jessica and Lara."

"I know, I know that, okay?" Adam says, his voice taking on a whiney tone. "But the thing is, that's not really what you're doing."

"What?"

"You killed Whitby, man, wasn't that enough?"

"No," Caleb says, "no it wasn't." What the fuck is wrong with everybody?

"Shit, fifteen years ago when you killed that sack of shit, I was thrilled. You did what anybody would have wanted to do. The difference is you had the balls to do it. That's why . . . it's why I can't blame you for Lara killing herself. I can't blame you because I'd have done the same thing. I hate you for it, but I don't blame you for it."

"Then help me now."

"What you're doing is wrong."

"Help me and the last girl won't have to be hurt. I promise, I'll be letting her go soon," he says, and even though Katy is still watching the cats he can tell she's more focused on what he's saying. If he's not careful, she'll make a run for it. "If the police find me first, there'll be a fight. She could get hurt. If I have somewhere to stay for the night, somewhere safe, then she will be safe too."

"You really let another one of them go?"

"Yes. She's safe."

"Then why not let the last one go too?"

"I'm going to—just not yet," he says. Jesus, is he going to have to go through every detail with anybody he asks for help?

"And her father?"

"I'm going to let him go too."

"You're lying."

"Actually, Adam, I'm not lying. I have no intention of hurting him."

Katy turns to look at him.

"I don't understand," Adam says.

"You don't need to. You just need to give me somewhere I can go so I can make sure the last girl will be safe. And you have to promise me you won't call the police, because if you do people are going to be needlessly hurt."

Adam goes quiet.

"Adam . . ."

"Okay, okay. Let me think a second."

"Adam . . ."

"Just a second, Caleb, okay? You owe me the chance to think about it."

Caleb looks at the cell phone, wondering if it can be traced, suddenly wondering if the police are at Adam's house listening to the conversation. This was a mistake. He should hang up and throw the phone out the window and leave.

"There's this house, I guess," Adam says. "We put furniture in it yesterday. Real estate agent is away and won't be back till the weekend. So that gives you a few days at the most. But if the neighbors get curious and call the police, you sure as hell can't mention my name, you got that?"

"I appreciate it," Caleb says, not feeling bad that soon he'll want the police to find him there.

"No, you have to do more than appreciate it, Caleb. You have to promise me. With the recession, things are tight, okay? If I lose my job, then I lose my house. You're in and out of there and any mess you leave we put down to a burglar. Okay? And promise me again you're not going to hurt anybody."

"I promise," he says, and it's a lie but it's for the greater good. One day Adam will understand. "To both things."

"Don't make me regret it," Adam says, and gives him the address, then hangs up.

Caleb switches off the phone. He starts the car and all the cats scatter.

"Is that true?" Katy asks. "Are you going to really let my dad go?"

"It's true," he tells her. "Listen," he says, the car still idling against the curb, "I'm going to need you to take these for me," he says, and reaches into his pocket.

"What are they?"

"Sleeping pills."

"I don't want to sleep."

"You need to," he says, "because I don't want you talking to your dad again before this is over."

"Over?"

He nods. "Take these, and when you wake back up you'll be with your dad again and everything will be fine," he tells her, and he feels much worse about lying than he thought he would.

He shakes the juice box Octavia was drinking from before and there's maybe a mouthful left inside. Katy uses it to wash down two of the pills, and then he hands her a third. It'll keep her knocked out for about twelve hours, he figures. Nothing will wake her.

There are some drops of rain on the windshield but not enough to worry about as he begins to drive. He drives into New Brighton, a beach suburb that he knows reasonably well because he used to have a flat here when he was in his early twenties. This was where he was living when he met Lara. It was his flatmate's birthday and Lara came along with one of her friends. Caleb had met her and chatted with her for a few minutes, then didn't think of her again until he ran into her a week later at the cinema. This time they chatted longer and he wondered what it was about her that he saw this time that he hadn't seen the first time. He never did figure it out. Two years after meeting her they were living in the nice house that he no longer owns.

He drives with the window down and can smell the salt air from the ocean. The rain picks up for a few seconds, a sudden violent pummeling of it against the car, then just as quickly dies off before he can reach the button to close the window. His right arm is soaked. He can hear the waves breaking against the shore. He hasn't seen the ocean in a long time. He drives parallel to the sand dunes. Part of him wants to park the car and climb them and stare out at the moon hanging over the water before the cloud cover conceals it. Instead he keeps driving. He makes a right turn and half a block away he finds the house Adam told him about. A real estate sign has been pounded into the ground in the middle of the front lawn. *Open House—Saturday 1:00–1:30.* The words are below a picture of a smiling man trying to look like he could be your best friend.

Katy has fallen asleep, her chin resting on her chest. He pops the trunk. He hauls Stanton over the edge of the trunk until the balance is on his side of it, then he lets him go so he piles onto the ground. He bends down and gets one of Stanton's arms around his neck and manages to stand up, then he walks him toward the house. He can barely hold on to him his joints are aching so much, but he deals with it, the same way he's dealt with everything over the years, only it's easier this time because he knows he doesn't have to put up with the pain for much longer. Stanton is semiawake and manages to contribute some steps but not all. He rests him on the steps before trying the door. It's locked. He puts the blade of the knife beneath the bathroom window and levers it upward until the latch strips out of the wood. He climbs through and loops around to the back door. He drags Stanton inside. The carpet in the house is new and spongy, making it harder to drag Stanton to the bedroom furthest from the street. He puts a fresh set of plastic ties around Stanton's feet and leaves him on the floor.

He flicks on the bathroom light for a brief second to make sure the house has power. Enough light spills into the hallway and two bedrooms to see the furniture is all modern, that there are nice prints on the wall too, everything in its place to make an empty house feel like a home, an illusion that will help the owner fetch more money when it sells. He brings Katy inside, lifts back the showroom covers, and puts her in the showroom bed, placing the showroom pillow beneath her cute little head. He tucks her in.

There's a nice looking LCD TV in the living room, which he carries down to a different bedroom, worried the glow in the living room would alert the neighbors. It's amazing how much lighter TVs are since he last owned one. And flatter. He watches the news. His picture comes up, taken the day he was booked for murder fifteen years ago. Then there's a photograph of him standing next to Lara, Jessica between them, taken when Jessica was six. They had taken her to a costume party for one of Jessica's friends. Lara had worked all week to make an outfit for her because for the week prior to the party Jessica had kept coming home saying she wanted to go as a bat. Lara had made the outfit in secret, promising Jessica it would be ready on the day, which it was, and it looked great, with its wings and pointy ears, made from gray bedsheets Lara had specially bought. When Jessica saw it, she had asked what it was. They told her it was a bat. Jessica told them it wasn't. *But it doesn't even look like a cricket bat,* Jessica had said, and that's when the problem revealed itself. Jessica had cried at first, but with some coaxing had agreed to wear the outfit. An ice cream later, she was smiling enough for the photograph. Later that night when Jessica was asleep, Caleb and Lara had shared a bottle of wine on the porch outside and laughed about the misunderstanding.

The photograph disappears, replaced by one of James Whitby, and then there are pictures of the people he's killed over the last four days. Then his mug shot. Next to it is an illustration of how he looks now.

A lot has happened to that man.

The reporter telling the story is standing outside the police station. The front is lit up, the walls stained with the exhaust fumes of years of passing cars, stained with bird shit and probably stained with all the bullshit too from the reporters being so close. There is movement off to the side of the camera; other media outlets are hanging around the scene. He guesses it's a good day for them. It is this reporter's certain understanding from inside sources, so the reporter tells him, that the police have Judge Latham and Mrs. Whitby under guard, along with others involved with the case fifteen years ago. She goes on to say that Dr. Stanton and his two youngest daughters are still being held captive, and that Melanie Stanton was found earlier today and is undergoing a battery of tests. When asked by the anchorwoman whether Melanie Stanton was sexually assaulted, the reporter says it's too soon for the police to release that information.

He throws the remote control at the TV. His aim is off and it hits the wall, the back cover popping off and the batteries disappearing into different corners of the room. The TV is still going. He rips the power cord from the wall. What the hell is wrong with people?

He goes back through to the bedroom where Stanton is

sitting with his eyes wide open. He removes the tape from his mouth, peeling it quickly. The doctor doesn't flinch.

"Where's . . . where's Octavia?" he asks, his voice sounding like a cartoon mouse asking a cartoon cat not to eat him.

"I let her go," Caleb says.

"Where?"

"I left her with a friend."

"Is she okay?" Stanton asks, his voice wavering.

Caleb shrugs. "I guess that depends on your definition of okay."

Stanton starts to cough, then swallows loudly. He sounds out of breath when he talks again. "What does that mean?"

"It means she's at peace."

Stanton slowly shakes his head. "Did . . . did you . . . hurt her?"

Caleb shrugs. "I can't remember."

"Answer me," he says quietly, then louder he says, "answer me, you piece of shit."

"Listen, Doctor, I'm really sorry for what I've done, but I'm better now," Caleb says, turning his palms upward and shrugging a little. "I'm good and want to be part of society once again, so give me some pills that I'll try to remember to take and half an hour of counseling and I'll be fine. Isn't that what I need to say for your forgiveness?"

"Jesus, it isn't like that! It's not fucking like that, Caleb. We work, we try our hardest to make people better."

Caleb ignores him. "It wasn't my fault, I was raised wrong, I couldn't help myself, just give me some antidepressants and I'll be fine. See? You believe me, right? You believed James Whitby. Would you have believed him if it had been your daughter he fucked and wanted to kill? Let's see, I've killed one of your daughters, maybe two—I can't quite remember—"

"You . . . you've . . ."

"—because I have a mental problem and get confused real easy. Will you defend me, Doctor? If I turn myself in, will you get up on the witness stand and tell the world it wasn't my fault?" He reaches into his pocket and pulls out his phone. "You're happy to defend people, aren't you, when it's not your family who's been hurt."

"Is that . . . is that what all of this is about? You want me to get up on the stand and defend you, to what, to prove that I'm a hypocrite? Because you think that I think it only matters when it's my family?"

"Doesn't it?"

"No, of course not."

"Well, it doesn't matter anyway, because that's not what I'm asking. You don't get to replay that moment from seventeen years ago, Stanton. You get to replay my moment from fifteen years ago."

"Please, please, don't hurt my family," Stanton says, crying again.

"When you let him out, why didn't you put him in a house on your street?"

"Please . . . please don't hurt anybody else."

"Well, it's late now," he says, playing with his phone. "And I'm tired, and if I don't get enough rest I won't have the strength to deal with your third daughter tomorrow. See this?" he says, holding up the phone. "Cameras have changed a lot since I've been in jail. Last time I used a camera I had to take the film into the store to get developed. You always had to pick and choose when you were going to push that button, because every snap cost you money. Now every cell phone has a camera in it, now everybody is a photographer, every camera has a hundred functions, but no matter how you shoot a dead baby it's always going to look dead."

He turns the screen toward Stanton so he can see it. The glow lights him up.

"Take a look," Caleb says, and he grabs Stanton's hair and twists his head until his face lines up with the screen. The picture is of Octavia lying on the floor facedown, her body surrounded by blood. There's a bloody knife lying next to her.

"You . . . you stabbed her?"

"Just the once," he answers, "and I sedated her before she died." He slips the phone into his pocket, then puts the duct tape back across Stanton's mouth. "I suggest you get a good night's sleep—tomorrow is going to be an important day for you. Tomorrow you're going to have to convince me not to kill Katy because I like her, and you like her too. It's obvious she's your favorite because she's the one you never picked to die. You see, Stanton, all of this, this is just me warming up. The best part . . . ," he says, "the best part is still to come."

CHAPTER FORTY-THREE

Tabitha Jenkins has her wrists tied behind her, her feet bound, and duct tape across her mouth. Her eyes are closed. She looks dead, except for the slight rise and fall of her chest. On the floor next to the bed is a baby that looks like Octavia, though I've found that except for my own daughter, all one-year-olds look the same. She is strapped into a car seat. Her eyes are wide open and she's staring right at me with a very confused look on her face. There is tomato sauce all over the front of her one-piece pajama outfit.

The knife is no longer down by my side. Instead it's in front of my body. My heart is racing and I want to rush into the room. I want to scoop Octavia up and shout out with excitement. I keep hold of those desires and stay calm and move in slowly, looking left and right, waiting for Caleb to appear like he did earlier today. Only he doesn't, and I reach Octavia and crouch down next to her and give her a big smile.

"Hello, Octavia," I tell her. "My name is Theo."

"Hello-zies," she says, smiling back.

"Is there anybody else here?" I ask her, knowing I could probably get more information from the seat she's strapped into than from her.

"Bufwiffy," she says, then her face scrunches up into a tight little ball and she turns red for a few seconds before relaxing, sending out a stench that makes my eyes water.

"Jesus," I say, standing back up.

I shake Tabitha and she stirs but only a little. I cut her bindings and remove the duct tape, then make my way back through the house, checking the same rooms, the hallway, the living room, back the way I came in and passing the tomato sauce on the floor that now makes sense. Caleb has faked killing Octavia. I check to make sure the doors are locked and I secure the dead bolts. When I'm satisfied we're alone, I head back down to the bedroom. I pick Tabitha up. She's heavier than I thought she would be for somebody so slim, or maybe I'm just a lot weaker than I remember. My leg hurts from the dog bites as I walk down to the bathroom and my back threatens to slip a disc as I lower her into the shower. Her eyes open a little wider and her body flinches when I turn on the water. It's cold for ten seconds before warming up. I stand back, not wanting to get wet. Her hair is pasted to her face and her clothes cling to her skin and she has her face pointing at the floor. Slowly she raises her head a little and puts her hands over her face.

"I'm awake," Tabitha says, but she doesn't sound it.

"Tabitha, my name is Detective Inspector Theodore Tate," I say, talking loudly to be heard over the shower. "Can you understand me?"

"Understand me," she repeats, the water splashing off her face.

"Tabitha? Where is Caleb?"

"Caleb," she says, "he's not a bad man."

"How long ago was he here?"

"He's just doing bad things," she says, blinking heavily.

"Tabitha? When was he here?"

"Don't know."

"Is he coming back?"

"Don't know," she says, and she focuses on me for the first time. "Who are you? A cop?"

"Yes. My name is Theodore Tate."

"It was an accident," she says. "I didn't mean it."

She rests her head against the wall of the shower and holds her hands above her eyes like a visor, shielding them from water. She wraps her arms around her legs and rests her chin on her knees.

"Tabitha," I say, and she looks up at me. "Is Caleb coming back? Do you know where he is?"

"No," she says, staring at her feet. "He didn't say."

I step into the hallway. I check on Octavia and think about opening a window to help with the smell, but don't want to give Caleb an outlet to sneak inside, not that I think he's coming back. Octavia is okay and seems to be enjoying the smell as much as she seems to enjoy staring at her fingers, which in this case is a lot. I grab my cell phone and call Schroder.

"I've found Octavia Stanton," I tell him.

"You what? Where?"

"At Tabitha Jenkins's house."

"What? You . . . what? What are you doing there? Is the girl okay? What about the others? What about Cole?"

I update him, telling him I wanted to speak to Tabitha on the chance that Cole had approached her, not mentioning the real reason, and Schroder is happy to believe it.

"So it was a lucky break," I tell him, "nothing more."

"You have a thing with lucky breaks, Theo. That's great you've found her, it really is," he says, and I get the sense he's shaking his head or nodding, or maybe even fist-pumping the air. "Two girls safe and sound," he says. "We're doing this," he adds. "We're going to nail this guy and we're going to get everybody back. I can feel it. I'll get some backup sent right away."

"Wait," I tell him. "Don't send backup."

"What?"

"Just come here with a couple of other people, and that's all," I tell him, "and make sure one of them is a paramedic to check Tabitha out—she was drugged. She doesn't know if Cole is coming back, and if he is we can use this place to ambush him. And if he isn't coming back, he's already long gone, so there's no point in sending every available officer."

"Yeah, yeah, good thinking. There's no way you're not going to be one of the team again, Tate. This is great stuff. Great stuff! Okay. We'll see you in a few minutes."

I hang up. Tabitha has reached up and turned off the shower. She gets to her feet and leans against the shower walls.

"You said you were a policeman?" she asks.

I pass her a towel and then show her my badge. She doesn't look at the badge and buries her face in the towel.

"I'm looking for Cole," I tell her.

"What?" she asks, pulling the towel away.

"Caleb Cole. I'm looking for him."

"Give me a minute," she says.

I leave her in the bathroom and head into the kitchen. I switch on the kettle but flick it off before boiling point, then make a strong coffee. It's ready and sitting on the coffee table on a coaster when Tabitha comes into the lounge. She's dried off and changed into dry clothes: a pair of jeans and a fleece jacket into the pockets of which she has her hands buried deep.

"Drink this," I say, and I hand the coffee over to her. "It's not too hot."

Tabitha drinks half of it in one gulp, then hands me back the cup. "I feel sick," she says, and she moves quickly into the kitchen and throws up into the sink. She turns on the faucet hard enough for the water to splash back at her. She rinses the sink, then eases the pressure and lowers her face beneath the tap. She takes in a mouthful of water and spits it out, then another and another. When she's finished, she turns around and leans against the wall, the front of her fleece sprinkled with beads of water.

"That has to be the worst review I've ever had for coffee I've made," I tell her.

She smiles. "I hate coffee. I'm a tea drinker."

I smile back. "You're feeling okay? You don't need to sit down?"

"I'm fine," she says. "Just light-headed is all."

"How long ago did Caleb Cole leave?"

She picks up a tea towel and wipes her face with it. In the process she moves her hair behind her ear, revealing a scar pale against her tan.

"What's the time now?" she asks.

"Ten thirty."

"Then an hour ago."

"He tell you where he was going?"

She balls up the tea towel and tosses it into the sink. "No."

"Is he coming back?"

"No."

I put the half-drunken coffee down on the bench. "Listen, there's something I need to tell you before the police get here."

Her face changes at the change of tone in my voice. "What kind of something?"

"I know about Victoria Brown."

"What?"

"I know it was you that hurt her."

"Oh Jesus," she says, and looks down.

"Listen to me," I say, and I put a hand on her forearm. "Nobody else needs to know. It's going to be okay, but you need to trust me. I want to find Caleb Cole before he hurts anybody else, that's all."

"I didn't mean to hurt her that badly. I wasn't even thinking about hurting her at all. I just came out of the stall and there she was, just standing in front of me. I don't even remember thinking about it."

"It's okay," I tell her. "It's going to be okay."

"It . . . it just happened," she says, and she reaches back for the tea towel and dabs it at the bottom of her eyes. "I ran. I left her there and I ran and maybe if I had gone for help the doctors could have done more for her."

"I know you feel bad about it," I tell her, "and I'm glad you do. You should feel bad, and that's what makes you a good person. But your life will be ruined if the police find out."

"That's what he said," she says, "Caleb, back when I went to see him in jail."

"And he was right. Tabitha, why did Caleb come here? Why did he tie you up? Why did he leave Octavia here? Did he hurt you?"

Before she can answer any of my questions, there's a soft knocking from the back door.

"Your visit with Caleb, you told him about Victoria Brown," I tell her.

"Oh," she says.

"Don't let it get any further, because you'll end up in jail," I add, and I open up the door and let Schroder and the others inside. He has a phone to his ear, and a stunned look on his face. He comes inside, nods a few times, says *okay* a few times, then hangs up.

"Jesus," he says, "you're not going to believe this. But I'm off the case. I've just been suspended."

CHAPTER FORTY-FOUR

The paramedic looks over Tabitha and gives her the all clear. He suggests a visit to the hospital for observation, a suggestion that Tabitha disagrees with.

"What would I know," the paramedic says, "I'm only the expert," he says, then walks off to the living room and sits down, putting his feet up on the coffee table. He pulls out a cell phone and starts playing on it.

Me and Schroder sit in the living room with the TV on while Tabitha volunteers to change Octavia's diaper in the bedroom. Detectives Hutton and Kent have shown up, along with two officers, one of whom was the guy who first approached me at the retirement home when we went to visit the late Herbert Poole. The other is a guy I haven't seen before. The four of them hang out in the kitchen. There are other officers in unmarked cars sitting at various points in a four-block radius. On the TV is footage from Lakeview Homes. It's shaky but clear, shot from somebody's camera, either by one of the residents or by a family member who was there at the time. There is footage of a windowsill, a curtain, then the lens focuses past the window and to the first of the minivan cabs. It comes to a stop, the door slides open, and detective after detective steps out of it. It's like watching clowns at a circus climbing out of a small car, only these clowns are drunk, racing off into the fields and watering the trees before trying to figure out who killed the ringmaster.

I look at Schroder whose face is blank as my car pulls up behind the first minivan and as we both step out of it. He walks off to take a leak and I walk toward the unit with the dead body. The camera operator follows neither of us, but instead focuses on the next van, more circus performers, and then a few close-ups of some of the detectives I've worked with over the last twenty-four hours, including a tight close-up of Detective Kent who never leaves the proximity of the minivan.

Schroder flicks off the TV and hangs his head in his hands.

"It may not be as bad as you think it's going to be," I tell him, but of course that's not true—it's going to be bad. The media is going to make sure of that.

"I should have listened to you."

"I . . . ," I say, but don't know what exactly it is I want to say. What is there? I wait a few beats, then ask the question I've avoided for the last few minutes. "You've been suspended?"

He shrugs and looks over at me. "At the least," he says, "but after seeing that I don't see how I can keep my job," he says. "That was Stevens on the phone earlier. He said he has no option but to suspend me. He said any further action isn't up to him, but yeah, somebody has to fall on their sword, right? And it's going to be me."

"I'm sorry," I tell him.

"Yeah, well, you don't need to be. You're the one who told me at the time I was fucking up. I just didn't listen."

"So what are you going to do?"

"What have you learned from Tabitha?"

"Carl . . ."

"What am I supposed to do? Go home and do nothing?"

"Exactly."

"Maybe you're right, and tomorrow we'll know for sure, but right now we still have one missing girl and her father and no way to find them. Then tomorrow—yeah, tomorrow is a new day, huh? Remember this morning at the morgue? Remember what I said about maybe it being time to move on? Hell, could be this is for the best."

He stands up and steps past me. I follow him to the bedroom where Tabitha is finishing up with the diaper change. Cole left behind the diaper bag.

"Tell us what happened tonight," Schroder says.

She hands Octavia a small teddy bear, and Octavia throws it away from her and then crawls after it. Tabitha sits on the edge of the bed and starts telling us. Octavia picks up the bear, brings it back, and hands it to Tabitha. Tabitha hands it back to Octavia, who throws it again, then crawls off after it.

Tabitha tells us she was reading a book when there was a knock at the door. She answered it. Caleb Cole wanted somewhere he could stay for a day or two. She told him he couldn't stay there.

"Did he say why he came to you for help?" Schroder asks.

"My guess is he's desperate, and he thought Tabitha would be on his side," I say.

Tabitha is looking at me carefully. We both know Cole came to her because of what she did to Victoria Brown. Schroder sees the look, then gives me a similar one.

"I told him to leave the girls and their dad with me, and he said no," Tabitha says, drawing our attention back to her. She's a confident talker, no pauses, no backtracking. "He asked if I would call the police, and I said yes. In the end we came up with a deal. He said if I took some sleeping pills, he would leave one of the children with me. He knew my girlfriend would be home tomorrow. I took the deal. It was either that, or he walked out with both children."

"You saw him the once in jail," Schroder says. "Why?"

She looks surprised, and I feel surprised. Sometime in the last few hours Schroder must have checked Cole's visitation records.

"Why? It's hard to say," she says, "and, well," and now the pauses are there, her comfortable way of talking a lot less comfortable. "I felt bad for him. Of course I did. He killed the man that hurt me, and I . . ." she pauses and her pause backs up what she said about it being hard to say.

"You thanked him?" Schroder asks.

"Umm . . . no . . . not really," she says, shaking her head. Schroder raises his eyebrows at her. She carries on. "Well, okay, maybe I did. He's suffered more than you'll ever know," she says.

"Tell us about his plans for Dr. Stanton," I say. "Did he mention him much?"

She pauses, her eyes shift up and to the left, and she's remembering something that happened. I look at Schroder and he looks at me and we both wait. It takes her a few seconds, but she gets there. "This is weird," she says, "but the thing is, he said he isn't planning on hurting Dr. Stanton."

I move forward, and Schroder does the same thing. Octavia picks up the teddy bear and throws it further, then chases after it. "What makes you say that?" I ask.

She slowly starts to nod. "He said he was going to let him go. He promised he wasn't going to hurt any of them."

"Did he tell you what he meant by that?" Schroder asks.

She shakes her head. "I believe him too. He's got no reason to lie. I mean, why would he? And he held up the promises he made me tonight."

Schroder is shaking his head now too. "Doesn't make sense," he says.

I start nodding. We all have our heads moving, just not in the same direction or at the same speed. "I agree. There's just no way he's going to let Stanton go."

"He's going to," she says, and she really believes it, nodding firmly now. "Also, he said something else. He said he wanted Dr. Stanton to walk in his shoes for a while."

"That's why he's pretending to kill the children," I say.

"But when he lets him go," Schroder says, "Stanton is going to find out he's been lied to. It doesn't make sense. It's a lot of effort to go to to make the doctor think his kids are dead for only a matter of hours."

Before now, it made sense because we thought Cole was putting Stanton through this in order to kill him. But if he lets him go . . . Schroder is right, it doesn't line up.

I realize I'm still shaking my head. So is Schroder.

"He's going to let him go," Tabitha says, and she says it so calmly and so positively that it's hard not to believe she's right.

"And then what?" Schroder asks.

"And then, well, then I think he's going to kill himself."

I look at Schroder and he's giving me the same look back.

"He told you that?" I ask.

"He said all he has to live for is justice, and once he has it, there's nothing left. I asked him if he was going to kill himself and he said no, but he also said he won't go back to jail."

"And you didn't believe him," I say, setting up the next question for Schroder.

"No. I could tell he was lying."

"Then what makes you so sure he's been honest about everything else?" Schroder asks.

She looks back down at her hands. "I could just tell," she says.

"Because in your life you've spent two hours with him," Schroder says.

"I just don't know what else to tell you," she says, sounding frustrated.

We step back out into the hallway and Tabitha goes back to playing with Octavia. Detective Kent wanders down to join us.

"Anything useful?" she asks.

"Not much," Schroder says, and fills her in.

"What do you think?" I ask, directing the question at both of them. "He wants to die?"

Kent shrugs. "It wouldn't exactly be a surprise."

"I don't know," Schroder says. "Let's call Barlow and get his take on it."

I lean against one hallway wall and Schroder leans against the other one, and suddenly I'm aware that I've hardly slept in two days. I feel like sinking down into the floor.

Barlow answers on the third ring. He's still at the station, still talking to Melanie and her mother, trying to mend fences that I can't imagine ever being mended.

"First things first, Detectives," he says. "Good job on getting the girl back."

"It's not over," I tell him.

"I know it's not over, but you have to acknowledge a victory when you have one."

"I'd rather celebrate when . . ."

"Yes, yes, of course, when everybody is back safe. But let yourself be proud of what has just happened here, Theo. You've gotten another of the girls back. Take heart in that. You need to let these moments drive you more than the dark ones."

We update Barlow. He says nothing as we talk, just absorbing the information until we're finished.

"Makes sense," he says. "Whatever he has in mind, he probably figures once it's done he has nothing left to live for. I've been thinking about what we spoke about earlier, about trying to use the media against him. Perhaps, if the media hasn't reported you've found Octavia, we can use this situation somehow. I should know more once I read those letters."

"Can we set up a story to lead him back to this house?" Kent asks.

"That's what I'm thinking," Barlow asks. "But I'm not sure how."

"I might know how," I say. "We know he doesn't want to hurt the kids, right?" I say.

Now Schroder is nodding faster. So is Kent and so am I. Kent was right—we should hire a masseuse to follow us around. We're all going to have sore necks in the morning.

"Yes, yes, exactly," Barlow says, and I can imagine him caressing his chin with his thumb and forefinger, his other hand supporting his elbow as he's deep in thought. "I see where you're going with this, and yes, yes, I think that if Cole believed Octavia was in danger he would either return to the house or he would call the police and tell them where she is."

"We make something up," I say, excited now.

"What could we say the baby could be in danger from?" Barlow asks. "Another person?"

Detective Kent shakes her head. "It's simpler than that," she says. "We're gonna need Stevens to help us out, but I think I have the perfect angle."

CHAPTER FORTY-FIVE

What was supposed to take one night or possibly two now has the potential to take three. Or even longer.

The doctor is asleep again with the help of more pills, and Caleb is envious. He wishes he could just lie down and get some sleep. His body is exhausted but his mind is buzzing and it's all, he realizes, just becoming too much for him. He could take pills too, but he needs to stay sharp. His fingers are aching and his right shoulder is hurting like a bitch after all the lifting he's been doing. He paces the house. It doesn't feel like a home, it feels like a show house. It's a shame the nice fridge in the freshly painted kitchen hasn't been filled with fresh food. He's not sure why, but he starts thinking about how Octavia felt in his arms. He liked the way she would rest her head on his shoulder, the way her breath would tickle his ear. He's not sure why he misses her, all he knows is that he does. He doesn't miss the way she smelled, and that only would have gotten worse unless he bathed her, but it was nice the way she would look at him with eyes that didn't judge. His own daughter used to look at him the same way.

He paces the rooms for another minute before settling back down in the bedroom with the TV plugged back in. He watches the stupid news and the stupid presenters making shit up about him. He hates that they can do that, and at the same time he knows they do have their uses—after all, it was the media that warned him earlier he needed to leave the slaughterhouse.

He stares at the TV but really he's thinking about Mrs. Whitby. He's thinking about what he said earlier to Tabitha, about threatening the children and making her help him. Maybe there is something in that. Not with Tabitha, but with the police. He doesn't have long until the police find him, he knows that. A day or two at the most. He looks at the knife on the bedside table.

If he wanted to, he could pick that knife up, wake the doctor, and put an end to all of this now. Phone the police, phone the media, get them all here earlier than he wanted. It's not that bad an idea, not really. He's tired and can't sleep. He can't get the judge. He can't get Whitby's evil mother. They're under guard and getting to them is going to be so fucking difficult, unless he can force somebody to help, or unless he can hide for the amount of days or weeks it would take for the police to let down their guard. So yeah, fuck it, he's sick of waiting, why not grab that knife and put an end to all of this cutting?

He picks up the knife.

He visualizes how it will go—waking up the doctor, showing him the knife, and yeah, by God, he will do it. He's going to fucking do it right now! He told Tabitha the doctor would be free to go, but it's not quite that simple and certainly not that accurate.

The mother, the judge—maybe he'll get them in another life. If James Whitby is in that next life, he'll get the bastard there again too. In this life Caleb has been fucked by fate. His car battery dying like that, shit, that's the reason the judge and the mom didn't get the ride out to the slaughterhouse along with a guided tour. Okay, that and killing that other guy. He rotates the knife in his hand, studying the handle, the blade, the sharp edge. Fate. Well, it's not like he shouldn't have seen it coming. When was the last time fate was any good to him?

He moves to the door. This is it. He's really going to go through with it. He's going to let go of everything—the anger, the hate, the disappointment. He doesn't know whether to smile or cry or laugh, all he knows is that in ten minutes' time everything will be okay. He's going to leave all that shit in this life and move on.

Weeks ago he put the phone numbers of the reporters he wanted to contact into his phone. He cues up the first one and presses send. It starts to ring. He stands in the doorway staring at the doctor who is still asleep. So is Katy. All three girls will be better off with their dad no longer around.

"Hello?"

"Yes, is this . . ." he starts, but he can hear the TV from the next room, and it grabs his attention as the tone of the anchor changes.

"We have a live, urgent plea from Superintendent Dominic Stevens to Caleb Cole. Let's cross to him now."

"Hello?" the voice says again.

Caleb hangs up and moves into the bedroom. The camera zooms in on Superintendent Dominic Stevens who is standing in front of a podium. There are other microphones and cameras in the picture. Stevens is gripping the edges of the podium and looking down at some notes.

He coughs softly into his hands a couple of times and the room goes quiet. He looks up at the camera, straight at the lens, right at Caleb. His stare is so forceful that Caleb actually glances behind himself to make sure nobody is standing behind him.

"I have a prepared statement," he begins, "after which I will not take any questions. As you know, we are looking for Caleb

Cole, a man we would like to question about four murders over the last two days, along with the abduction of Dr. Stanton and his family. We have an appeal to Caleb and we hope that you are watching. Less than an hour ago we were contacted by Octavia's family doctor and informed of a heart condition she has had since birth, for which she requires constant observation and medication. Please, Caleb, Octavia is only one year old, she's scared, and, without her medication, is in considerable risk of heart failure. We beg you to think of just how vulnerable she is. We ask that you turn yourself in so we can help her and Katy. Please, Caleb, if not that, then at least take her to a hospital and drop her off so she can be helped. She takes medication every twelve hours and already missed one very important dose. Check her pulse, check her skin color; is she clammy, is her heart rate slowing? You can't afford to wait, Caleb, she needs help now. You're a father, I'm a father, and as a father I'm begging you, don't let this be your legacy. Don't become the man who is remembered for killing a one-year-old baby."

Stevens picks up his cue cards and taps them square. "Thank you," he says, and steps away from the podium. A dozen questions all come at once, none of the words distinguishable over any other. Stevens keeps walking.

Cole turns off the TV. His skin has broken out in goose bumps and his blood feels like it's turned arctic. Even his mouth is tingling.

"Fuck," he says at the dark room. "Fuck," he repeats, as he stares at the small red standby light on the TV screen.

He goes through to the other bedroom and shakes Stanton, but the man won't wake up, and after a few seconds he realizes that's a good thing. If he were to ask the doctor about his daughter's medical condition, then he'd be telling him she was still alive. But why the hell hadn't Stanton mentioned it already? Or the sisters?

It's obvious. The police are lying. They're trying to get him to give up another of the girls—yet that doesn't make sense either, because they must know the fact he didn't harm Melanie means he won't harm the others either.

So if that doesn't make sense—then what does? Is it possible with all that's gone on that the girls, the father, that they've simply forgotten to tell him that Octavia has a medical condition?

"Katy," he says, looking over at the little girl, "I need you to help me help your sister."

But Katy won't wake up either.

Easiest solution is to call the police. He starts to tap the number into his phone. He was going to call them anyway, so it's not that big a deal. Stick with the new plan. Only he can't. He can't go to his grave not knowing whether the girl lived or died.

He has to go back to the house.

And if the girl is dead? Then he has to see it. He has to put himself through the knowledge of that. Tabitha was right—he has been hurting the children.

"Fuck," he says again.

He can still hear Stevens's words. *You're a father, I'm a father, and as a father I'm begging you, don't let this be your legacy.*

He doesn't care about his legacy, people can say what they want about him, but he doesn't want to let a baby girl die.

"I have to go out for a bit," he tells Katy, but of course Katy doesn't answer him. He uses the tape and the plastic ties to make sure she's not going to go anywhere if she wakes up while he's gone.

You're a mean man, she would probably tell him right now if she could. *A mean, mean man.*

And he is a mean man. He knows that now. He's a mean man who may have just killed a one-year-old girl, and God how that hurts, how it makes him feel sick, and if that is what has happened—then what?

He puts duct tape over Katy's mouth. He supposes he is hurting her too.

He heads out the back door to the car, taking his knife with him.

CHAPTER FORTY-SIX

"I think I sold it," Stevens says, his voice coming through clearly on the speakerphone.

Detective Kent is nodding. Detective Hutton is eating part of a chocolate bar he found in his pocket, and Schroder is sitting on the couch still staring at the TV. The two officers are peeking through the curtains. I'm the only one not carrying a gun. There are no cars outside, nobody hiding in the bushes either. We're hoping Cole is going to come charging back through the door. If he does, there's nobody to spook him on the way. Tabitha and Octavia have been taken back to the police station along with the letters Mr. Chancellor gave me, minus the last one. The paramedic has been dropped off along the way.

"It was perfect," I say. Tabitha's TV is still on and there's a reporter from the scene recapping into the camera what they were all just told. It'll be similar across all the channels, reporters excited as the case continues to build. If Cole saw it, then hopefully he'll be on his way. We could have him in custody within the next ten minutes. This could all be over soon.

"Question now is, will it work?" Stevens asks.

"Let's hope so," I say, "because it's all we have."

"Well, let's hope you're right," he says. "Listen, Tate, you and Detective Kent have both done good jobs today, but don't drop the ball now, huh? And I'm sure if I ask if Schroder is there," he says, and Schroder looks over at the mention of his name, "you'll all tell me that he's gone home for the day?"

"Exactly, sir," I tell him.

"Good. I'd hate to think you were lying, Tate, because that would put things on the wrong foot. So for the sake of argument, right now I'm going to believe you and not ask one of the others. And if Schroder were to call me from his house in say . . . fifteen minutes, that would help."

He hangs up. The media is no doubt downstairs at the police station waiting for the next sound bite. Stevens is hoping to be able to provide that to them within the hour. He's hoping to tell them we have Caleb Cole in custody and that Dr. Stanton and his remaining daughter are safe.

There are six unmarked patrol cars spread in a diameter around us, all parked between four and six blocks away, the drivers all hunched low in the seats, all of them no doubt uncomfortable and keeping an eye out for Stanton's car. Of course we don't know if Cole is still using Stanton's car. The same house lights that were on when I found Tabitha and Octavia earlier are still on. It's an hour away from midnight and everybody is tired and I never did get around to eating. The packet of cookies Tabitha left out are all gone, Hutton and the two officers having made it their first assignment. I open the fridge hoping to spot some cold pizza or chicken or maybe a chocolate bar and end up finding only fruit and vegetables.

"It's a lesbian thing," one of the officers points out, nodding toward the fridge and smiling.

"What?"

"They don't eat meat."

I get the joke but don't feel like laughing, even though his partner does. Detective Kent rolls her eyes and smiles at me. I grab an apple.

"You reckon he saw the news?" Schroder asks, and he looks like he's just waking up. The question is identical the one we've all been asking each other for the last thirty minutes, the only difference is the tense. *You reckon he's going to watch the news?* We kept reassuring ourselves that he would to the point where we were convinced of it. On this side of the bulletin it's all so very different.

"If he didn't see it, it'll be online soon enough," I say, talking with a mouthful of apple. The apple is making me think I should make an effort to eat more apples. Scientists say apples are good for you, but they also say that coffee is bad, so I don't really want to listen to scientists. I must look like I'm enjoying it because Detective Kent also goes to the fridge and grabs one. "If he is staying up-to-date, then yeah, he'll see it. Question is when will he see it? And will he take the bait?"

"Stevens was pretty convincing," Kent says. "He really did make it sound like Cole still had the girl. If Cole is convinced, he might just make an anonymous call to the police with the address."

But the only convincing thing is how desperate we are to believe what we're saying. It was always the weakest part of the plan, even though Barlow thinks otherwise. After reading the letters, he's convinced Cole sees himself as a father figure to Ariel Chancellor. He was the one who told Stevens to use the father-to-father line. He told us there was still enough of a caring father figure inside of Cole to check on the girl himself, to check that he hadn't hurt her. *It will be important for him to come back,* he told us, *and he will, as long as he saw the bulletin.*

"Don't suppose anybody's up for splitting some pizzas?" I ask.

Hutton looks like he is, even though he knows I'm only kidding. Only I'm not so sure that I am. The others all ignore me.

My cell phone rings. I look at the caller display. I don't recognize it. I walk into the hallway and answer it.

"Theo, it's Carol Hamilton," she says, her words are urgent and she sounds out of breath and I suddenly feel like I'm going to be sick. I can hear the sounds of traffic in the background. She's not calling from the nursing home.

"Has something happened to Bridget?"

"I'm on my way there now," she says, "and I suggest you do the same thing. She's woken up."

My body temperature plummets, it touches on freezing point just long enough for my back and neck to break out in a violent shiver. My legs actually wobble and I have to grab hold of the wall. "What?"

"Dr. Forster is on his way too. I'm about ten minutes away."

"Wait, wait, you said she's awake?"

"Yes."

"Bridget is awake."

"Yes, Theo, she's awake."

"I'm . . . I'm on my way," I say.

I hang up and move into the living room. I feel light-headed. My mouth is dry. I fumble with the phone and actually miss dropping it into my pocket and it hits the floor, then I almost step on it.

"Theo?" Schroder says.

I'm scared Nurse Hamilton is going to call back and tell me she was just joking, I'm excited that for the first time in a long time a life changing phone call is going to be a good thing rather than a bad one. Schroder is looking at me. My hands are shaking.

"Theo?"

I open my mouth to answer him, but it's so dry that the words just get caught at the back of my throat. I try to build up some moisture.

"Theo? What is it?"

"I have to go."

"Go? Go where?"

"Bridget—she's . . . she's out of her coma."

"Jesus," he says, and he stops himself from coming forward and putting his hands on my shoulders. "Theo, that's . . . that's fantastic."

I head for the door.

"Wait," he says, following me.

"What?"

"Oh Jesus, there's no way to say this without sounding like a prick, but you can't leave."

"What?"

"You can't compromise the investigation."

"What?"

"We got headlights," one of the officers says. He's crouched behind the living room window. He's holding the curtain back about an inch. "They're slowing down," he says. "Wait, wait, it's coming to a stop. About three houses away. It's just sitting there. No movement."

"He knows you, Theo," Schroder says to me. "If Cole is on his way, if he sees you walking out that door, or walking down the street, it'll ruin everything."

"I have to go," I tell him.

He nods. "I know," he says, "I know you do. But you can't. Not yet. Soon, but not yet." He puts his hand on my shoulder and I shrug it off.

"I swear, Carl, if you try to stop me, I'll fucking hit you."

"Ladies," Detective Kent says, also looking through the curtain now and glancing back at us, "the car is still there. It might be showtime."

"The headlights are still on—I can't even tell what kind of car it is, and I can't tell how many people are inside," the officer says. "Should we send someone out there?"

"I'll go," I say.

"No. Not yet," Schroder says. He turns toward me. "Theo, it's been three years. I'm just asking you for another few minutes."

"Do you even know how that sounds?"

"Yes," he says.

"Carl, right now I don't care about Caleb Cole, I don't care about the case, all I care about is seeing Bridget."

"Think of Katy Stanton," he says, and I do, and it works.

"Five minutes," I tell him. "And if that isn't Cole out there now, there's no way you can stop me from leaving."

He nods, but I'm pretty sure he thinks between the five of them they can stop me from doing anything. I don't think they can.

"Let's just go out there," I say.

"I don't want to spook him, and we don't even know if it is Cole. Could be he's sent somebody else, another pizza boy even," Schroder says, and then he gets on the radio and tells two of the unmarked cars to move in a few blocks. "If he takes off, we'll still get him," he says.

"Whoever it is," Detective Kent says, "they're still in there. If it were a neighbor they'd just go up the driveway. If it's a friend they'd have gotten out by now."

"I agree," I say to Schroder. "We can go out there, sneak up from behind and—"

"Hang on," the officer says. "The lights just switched off. Still no movement though. It looks similar to the doctor's car but it looks similar to about a thousand cars. Damn it, I can't tell from here, but I can see a partial plate. I don't think it's a match."

The comment seems to take the tension out of the room.

"Do you see that?" Kent asks.

"Yeah I do."

"What?" Schroder asks.

"The door has just opened, just the driver's door," Kent says. "One person inside. Male. Caucasian. Can't get a good look at him. Could be our suspect."

"Who else could it be?" Hutton asks.

"He's getting out," the officer says. "Now he's standing by the side of the car looking at the house. He's just closed the door."

The tension comes back.

"Make sure he doesn't see you," Schroder says.

"He's not moving anywhere. Now he's turning a full circle, looking at the other houses. Now he's coming forward," he says, his voice getting quicker with excitement. "He's coming this way, walking slowly. Jesus, my grandmother can walk faster than this guy."

"Is it him?" I ask.

"I don't know."

"I'm going out there," I say to Schroder.

"Just wait," he says. "Stick with the plan, Tate. Let him come to us," he says, and he's right but that doesn't dull the desire to rush out there. "We have to be careful. If Stanton and his daughter aren't in the car, then they're somewhere else, and we need Cole to give up their location. If Tabitha is right about Cole wanting to die and we go running out there, for all we know he might jam a knife into his own throat."

I nod. I get his point.

"He's coming straight for us," the officer says.

"You and you," Schroder says, pointing to the other officer and Detective Kent, "circle out the back door and around the side of the yard but don't approach the suspect. Just be ready to cut off his escape route. Tate, get ready, the moment he reaches the doorstep we're on him, okay? Not before then. Let's—"

"We've got another vehicle," the officer says. "The guy is still coming toward us. The other car isn't worrying him. Shit, we've got two more vehicles. They're both slowing down. Our suspect is pausing, he's looking back but not going anywhere. They're not cars, they're vans."

"What the hell is going on?" Schroder asks.

"They're parking right outside. Shit, our suspect is heading back to his car."

"We have to go," I say.

"Go, go, go," Schroder shouts, and we all rush toward the

door while the two who went out the back rush around the side of the yard. All we can hear is footsteps as our feet pound into the floor. The door is already unlocked and I'm the first one through it.

We all converge on the man at the same time. People are getting out of their vans. They're holding lights and cameras. Shit. Schroder is the first to reach Caleb Cole, who is now looking at us without an ounce of surprise on his face and, who, it turns out, isn't Caleb Cole at all.

"What the hell are you doing here?" Schroder asks, grabbing him by the collar.

"I saw the news, Detectives," Jonas Jones says, looking from Schroder to me, all of it caught under the harsh glare of the camera lights. Schroder glances at the cameras and lets go of the front of Jonas's shirt.

Jonas takes a step back, then straightens it, then runs a hand over his hair, making sure it's all in place. "I know how much Octavia Stanton needs her medication," he says. "I knew it before it was even on the news. The thing is, Detectives," he says, adjusting his shirt one more time, "this is where Jessica Cole told me I would find her."

CHAPTER FORTY-SEVEN

The camera lights wake up the thing living inside my head, it rolls over and taps at the walls briefly before falling back asleep.

"You need to get the hell out of here!" Schroder yells, directing the words at everybody on the street. He pulls out his handcuffs and seems to realize two very important things. The first is that there is nothing he can arrest Jonas for except being a weasel. It's a public street and Jones hasn't broken any laws, and the same goes for the reporters sending out a live feed to the rest of the country and a warning to Caleb Cole.

The second thing Schroder seems to realize is that he has no authority. He's on suspension, he can't make an arrest, and the question is whether or not anybody else here knows that.

It's a question that isn't posed for long.

"I'm pretty sure you've been suspended, mate," Jonas says, "and therefore I don't have to answer to you."

"Is this true?" one of the reporters yells, and upon hearing it the others all follow suit.

"Detective, can you comment on the actions of a department who would continue to have a drunk detective run a very
important—" "Are you drunk now, Detective?" "How long has
this drinking problem been—" "Is everybody drunk?"

Jonas holds his hands up and all the reporters go silent, staring at him as though he is about to do a magic trick, or receive
a message from God. "Please, everybody, we're here to save
the girl," he says, bringing the attention back to him, which is
where he likes it the best. "This is where she is, isn't it?"

"This is bullshit," Schroder says. "You're here to sell your
books. If you thought she was here you'd have called it in."

"First of all you never take my calls," Jonas says, "and second
of all if you're already here, then the girl must be here too. Although . . . now I'm here, I'm sensing that like your job, she's
gone."

"Is that correct, Detectives?" a reporter asks. "Was Jonas's
vision accurate? Did you find Octavia Stanton here? What is
her condition?"

Then the questions start coming again. "Is she still alive?"
"Was she molested?" "Was Melanie molested too?" "Is there
any hope of finding Caleb Cole before he kills again?" "Is Octavia Stanton dead?"

"I sense she's alive," Jonas says.

"Is that true, Detectives? Did you find her alive?"

I sense by the end of the night Jonas isn't going to be able to
use his legs anymore.

"Is her father here too?" "Just what did you find here at the
scene?"

Schroder is looking mad and uncomfortable. His face is
turning red and there's a vein near the middle of his forehead
that's standing out like a worm buried just beneath the skin. He
looks like he's about to have a stroke. If he holds the handcuffs
any tighter he may actually bend them. I want to reach over,
punch Jones in the mouth, get into the nearest car, and speed
to see my wife.

"You need to clear out of here," Schroder says, keeping his voice low, unable to hide the anger in it. "All of you," he says. He sounds like he's wondering if he has enough bullets to put an end to their questions. "This is an ongoing police investigation, you need to leave," he says, but it's too late. He knows it. Somehow I think Jonas knows it too. The camera crew keep filming. Large microphones fill our vision.

"We don't have to do any such thing." "The public has the right to know if Octavia Stanton is safe." "Are you saying you're still part of this police investigation?"

"She was here, though, wasn't she," Jonas says. "That much we know for sure, thanks to Jessica Cole. She told me."

"Then why doesn't she tell you where her father is?" I ask.

"She doesn't want him caught, that's why," Jonas says. "She just wants the girls returned safely."

"Then where is Katy?" I ask.

"Only Katy? Not Octavia too?" Jonas asks, and I realize my mistake, and it confirms to everybody that we have another of the girls back.

"Fuck this," Schroder says, and he reclaims the step between him and Jonas. I head toward the cameras, ready to put my hands in front of the lenses in case Schroder wants to take a swing, but there are so many lenses I'd need hands the size of a couch. Kent is by my side, figuring out the same thing.

"You slimy son of a bitch," Schroder says, leaning in toward Jonas. "How did you know? Who told you?"

"Jessica Cole told me," he says. "I talk to the dead."

"Turn around," Schroder says.

"What?"

"Turn around. You're under arrest."

"What for?"

"Yes, Detective, what are you arresting him for?" one of the reporters asks. "And can you arrest him? You have no power."

"I said turn around, Jones," Schroder says, ignoring everybody.

"No. You have no authority to arrest me."

"Turn around, dipshit," Detective Kent says, pulling out her own set of handcuffs. Jones stares blankly at her, then a small grin touches the sides of his lips. He could never buy this publicity. Kent sticks the handcuffs on him, and as they click into place I think she realizes the same moment that I do that this is exactly what Jonas wanted.

"You have no right," Jonas says, looking at the cameras when he says it and flashing a whole lot of white teeth. "No right at all."

"We have every right," Schroder says, "and nobody here is buying the act. You're loving every second of this."

"What grounds are you taking him into custody on?" "What is the condition of Octavia Stanton?" "How many of you have been suspended?"

"Only somebody working with the killer could have known where Octavia was being kept," Schroder says. "That gives us the right to take him into custody."

"So you don't believe in Jonas's psychic abilities?" "Is that the police department's official stand on psychics?" "Are you charging Jonas Jones as a suspect?" "Where is Katy Stanton?" "Where is Octavia?"

"I believe it wasn't hard for him to predict you would all show up to give him everything he's after," Schroder says to them all.

I want to put my hand on Schroder's shoulder and lead him away. I want him to shut up.

"Jessica told me," Jonas says, looking into the camera. He sounds calm. "She told me that Octavia would be fine."

"Is she fine, Detective?"

"No comment," I say for Schroder as his mouth starts to open, and he knows it's time to accept defeat. We turn Jonas away from the cameras. Kent and Schroder walk on each side of him, marching him toward the house. I follow a few steps behind. The cameras follow us right up to the door.

"You're on TV," Hutton says as we step inside, the TV switched on in the lounge showing the live broadcast of the house, zooming in on the windows of the living room and on the now shut front door. The officers who were here are still out there, trying to push everybody back.

Kent throws Jonas onto the couch.

Schroder stares at him. "You piece of shit," he says. "You blew it, you blew our chance to get him."

Jonas lands on his side, his arms pinned behind him. He looks unsure of himself. He's noticing for the first time that he's in a room with four extremely pissed off people and nobody to verify he didn't walk into a door fifteen times. "Get who? Cole? He's already been here. He's been and gone."

"Yeah? How do you know that?" Schroder asks.

"Jessica told me," he says.

"I hear your new book is doing badly," Schroder says. "It seems people don't believe in you, Jonas, and I'm one of those people. Coming here tonight, this was just a stunt for you, wasn't it? You're just trying to drum up business. This is fantastic publicity for you, isn't it? Only a real bottom-feeder would use kidnapped girls to sell his books."

"You knew we were here," I say. "There was no surprise on your face at all. You wanted to get arrested."

"You selfish bastard," Schroder says. "You fucked our best chance of saving these people."

"If we don't get them back alive, that's on you," Kent tells him.

"No it's not. I'm trying to help," Jonas says.

"How'd you know we were here?" Schroder asks.

"I told you already."

"Are you paying somebody for information?" Schroder asks, and it has to be—it's also how he knew Schroder had been suspended and not fired, though anybody who saw the news probably would have drawn the same conclusion.

"I'm psychic," Jonas says. "It's a gift."

Schroder curls his right hand into a fist. Jonas sees him do it, so Schroder curls his left one into a fist too.

"Go ahead," Jonas says, looking at Schroder. "Let me walk out of here with bruises on my face. See what the media says about that," he says, only he doesn't sound that sure.

"Don't think I'm not willing to try," Schroder tells him. "You deliberately interfered with a police investigation. When we prove you've either been following us or paying somebody for information, you'll be charged. If Stanton dies, you'll be an accessory to that."

"That's bullshit," Jonas says, "and even if it weren't bullshit, you can't prove anything. Jessica told me to come here. I asked her, and this is where she led me."

"Oh, we can prove it," Schroder says. "It's an online world, Jones. We're going to track where your cell phone has been today, we're going to check traffic cameras, we're going to talk to witnesses—we're going to dig up all of your dirty little secrets."

Jonas is shaking his head. "No way, that's not what happened. I talk to the dead. That's what happened. You just have to open your mind."

"And you know what?" Schroder asks. "I'm looking forward to doing it. Hell, even if I don't have a job to go back to, I'm going to make it my mission to prove what an asshole you are. I might even write a book about it. What do you think, Theo?"

"I think you'd have to market it as a comedy, because this guy is a joke."

"Very funny," Jonas says.

"You phoned the media," I tell him.

"The whole country is worried about Octavia," he says. "I was trying to put them at ease."

"With your gift," I tell him.

"Exactly! I was right about the stab wounds too, wasn't I?" he asks me.

"Definitely have to write it as a comedy," Schroder says. "Or perhaps even a tragedy, because the main character doesn't see how fucked up he really is."

"Don't people die in the end of tragedies?" Detective Kent asks.

"They do," Schroder says, reaching into his pocket and pulling out his Wake-E pills. "Isn't that right, Jonas?"

"Fuck you," Jonas says.

"You might have a fan base who believe that shit you're sprouting," Schroder says, "but unless they're on the jury, you're going to jail for what you've done here."

"You've got nothing you can prove, and no real reason to arrest me," he says. "I'm a real psychic," he says.

"Good," Schroder says, tossing a tablet into his mouth, "because then the shit that happens in jail to you won't come as a surprise."

"I want my lawyer," he says. "Until then, I'm not saying anything else."

The two officers come inside, beaten back by the media. We leave them to watch Jonas and I head into the kitchen with Schroder and Kent and Hutton.

"What was he talking about?" Schroder asks me, "when he mentioned the stab wounds?"

"He figured out the victims had nineteen stab wounds. He told me just before the briefing. He figured it out before the rest of us."

"And you didn't tell us?"

"I didn't think it made him a suspect. If anything, it made him either a great detective or very lucky."

"So that was his idea," Kent says, "about the stab wounds. Not yours."

I feel myself turning red. "According to Jones, it wasn't even his—a dead person told him."

"Maybe he really is psychic?" Hutton suggests, proving that with questions like that his body-fat index is higher than his IQ. We all stare at him. "I mean, he did know the girl had been here," Hutton says. "Come on, a million psychics in the world, a few of them have to be genuine, and that'd explain how he knew about the stab wounds. Some of the stuff they come up with, it's way too accurate just to be a guess. My sister, she went to a psychic a month ago and he told her—"

"Jesus, Hutton, we get it, okay? You believe in psychics," Detective Kent says.

"I'm just saying, is all," he says, and shrugs.

"So what the hell do we do now? It's already over the news," Schroder says. "Caleb isn't coming here. No chance of it."

He looks at me to agree with him, and I slowly nod. He's right. And that's not good for Katy, her father, or for Schroder's career and future children and victims he could have helped. He's been caught working a case while suspended, and I've been caught lying to Stevens that Schroder wasn't here. Jonas Jones has fucked us all.

But right now none of that matters.

"I need a car," I tell him. My car has been driven back to the station, well away from the area since Caleb knew what it looked like.

He hands me his car keys. "It'll be here in two minutes," he says, then reaches for his phone to call for it.

CHAPTER FORTY-EIGHT

Caleb was halfway to the house when it unfolded. It was breaking news. The media and the police had shown up at the house where he had left Octavia. He had pulled over and listened to the report come in, then he had done a U-turn and come back.

In the bedroom now with the TV going, he's in time to see two cars pull up outside Tabitha's house. Seven people step out the front door and climb into them. At first he doesn't realize what has taken them so long, but then he figures out that it's a replay. All of this happened twenty minutes earlier.

So, the police had lied after all. But he had never thought of the possibility of a trap. Somehow they had found Octavia. They were using her to draw Caleb back to the scene. They were using children to try and get to him, and he understood that because he too was using the kids as tools.

He's relived that Octavia is fine. And just as equally, he's concerned. How did the police find her? Is he leaving a trail? If so, will the police come here? Or did Tabitha manage to escape? Should he move to a new location? Where would he go? What difference would it make?

He stares at the TV, studying the man he recognizes from his earlier fight and from the cemetery last night. There's another detective he's seen on the news over the last few days, and then there's Jonas Jones, the psychic he's seen on morning breakfast shows, the psychic he's wanted to see more than any of the others. When he started seeing them, Caleb contacted Jones only to learn the man was backlogged with clients and also charged more than Caleb could afford.

He sits on the edge of the bed with the knife back in his hand. He watches the news as it goes back in time, showing men running out of the house and approaching Jonas Jones. He is fascinated with Jones—is it possible he is looking at a true psychic? There is a confrontation. Jones starts explaining why he's there.

Caleb tightens his grip on the knife at the sound of his daughter's name.

Jonas Jones is saying it was Jessica that sent him there!

Why would Jessica do that?

As if to answer his thought, Jonas tells the police and the cameras that Jessica sent him there to protect the girl.

Caleb lowers the knife onto the bed. Would she really do that? He thinks that she would. Jessica was hurt—and the last thing she would want would be for another girl to be hurt too. Jesus, has he slipped so far that even his own daughter doesn't have any faith in him?

Jones is put into handcuffs and dragged back into the house. The police look angry enough that Caleb spends the next ten seconds waiting for a gunshot and a flash of light, but it doesn't come. The camera cuts away, and the scene is given a live update. He listens to what the reporter has to say, then switches between channels to get different perspectives on what happened, but the reporters are all saying the same thing—Jonas Jones led them to Octavia Stanton through a vision he had

had where Jessica Cole, the ten-year-old girl who was murdered fifteen years ago, came to him.

Jessica. His daughter is trying to protect a girl from him.

It makes him feel sad at the thought.

And if Jonas is like the other psychics, then it makes him angry if he is using Jessica's name to gain publicity.

But what if he's not like the others?

There is no word on Octavia Stanton's condition. The reporters have not seen her come out of the house, and with the police obviously having wound down the operation, there is doubt that she was ever there. Yet Jonas certainly got something right—just not the timing. On this the reporters also agree.

Caleb isn't sure if that makes him any less genuine.

"It's not a science," one of the reporters says, "it's a gift."

Then it goes back to footage of the man he fought with. Theodore Tate. The anchor goes on to tell the country a little bit about Theodore Tate, which includes a drunk-driving conviction for which he spent four months in jail, the apprehension and deaths of two serial killers, and the loss of his own daughter. The man who killed Tate's daughter fled the country.

Caleb turns off the TV. Exhausted, he strips down to his underwear and climbs into bed. He stares up at the ceiling, exhausted but unable to fall asleep as he thinks about Jonas Jones, Mrs. Whitby, and most of all he thinks about Theodore Tate.

CHAPTER FORTY-NINE

I light up the siren in Schroder's car on the way to see my wife, my wife who is now awake and more alive than she has been in three years. I speed through the streets of Christchurch with my hands clenching the wheel and the window down with the breeze whipping at my face. There isn't much in the way of traffic, but there is lots in the way of red traffic lights, which I get to race through. There is a smile on my face that I don't think is going to disappear for a month. Images of my future are playing out in front of me. I can almost see them against the windshield, as if my imagination is the projector and my eyes the lenses. It will be hard in the beginning. Bridget won't know our daughter has been dead for three years, that gas costs three times as much, that hip-hop music is taking over the planet. She'll be waking into a new world but the last yesterday she remembers was three years ago. In her reality she's a younger woman with a future and a family. There are going to be tough times ahead, but then there are going to be better times. Amazing times. The future we always wanted won't be the same, but there will be a future nonetheless. The house won't be empty anymore. We can get another cat, we can maybe have another child. . . .

Another child.

I'm not even sure where the idea has come from. It's not something I've even thought about. Another child. No, no way. I've seen what happen to children in this world. There's no way I'm going to bring another one into it.

Still . . .

I'm getting ahead of myself. First we have to get through the sorrow. Any thoughts of the future have to be put on hold until I've explained the present. Sitting her down and telling her about Emily, holding my wife in my arms as she cries at our loss, the painful days ahead turning into painful weeks and months, taking her to the cemetery to show her our daughter's grave. I shake my head.

The waitress's shirt in Froggie's Diner summed it up perfectly.

Yet the smile is still there, fixed on my face, and I keep my foot on the accelerator and God it feels good, it feels so good to be racing to a destination that isn't the scene of death and despair.

When I get to the nursing home there is still a police car out front, a leftover from the previous night, an officer inside it on watch. There is an ambulance there too, and a late model BMW next to it. The lights on the ambulance are flashing and I'm not sure why that would be.

I park next to the BMW. Forster is standing by the back of the ambulance. He's a guy in his mid-fifties with dark brown hair and designer glasses, his tie is loose and his sleeves are rolled up, and he looks like the kind of guy who plays a doctor on TV. The ambulance doors are closed, there's an internal light going, and still I have the smile on my face.

"What's the story with that?" I ask, pointing my thumb at it.

"Let's go inside," he tells me.

I shake my head. "I'll go inside and see Bridget in a second," I say, "but how about you tell me about the ambulance?"

"Theo . . ."

I shake my head. "She's awake, Doctor. She's awake and she's fine."

"Please, let's go inside."

"No. Not until you tell me she's okay. Not until you tell me the ambulance isn't here for her," I say, and the smile, that stupid fucking smile is still on my face. I'm keeping it there, and as long as it stays my wife is going to be okay. The ambulance starts to roll forward.

"Theo . . ."

"Damn it," I say, and I push past him and put my hand on the handle of the back door.

"Theo, don't," he says, reaching for my shoulder, but I do.

I open the ambulance door and that smile is finally gone. Bridget is lying in there with an oxygen mask on her face and two men crouched over her. The driver brings it to a stop.

"What the fuck," one of them says as I try to step inside. "Get the hell out of here."

"Theo," Forster says, this time reaching me and pulling me back.

"What's going on?"

"Get him out of here," one of the paramedics says, while the other one is pressing on the bag to provide oxygen to my wife.

"What . . ." I say, and it's all I can say. Bridget's eyes roll toward me, her blue eyes wide open, they stare at me and lock onto me for the first time in three years. Her right hand reaches a little toward me. She knows who I am. She can see me and she knows who I am and I reach out toward her, and she looks at me and through me and into me, and she's in the process of dying and I stand in the back of the ambulance with Forster dragging me back and the driver slowly starting to roll forward again.

"Get out," the paramedic says, and this time he reaches up and shoves me in the chest. I fall into Forster and we both tip into the driveway and land heavily against it, Forster breaking most of my fall, but not enough of it to stop the headache waking back up. The ambulance door closes and it pulls away. It races down the driveway out of sight, and when it's out on the road the sirens start wailing.

"I'm sorry," Forster says.

"Tell me," I say, rubbing the side of my head, only the words don't come out that way. They come out all beaten up and slurred.

"What?"

"I thaid thell me."

"Are you okay?"

I rub at my head and I squeeze my eyes closed, and in the darkness there are some fading fireworks. I focus on the words. "I'm thine," I say. Then I try again, focusing on each word. "I'm fine. Tell me about Bridget," I say as the fireworks start to fade.

"You're not fine. Did you just knock your head?"

"Goddamn it, Doctor, just tell me!"

"Your wife," he says, "Bridget, as you know, she came out of her coma forty-five minutes ago. She didn't say anything," he says, and his head is moving slowly from side to side, a slow shake of his head, a slow bad-news-is-coming shake. "She came to and she walked into the corridor. The nurse who found her thought it was another one of her walks, but then Bridget grabbed her shoulders and tried to speak but couldn't make any noise. She was highly agitated."

"Is she okay?"

"I was called and by the time I got here she had been calmed. She was sitting down drinking water. She was looking around, she didn't understand what—"

"Just tell me, is she okay?"

"She didn't know what was happening, but she was alert. We told her who she was and that she had been in an accident, and she began to get upset. We thought we were going to have to sedate her."

"Goddamn it, Doctor, is she okay?" I ask, and I can feel the bile at the back of my throat, and if he says no, if he says she's going to die, then he better run, he better run like the devil is after him.

He stands up and brushes off the back of his pants. He reaches down and takes my hand and pulls me up.

"She suffered a seizure," he says. "Before I could even start to look her over, she started convulsing. We couldn't get her to stop. We got an ambulance and then she went into cardiac arrest. They're helping her, and every second . . ." He stops talking. "It's serious," he says.

"You were going to say every second counts," I tell him.

"Theo . . ."

"You're telling me I just cost my wife twenty seconds."

"Don't look at it that way."

"I should have been here earlier," I tell him, thinking of Cole, of Jonas, thinking that this city owes me a favor, hell, a hundred favors. "Fucking hell, I should have been here!"

"There was no way of knowing it was going to happen, Theo, and even if you had been here, the same thing would have—"

"And all I managed to do was delay the ambulance."

"Theo, you can't have known. . . ."

His words fade out as I race back to my car, each heavy step echoing in my skull. I feel like I'm going to throw up again.

I drive to the hospital hitting speeds I've never hit before. People pull out of the way. The headache comes and goes like waves smashing against a cliff, each wave a little less powerful than its predecessor but still damn strong. When I get there I park by the main doors and run into the emergency room. I push my way ahead of two other people at the counter who bitch at me, and I flash my badge at the nurse behind it and I demand that she buzz me through the security doors between the waiting room and the operating rooms. She does. I go through and a doctor approaches me and tells me to calm down, then asks what the problem is. I tell him. He tells me to follow him, and I do, and he leads me to the same waiting room I was in yesterday with Schroder when we were talking to Mrs. Hayward. This time I'm the only one in there. I pace the room a few times, sit down for half a minute, then pace the room some more. Over the years people have gotten the best news and the worst news in this room. Their lives have changed. After five minutes I head into the corridor. I pace it up and down, looking at other people in different stages of pain. I stare at a young woman on a gurney whose eyes are open and blank, there is vomit down the side of her face and on her neck, a tube hanging out of her mouth that's been disconnected, a nurse pulling a sheet up over her face.

"What happened to her?" I ask.

The nurse turns toward me, and I show her my badge.

"Overdose," she says. "By the time she got in here there wasn't much we could do. It's sad," she says, "it's always sad."

I start pacing the corridor again and haven't gotten much further before Dr. Forster finds me. There are cuts and grazes in his palms from where he broke our fall.

"Theo," he says, and he's puffing slightly as if he's been running around looking for me. "I've spoken to the doctors," he says. "Bridget's blood pressure has plummeted and her heartbeat is erratic, but they are in the process of stabilizing her vitals," he says.

"What the fuck does that even mean?" I ask.

"It means her body is crashing and they're trying to save her."

"Why? I don't get it—she was awake, wasn't she?"

He shakes his head. "She was, and now she isn't. I don't know why. We'll know more when she stabilizes and we can look her over."

"But she'll be okay, right? And when this is over, she'll be okay again? She'll be normal?"

"I—I don't know."

"I want to see her."

"You can't. They're working on her. There's nothing you can do here," he says.

"I'm not going anywhere."

"I know," he says. "I'll keep you updated."

He leaves me alone. I grab my cell phone and see I've missed two calls from Schroder. I never even heard it ring. I call him back.

"How is she?" Schroder asks.

I start to tell him, and I have to sit to get through it all because my legs are ready to collapse. He listens without interrupting me, and then at the end he tells me he's sorry.

"What's happening with Jones?" I ask him.

"Are you going to be okay?" he asks.

It's a dumb question but one he had to ask, and I give him the response he needs to hear. "I'll be okay. And Jonas?"

"I don't know. I was given a lift home. I'm out of the loop," he says. "I had a call forwarded to me earlier from the hospital," he says. "Apparently you've got a head injury you're keeping to yourself. They were in the process of admitting you and you walked out. They want you back."

"As soon as this is over," I tell him.

"Theo—"

"I promise," I tell him.

"It's your brain," he says. "Do what you want, and if you want to update the department before you die, call Detective Kent," he says, and hangs up.

I give Kent a call.

"How's your wife?" she asks.

"She's fine," I tell her. "What happened with Jonas?"

She pauses for a few seconds. "I'm thinking Jones must really be psychic," she says, "because he already had his lawyer at the station waiting for us, which, unless his lawyer is psychic too, is pretty clever since we hadn't let him make a call. Jones, according to the lawyer, has proven himself time and time again to be as he claims, a genuine psychic who wants nothing more than to help the community, and in his role as community helper, Jonas was trying to use his tremendous gift to save a young girl's life. No man should be held accountable for attempting such a feat. And no, Jonas had no idea he was stumbling into an ambush."

"Wow, I guess we all should be thankful the world has Jonas Jones in it," I say.

She gives a small soft laugh, the kind my wife used to give on the phone sometimes. "We should be, according to Jones and his lawyer. So we took a run at him for fifteen minutes and got nothing. That's when Stevens came in and got us. Told me and Hutton to cut loose Jonas Jones, humanitarian slash psychic. Hutton pointed out that Jones cost us catching Cole, and Stevens pointed out we didn't know that for a fact, that there was nothing more we could do, that we had every right to be pissed off but we needed to focus on finding Cole and not focus on pissing around with a guy who speaks to dead people."

"Listen, I found Ariel Chancellor," I tell her.

"What? Where?"

"She's here," I tell her. "At the hospital."

"You've spoken to her?"

"No. That's more Jonas Jones's domain now," I say, and explain the overdose. When I close my eyes I can see the tube hanging out of her mouth, the vomit on her neck, I can see her the way she was in her flat this morning telling me about her life. *She'll die on those streets* her father told me, and the timing of it all—she may have been dying when he said those very words. She's certainly been dying since the day James Whitby chased two scared little girls through a park.

"I'll send somebody down to get the details," she says. "Anything to do with Cole?" I shake my head even though she can't see me. "You think she did it deliberately?"

I keep my eyes closed, pinching the bridge of my nose at the same time. I keep watching Ariel in her flat, taking a drink, telling me she was living the dream. "Who knows," I tell her. "So what's the next step?"

"Now we call it a day," she says. "All we can do is fill the streets with as many patrol cars as we can. What else is there? Knock on every door in the city?"

"Maybe you should call some of those psychics back that were calling Schroder."

"You think there's a term for a collective of psychics?" she asks. "You know, like a herd of cows, a murder of crows?"

"I'm sure there is," I say, and I look for a one-liner, something clever, but my brain is too busy being clever by holding the headache at bay.

She says nothing for a few seconds and I get the feeling she's building up to something.

"There a problem?"

"The psychics," she says. "The thing is we started calling them back, you know, just because we have to be doing something, right?"

"Right . . ."

"Well, they weren't ringing because they were having visions or speaking to the dead. They were ringing because they were all witnesses. Caleb Cole has been visiting them. He's been trying to talk to his wife and daughter."

"Jesus," I say, wincing at the information.

"If we'd called them earlier . . ." she says, but adds nothing.

The problem is it was Schroder's job to call them, or his job to have somebody else call them. The thing with psychics is that as soon as they call whoever is talking to them just switches off, they don't hear what's being said and barely make the effort to even take down a name and phone number. These people were probably saying they were seeing Caleb Cole and whoever was on the other end of the phone all thought they meant they were having "visions" of Caleb Cole. But no, that wasn't it—*they all wanted some credit*, I remember Schroder saying that.

"Is that something we can use?" I ask.

"We're contacting other psychics. We're on it. And we'll keep an eye on Jonas in case he's a target. What do you think is going to happen to Schroder?" she asks.

"I don't know," I say, and right now I'm just way too tired to look that far into the future. Maybe she should ask Jonas Jones.

"You think he'll lose his job?" she asks.

"I don't know."

"I hope not," she says.

"I gotta go," I tell her.

"Listen," she says, and in that moment she sounds like Schroder, good ol' Schroder, who starts half of his sentences with either a *look* or a *listen*. "He wanted me to give you a message when you called. He said nobody was going to hold it against you if you didn't show up here for a few days. He said with what you've done, Stevens is impressed. He's not going to renege on his offer of letting you back on the force because you're staying with your wife, and he doubts Stevens will hold it against you for lying earlier to protect him."

"Okay. Thanks, Detective."

"Rebecca," she says. "And I'm glad your wife is okay. I'll talk to you tomorrow."

I pace the room a few more times until my sore leg suggests sitting is the way to go. I hold my head in my hands and stare down at the floor until my head suggests looking down isn't the best of angles because it makes my brain feel like it's pressing against the back of my eyes. On the other side of the door Bridget is fighting for her life. Or the doctors are fighting for it. A nurse comes by and offers me some coffee and I tell her that would be great, but she never shows up with it. After an hour a doctor walks out of the operating room. He walks toward me and I stand up and wobble for a few seconds in front of him, and in those seconds are a world of possibilities. This is the moment where my life changes, just like it has done for all the others who have stood here before me.

"Your wife is fine," he tells me, and everything is okay in the world. I almost hug him. I cry. And then I do hug him. He pats me on the back and pushes me away after a few seconds.

"We've stabilized her," he says. "We'll have to keep her for a few days, and I know Dr. Forster will want to run some tests and try to figure out what happened."

"What did happen?" I ask.

He gives a small shake of the head. "Honestly, we don't know. All we know is that her vitals crashed and for a while there it was touch and go."

"And the coma?"

He holds my gaze and doesn't flinch. "She's unconscious," he says, "but when she was with us she was unresponsive. I'm sorry," he says, "but I can't tell you anything more than that."

"But it has to be a good thing, right? Her waking up like that?"

"Brain injuries are tricky things," he says. "I've seen plenty of them over the years and in some ways they're like finger-prints—no two are identical."

"Can I see her?"

"We'll move her into a room soon, and you can see her then for a few minutes," he says. "We should know more tomorrow."

He turns and heads back into the room, and I collapse into the chair. Bridget is fine. Everything that's gone on, she's going to be fine. I lean back and my head touches the wall and imme-diately the room starts to sway. I'm hit with an overwhelming sense of exhaustion. The ceiling gets blurry, it swims in and out of focus for the next fifteen minutes until a nurse comes and gets me and takes me through to my wife.

CHAPTER FIFTY

Caleb Cole stares at the ceiling, then closes his eyes for a few seconds and stares at the ceiling again. The view between the two doesn't change much. He thinks about Jonas Jones. Whether or not the psychic is a fraud it doesn't matter. Jones is in custody. He's as impossible to get to as Mrs. Whitby.

He thinks about Mrs. Whitby, about how satisfying it would be to cut her into a thousand pieces. It's an idea he often falls asleep having.

Most of all he's thinking about the man from the cemetery—Theodore Tate. An idea is starting to come to him. An exciting idea that came from his conversation with Tabitha earlier when he suggested that she kill Mrs. Whitby for him.

He gets off the bed and walks to the kitchen, this end of the house getting some of the street light so he can see better. He fills a glass of water and sits in the living room and uses his cell phone to quickly go online. If the police didn't have his number before, they will have it after he phoned in for the pizzas. It's amazing how much technology can fit into one small phone, but it is a pain to use.

He looks up Theodore Tate. They were in prison at the same time—four months they were in the same complex, but Caleb doesn't remember ever seeing him. They must have been in different wings. An ex-cop, he would have been put into a section of jail where he didn't have the life kicked out of him every day. It would have been a good gig for him. At least comparatively. It meant he never would have had the real prison experience. Caleb is envious of that.

Three years ago Tate lost his daughter in an accident. A drunk driver ran her down, along with her mother, when they were walking out of a movie theater through a public parking lot. The mother survived, if that's what you could call it. The man who hit them was released on bail and went missing. He skipped the country, so the articles say.

Caleb keeps reading. There's the Burial Killer case from last year, where a psychopath was replacing interred corpses in a cemetery with fresh victims. Then there's the case from earlier this year where some whack job was kidnapping people and taking them to Grover Hills, the same institution James Whitby was taken to, only Grover Hills closed down a few years ago.

Theodore Tate. Ex-policeman turned private investigator, turned inmate, turned private investigator again, turned police consultant, and somewhere in there a killer of bad men.

The more he reads, the more he begins to relate, and the more he relates, the more his excitement builds. This is working out better than he hoped. Theodore Tate—husband and father, but so much more, perhaps even a man with his very own monster who hunted down the man who killed his daughter.

Yes. Theodore Tate will do quite nicely for what he has planned.

CHAPTER FIFTY-ONE

I drive through town, reaching intersections and having moments where I have no recollection of even driving there. I get caught for ten minutes in boy-racer traffic but I just don't care. Cars are tooting and cars are weaving in and out of the flow of traffic. My eyes are half-closed and all I want to do is get home and fall into bed. My head is hurting a little and massaging it isn't really helping. Schroder's car is an automatic and thank God it is, because if I had to spend mental energy on changing gears I'd break down and cry. When I do make it home I leave Schroder's car in the driveway.

I still have my keys, other than my car key, which is somewhere with my car back at the station. I fumble my way inside and the only food I can find is a loaf of bread in the freezer that has been there since last year. I make a few slices of toast and eat it while staring out the back window toward the spot in the ground where I had to bury my cat after some psycho killed it the day after I got out of jail. I force the toast into my body to stem the hunger pains. It's too late for coffee, too complicated to make it anyway, so I settle for water. I reach into my pocket for the painkillers the nurse gave me for the dog bite. I take two of them and tip the rest down the sink, not wanting to risk another addiction, not wanting to hide the symptoms in case there is something wrong inside of me. I can see my reflection in the window, I can still see the hospital room, I can still see my wife wired up to medical equipment like something in a science fiction movie the same way she was three years ago. I sat by her side and held her hand for the five minutes I was allowed, waiting for her eyes to open knowing they wouldn't—and they didn't. I finish the toast and head to the bedroom.

I climb into bed. I switch off the lamp and close my eyes and wait for the pills to take effect, feeling the absence of Bridget strongly tonight. The medical equipment, the tubes, all that science keeping her alive. Close—she was so close to being back. What's the next step?

Sleep. That's the next step. Tomorrow I'll figure out the rest.

I hear the footsteps outside the front door before the knocking. I look at the alarm clock and see that I've been in bed for two minutes. I close my eyes and wonder if I can just ignore it, then decide that I can't, even though I give it a good try. I pull the pillow over my head but the knocking doesn't stop. It's like I have a woodpecker inside my skull. I guess at quarter to three in the morning, it must be important. Then the idea hits me that it could be a reporter or, worse, a psychic. The wood-pecker confirms whoever it is they won't be ignored. I throw on some clothes and head into the hallway, dragging my feet and almost tripping over them. I can barely keep my eyes open. The knocking stops when I turn on the outside light. I've only been in the dark for two minutes but the light hurts. I put one hand against the wall to stay balanced.

"Who is it?" I ask.

"Theodore Tate?" a voice asks, and I recognize that voice, and my first thought is it's somebody from the hospital, that they've come to tell me in person what they should have told me over the phone. Only I get the feeling that's not where I know the voice from.

And it's a bad feeling.

"Yeah?" I ask, a little more awake now, but not too much more.

"It's Caleb Cole," the voice says, and the response makes my stomach clench and I take my hand off the wall and straighten up. "If you don't open the door in the next five seconds I'm going to dump a dead girl on your doorstep for you to deal with."

My cell phone is still in the bedroom. I don't have a weapon. All I have are two arms that I can barely hold up and eyes that blink open for split seconds rather than blinking closed.

"I mean it," he says.

I reach out and unlock the door. I swing it inward and, like he suggested, he's holding on to Katy Stanton. He's also holding on to a knife. The view wakes me up.

I take a few steps into the hallway and he follows. No matter what happens, it's time I moved and got an unlisted address— over the last year serial killers, madmen, lawyers, reporters, and also my parents have been showing up at my door. He kicks back with his foot and closes the door behind him. He doesn't give it quite enough power and it doesn't latch, and it swings back open an inch.

"I wish I'd never helped you with your car," I tell him. By helping him I helped him move on to his next victim. I helped him make his way to kidnapping Stanton and his kids.

He opens his mouth to say something, but he can't seem to figure out what that should be. He closes it, and gives a small acknowledging nod. "Turn on the light," he says.

I reach out and flick at the light switch. The hallway comes to life.

"Now what?" I ask.

"You have somewhere to sit down?"

I nod. "This way," I tell him, and I turn around and start walking.

"Don't try—"

"Yeah, I know," I tell him. "You said already." I lead him through to the dining room. "Here okay?" I ask him.

"Sure. Sit down at the opposite side of the table."

"You don't have to keep holding the knife against her," I say, looking at the blade that has taken so much from so many over the last few days. "I'm not going to try anything."

"Sit down," he repeats, "and we'll see what happens."

"Have you drugged her? Or is she asleep?" I ask, taking a seat.

"She's fine," he says, also sitting down. He rests her across his lap. "You're the one who found Octavia?"

I nod.

"How?" he asks.

"I went there to talk to Tabitha and she didn't answer the door."

"So you broke in?"

"Listen, Caleb, I'm way too tired and not in the best of moods, so how about you just tell me what you want?"

"You're not the only one who's tired."

"Yeah, but I'm the only one not holding a knife to a girl. What do you want?"

"Right now I want you to tell me why you went there."

"Because you sent Ariel Chancellor a letter saying that Tabitha was the one who put Victoria Brown into a coma."

He thinks about this, nodding slowly the entire time. "That was stupid of me," he says.

"You're right," I tell him. "And not just that, but this," I say, spreading my arms, "all of this is stupid. You're hurting all the wrong people."

"No. I'm hurting the right people. So far nobody innocent has died."

"What in the hell is wrong with you? Four people have died," I tell him. "Three of them were only doing their jobs, and the fourth—you didn't even know him."

"Well, they shouldn't have done their jobs as well as they

did," he says. "And that other asshole should have kept his dick in his pants. What is going to happen to Tabitha now that you know what she did?"

I shrug. "It's out of my hands," I tell him.

"Do you want her to go to prison?"

"No."

"Why?"

"Because it wouldn't serve any purpose," I tell him. "What she did was—"

"Illegal," he says. "She almost killed that woman. In a way, she did. And you want her to get away with it because it's revenge."

"That's not it at all," I say.

"Isn't it? Then why?"

I don't have an answer.

"It's the same with the others," he says. "For me. It's the same kind of revenge."

"What about Brad Hayward? What about his children. They deserve your revenge too?"

He doesn't have an answer.

"There's nobody left in my life," he eventually says.

"And her?" I ask, nodding toward Katy. "You'll hurt her for revenge?"

"If I have to. But if you help me out that won't have to happen."

"Help you how?"

"Did you kill the man who killed your daughter?"

"He fled the country."

"Did you kill him?"

"No."

"I don't believe you."

"I don't care what you believe."

"You've killed three people," he tells me. "I've killed five. They were all bad."

"I've killed one," I tell him, though technically it's four.

"You've killed six. One of them was a police officer. He was a good man."

"I know," he says, "and I regret that. I really do, and I've paid for it. We're not that different, you know. People who do bad things, we make them pay."

"Lower the knife," I tell him. "We're sitting at opposite ends of the table."

He lowers the knife.

"We are different," I tell him, not liking the comparison. "Very different."

"Maybe. Maybe not," he says. "If it'd been your daughter, you'd have done the same thing to James Whitby."

I don't give him any indication either way, but yeah, of course I would have. Only I'd have found a different way of doing it. Nobody else would have suffered. Nobody would ever know what had happened.

"It wasn't just James Whitby who killed Jessica," he says. "It was all of them."

"So what do you want from me?" I ask, knowing there's no point in arguing.

"You know what was done to James Whitby as a child? It's all in the transcripts from his court case after Tabitha Jenkins."

"I know his mother fucked him up," I say. "I know James Whitby never had a chance in life because of her. I know she's a candidate for worst mother of the century and that you want to kill her."

"Not anymore."

It's not the answer I'm expecting. "No?"

"No," he says. "I don't want to kill her. I want you to do it for me."

I almost laugh at the suggestion, but of course he's being serious. "Come on, Caleb, there's nothing in your file to say you're nuts. Why would you think I would do that?" I ask, and I look at Katy as I ask the question, and at the knife, and I have a pretty good idea about what's coming up, and it's bad.

"You want to do it because Mrs. Whitby's as responsible as anybody," he says. "You can't tell me with all that's happened that she deserves to be walking around free? That she gets a get-out-of-jail-free card? That's not fair. It's not fucking fair!" he says, and he slams his hand down on the table. Katy doesn't move. "I was hoping you'd see it from my point of view. I was hoping it wasn't going to come to this," he says, and he puts the knife back against Katy's throat.

"Caleb—"

"Phones these days, they are amazing things," he says, confusing me with his change in direction. "You can do so much with them. Here," he says, and he slides a phone across the table toward me. "It belongs to the doctor. I want you to have it."

"I already have a phone."

"Is it like that one?" Cole asks.

I look at the phone. No, mine is nothing like it. "Mine makes calls," I tell him, "not much more."

"Does it make video calls?"

I shake my head.

"Then take the phone," he says. "You have thirty minutes. That gives you time to drive to Mrs. Whitby's house and kill her, and when you do it," he says, "I want to see it happen. I'll call you in thirty minutes and you can show me on that phone what you've done, and it better be real, because if it isn't, if I think she's really still alive, I'm going to kill this little girl."

"No, you're not," I tell him. "She's just like your daughter."

He puts Katy's hand onto the table and holds the knife above it. He touches the blade against her finger.

"Don't," I tell him.

"You don't believe I'm going to hurt her," he says, frowning in disbelief as he shakes his head. "I can't blame you, because this morning I'd have agreed with you," he says, "but things are different now." He starts to push down on the knife.

"I believe you," I tell him, standing up, my legs no longer heavy and tired.

He points the knife at me. "Don't move," he says loudly, "don't you fucking move. Sit back down."

I sit back down. My legs are tight, ready to pounce, but they're shaking too. "You don't need to prove anything," I tell him.

"You're wrong. I'm alone in all of this. Tabitha wouldn't help and she was a victim. You've gone through something similar and even you don't want to help."

He pushes the knife back against Katy's finger.

"Wait, wait damn it. You've got it all wrong," I tell him. "You're hurting the wrong people—that's why nobody wants to help you, and if you hurt her you're . . ." He starts to press harder on the knife. "Damn it! Listen to me! Don't do this," I say, starting to move again.

He looks up at me. "I'm telling you, if you fucking move I'll kill her right now."

I don't sit back down, but I stay where I am, my legs against the chair. "Caleb—"

"I'm not fucking around here. Fuck, what is it with you people? You push and push and people don't want to help, they don't want to believe, so what else do I have?" he asks, his voice becoming high. "Huh? What else?" And before I can answer, he gives the answer he wants to hear. "Nothing. There's nothing else. So this, this right now is your fault!"

He pushes down hard on the knife.

"Caleb, you don't need to . . ."

There is resistance.

". . . do this."

There is a thud as the blade goes through her little finger.

"Jesus, Caleb!" I shout, banging my hip into the table as I start toward him. Blood is squirting up from Katy's hand. She doesn't wake up, she doesn't even flinch. She isn't just asleep—she's been drugged, just like Melanie was this afternoon.

He puts the knife against her throat, and when he moves Katy moves too, and her finger goes with her. It's still attached by some threads of skin that didn't break at the bottom. "Don't you fucking move," he seethes, and I stop a few feet short of him, my hip sore and my blood boiling.

"You . . ." I say, but don't know what to add. There isn't an expletive strong enough.

"Sit back down, sit back down or you'll see what else I'm capable of."

I move backward toward the chair, keeping my eyes on him, my hands hanging down by my sides. My legs hit the chair and I more fall into it than sit, the impact jarring into my head and almost waking the beast who has his hand on the headache button. I rest my arms on the table.

"Caleb . . ."

He sees her finger is dangling, so he puts her hand back on the table and slides the knife across the remaining skin. I can't look, instead I stare at my own hands with all my fingers intact. Stick a gun in those fingers and this would all be over. It's an effort for me to stay still. An effort to do nothing while listening to the blade dragging across the table. But what can I do? Make a move? No. A guy willing to cut off the finger of a tiny girl, well, a guy like that is capable of anything. That's his whole point.

"It's done," he says, and the finger has come free.

I don't have the strength to say anything. I just stare at him. Everything I thought I knew has just changed. Earlier I was sure we were getting all the girls back safely. Now . . . now I don't know what to think.

He stands up and points the knife at me. Blood is dripping from Katy's hand over the front of his shirt. There's a gouge mark in the table and blood staining it.

"Thirty minutes," he tells me. "I swear to God, when I call you in thirty minutes if Mrs. Whitby is still alive this little girl is going to run out of fingers, and it's going to get a whole lot worse after that."

CHAPTER FIFTY-TWO

Caleb puts the girl into the front seat of the car and climbs into the driver's seat. His stomach feels like it's grown a finger and is flicking at the back of his throat. His shirt is covered in blood and he got some on his face, and it's all over the front of the girl's dress. His hands are shaking so hard that when he tries to start the car he keeps missing the ignition with the keys. He looks over at the girl, at her hand, at the stump of the finger. He can see Tate standing in the doorway. He can feel the vomit coming.

"Hold on," he tells himself, and he gets the car started. He gets it into gear and turns around, and before he reaches the end of the street his stomach forces the bile upward. He doesn't have time to pull over and open the door—instead it gushes from his mouth and around the hand that he's put up to try and hold it, it sprays sideways, it's forced between his fingers, it covers his lap and the steering wheel, it hits the door and the girl, small chunks of it splatter the windshield. It burns his mouth and his throat and for a few seconds he can't breathe. He keeps driving, forcing himself to get around the corner before pulling over, not wanting Tate to get any indication of weakness.

"Christ," he says, and all the humanity that left him over the years is coming back. Everybody was right—he's hurting these children. The inside of the car stinks and he winds down the window. He looks over at Katy and he wipes the vomit off his chin and he shakes his head and starts to cry. "I'm sorry," he tells her, and he leans over and picks up her hand. The cut is neat, he can see bone, but it splintered on the edges. He looks around the car for something he can tie around it and can't see anything. He tries the glove compartment. Nothing. In the end he uses the knife to cut some of his shirt away, and he ties it as tight as he can around the rest of her finger and hand.

He doesn't want to keep hurting her. He doesn't have the stomach for it, but with no choice, well, what does he have with no other choice? She's lost her finger and she may lose a few more so an evil woman can be taken out of this world, and it's not a huge price to pay.

He drives another minute before he has to be sick again, and this time he's able to pull over. He opens the door and leans out. When he's done, he climbs out of the car and takes off his shirt. He wads it up and tosses it onto the street. He looks at his watch. It's been five minutes.

It takes him another ten to drive back to the house with its showroom furniture and tied up doctor. He parks in the driveway and carries Katy inside.

"Just so you know, this isn't a nightmare you're going to wake from," he tells Stanton, holding up the girl so Stanton can see his daughter's hand. Stanton almost retches into the duct tape. Sounds that are supposed to be words get caught in there somewhere.

"This is all your fault," Caleb says, "every bit of it, all your Goddamn fault," he says, and it's true. So very true. He steps back out of the room and carries Katy into another of the bedrooms. He lays her down carefully and rests her head on a pillow and drapes a blanket over her. Her hand has stopped bleeding. He's glad. When she wakes up she'll probably hum her fucked-up version of her ABCs for a few weeks while people smile at her and say *what a shame*, but she'll move on.

In ten minutes Theodore Tate will either kill Mrs. Whitby or he won't, and if he doesn't, he's going to cut more of Katy's fingers off, and he's going to keep cutting them until that evil old bitch is dead. He has to. He doesn't want to, but he has to—it's the only way. Mrs. Whitby has to be punished. And then it will end. It has to, because the only thing left is to finish this.

CHAPTER FIFTY-THREE

First thing I do is go into the bedroom and grab my cell phone. I get Schroder's number up on the display but I don't make the call. Can I kill Mrs. Whitby to save the life of a five-year-old girl? It's a simple question. Yes or no.

If yes, how am I going to do it?

If no, can I live with myself if Cole kills the girl?

I sit down in the same seat I occupied earlier in the dining room and I stare across the table at the finger no longer attached to Katy Stanton. Cole is gone and my headache is gone and I think about the lesser of two evils because that's what Cole is forcing me to do. I think about taking the life of Mrs. Whitby to save the life of Katy Stanton. In a logical world, the equation is simple. You sacrifice the older evil woman to save the innocent little girl. Mrs. Whitby beat her son within an inch of his life. She scarred his chest and legs with an iron. She used to put out cigarettes on his arms and lock him in closets for days at a time. She created a killer. So it should be a simple equation, and on paper it is.

But this isn't on paper. This is real life, you can't exchange one life for another, and even if you could, the person making that exchange is going to go to jail.

I load Schroder back up on my phone.

I set the phone on the table and don't make the call. Then I walk into the kitchen where there are still crumbs on the bench and I turn on the tap and cup my hands with water and splash my face. My eyes get a little wider but my mind stays just as foggy. Tired or awake or high on adrenaline, the solution wouldn't be any clearer.

In thirty minutes' time if Mrs. Whitby is still alive, will Cole kill Katy? All I know is that five minutes ago I didn't think he would cut her finger off. Any understanding I had for him disappeared when he pushed down that blade. So did any profile of the man that we'd built up. Cole is desperate. A desperate man can do anything. I splash more water on my face, grip the bench hard, tightening my grip until my fingers and thumbs throb, then push myself away, my reflection in the kitchen window doing the same thing.

I put on my shoes and put the two cell phones into my pockets, grab a jacket and my keys. I'm making my way to the front door when I hear the cat flap swing open in the dining room.

I back down the hall in time to see the neighbor's cat jumping up onto the table.

"Hey," I yell at it.

It jumps down and races back toward the cat flap, a look of utter panic on its face, the finger hanging from its mouth. I move to intercept it and it changes direction and goes back toward the dining room, then into the lounge. I go after it and it hides behind the couch. Jesus, I just don't have the time for this. The clock is ticking. I flip the couch over and the cat rushes past me back toward the door. I reach for it and miss, it looks back at me and runs into the wall, the finger falls from its mouth. It reaches for it again but I've halved the distance, so instead it hisses at me, then starts to growl. I clap loudly, it turns away and gets outside.

I pick up the finger. It's lighter than I'd have imagined, but I guess I'd never really imagined how much one would weigh before. I wrap it in a plastic bag and put it into the fridge. I figure it needs to stay cold if there's any chance of it being reattached and maybe the freezer will cause too much damage. I think the cells can crystallize or something—or maybe I'm just making that up. I don't know, but I figure the fridge is at least better than it getting munched on by the damn cat.

I get out to the car and put on the sirens, lights only. I don't know what in the hell to do. Call Schroder? Risk a girl's life? I don't know. I just don't know. All I know is that the car eats up the distance between my house and the Whitby house. I can still see that knife pressing down and cutting through Katy's finger, and the look on Cole's face, and it wasn't the face of a man who liked what he was doing. He was proving a point. Would he kill her to keep on proving it?

I don't know. If I call for backup, will Cole kill her?

If he does, can I live with that?

If I kill Mrs. Whitby, can I live with that?

Can I handle going back to jail?

Selfishly, that's what it comes down to. No, no I can't. Not with Bridget coming back to me.

I carry on driving, getting my cell phone out of my pocket. I hit the outskirts of town, and I hit them fast, coming out onto one of the main avenues where there have to be at least two hundred boy-racers all parked up on the road, blocking traffic. Fuck. I drive up over the medium strip and down into the oncoming lanes, which are empty. Up ahead I can see the lights of a fire truck and the orange glow of flames. I call Schroder. It rings a few times. He picks it up.

"Theo," he says, and I can hear his wife in the background and a crying baby. I can tell by the tone of his voice he's expecting bad news. He's expecting me to tell him that Bridget has died.

"I need your help," I tell him.

"What's wrong?"

"I don't know whether I'm calling you as a friend or as a cop."

"It's as a friend, Theo. I'm not a cop, not tonight. Maybe not ever again."

"Then it's as my friend."

"Okay, Theo, you definitely have my attention. What's happened?"

"Caleb Cole came to see me."

"He what?"

"Just now."

"And he's still there?"

"No. He left."

"You let him leave?"

I tell him what happened. It takes up three of the thirty minutes Cole gave me. In those three minutes I pass two burning cars, one group of people watching a fist fight, and a purple car driving very slowly also in the wrong direction, with two flat tires and sparks flying up from the rims where they are shredding away and flapping at the neon lights below.

When I'm done Schroder is silent, but I can hear him popping open his packet of Wake-E, and a moment later he starts munching on a tablet.

"Well?"

"Well, you should ring Detective Kent, or ring Stevens directly. And of course you can't kill her," he says. "How long ago did he leave?"

"Eighteen minutes ago," I tell him, "and of course I know I can't do it."

"If you knew that, you'd have called me eighteen minutes ago."

"Listen, Carl, I don't know why I didn't call right away, okay? But that's not the point here—the point is what do we do now?"

"Well, you can't kill her."

"I know, you said that already, and I've already told you I know that."

"We have to fake something. It's the only thing we can do. Make Cole think we've killed her."

"He's not going to fall for that. And when he calls, he'll get me to prove it. He's going to ask me to do something that we can't fake."

"Fuck, Theo! You should have called straightaway."

"I know. I'm sorry."

"Well, you can't kill her."

"Jesus, Carl, stop saying it as if I'm considering it!"

"Okay, okay, I'm sorry, but you can't."

"But if I don't, he's going to kill Katy. When he cut her finger off—shit, I just couldn't believe it."

"See, you are considering it," he says.

"Just tell me what to do."

"Where are you now?"

"About two minutes away from her house."

"Okay. I'm in the car now. I'm on my way."

"That's still not telling me what to do."

"I don't know. Shit, we need more time."

"I have to at least go there, right? Even if we're going to fake something, I have to go there."

"Okay. Listen, I'll call the officers at the scene and let them know you're coming. I'm ten minutes away."

"They won't listen to you, remember?"

"I'll make them listen. Goddamn it, Theo, you should have called sooner! I'll call you back," he says, and he hangs up.

Mrs. Whitby lives in a neighborhood full of nice homes, nice cars—nothing really expensive, but everything is tidy and well kept. It's the same kind of neighborhood my parents live in and where I grew up. Nobody rich, nobody poor, just people with families going through the daily grind of life, doing better than some, some not doing as good as others, but everything averaging out. There are no patrol cars in sight, and that's because the house is still being used as bait. There is no point in hiding the fact anymore that the police are here—Cole knows Whitby is under guard.

I park in the driveway. There are eight minutes left. You can do a lot in eight minutes, or you can do nothing. I knock on the front door. An officer opens it and lets me in.

"She's in the bedroom," he says.

"I need to talk to her."

"Detective Schroder said not to leave you alone with her."

"Detective Schroder isn't a detective at the moment," I tell him.

"Doesn't change the fact he told us not to leave you alone with her."

"Okay."

"And she's drunk," he says.

"Okay."

"Real drunk," he says. "Told my partner that for ten bucks she'd—"

"I get the idea," I tell him.

"I don't think you do," he says, shaking his head. "This way," he says, and he leads me down the hallway, the same hallway James Whitby used to walk up and down before he was violently attacked by his mother, before he violently attacked Tabitha Jenkins. We pass the officer's partner, who's sitting in the living room talking on his cell phone. There are no paintings on the walls, no photographs, just wallpaper that's coming away at the edges near the top. The décor through the house looks like it's been tired for about thirty years. The carpet is frayed up around the doors, the result of a cat living here at some point or still living here now.

My phone rings. It's Schroder. "I've made some calls," he says.

"And?"

"And I spoke to Barlow," he says, and he sounds panicked.

"I told him what happened. He said he couldn't believe it. He said it's outside of the box for what he thought Cole was capable of. He says cutting Katy's finger off throws everything we've come up with into chaos."

"What does he suggest?"

"He doesn't have a suggestion. I mean, why would he? He'd be putting his career on the line. I rang Stevens."

"And?"

"Stevens said you can't hurt Mrs. Whitby. That's all. He didn't come up with an alternative, probably for the same reason. Best to come up with nothing because coming up with something might lose him his job. He told me others are on their way to meet you. Told me not to show up."

"It's almost time," I tell him.

"I know. I know."

"He's going to kill her," I say. "He's going to cut off her fingers, and then he's going to put a knife into her chest."

"I know."

"We can't let that happen."

"Damn it, Tate, don't go in that room alone. That's an order."

"From a friend?"

"Just . . . just wait for me, okay? I'm almost there. Just a few more minutes."

"Okay."

"I'm serious, Tate. Wait for me."

"I will."

"Promise me."

"I promise."

"Hand the phone to the officer."

I hand over the phone to the officer. He takes it and listens, says "okay," while he nods, then nothing more before handing it back. "I've been dismissed," he says.

"What?"

"Cole isn't coming here. There's no reason for us to stay."

He gives me a relieved look. He has no idea what's going on, but he knows it's something bad, and he's just learned he and his partner don't have to be a part of it. He walks up the hallway and leans into the living room. I listen to him tell his partner the same thing, then he shrugs, and I can't make out what his partner says. A moment later they're both stepping outside. They close the front door just as another car pulls up outside.

I look at the bedroom door, then at my watch. There are three minutes left. The front door opens. Schroder comes in. I can see my car out on the curb. I have his, and he must have ended up getting a lift back to the station and taking mine. He's wearing shorts and his pajama top and he's in bare feet. He's puffing. Both his hands are shaking, but not like he's scared or cold, but like an electrical charge is going through him. He's chewing another tablet. He's also carrying a gun.

"We're alone?" he asks, his eyes darting left and right.

"Except for Mrs. Whitby. What's the gun for, Carl? Cole isn't here."

"She's in there?" he asks, nodding toward the bedroom door.

"Yep. The gun?"

"The girl," he says, still ignoring my question. "Is Cole really going to kill her?"

"I don't know. At the very least he'll take her fingers. I really believe that."

"So do I," he says. "If he can cut off one he can probably cut off ten. She's a bitch," he says, nodding toward the bedroom door again. "Mrs. Whitby. I remember her. I remember talking to her. She's as bad as they get," he says. "You saw the case file."

"She's a monster," I say.

"One of the worst," he says, and he's staring at me and I can almost feel the charge coming off him. The hairs are standing on his arms and he's still chewing at the tablet. His eyes are wide and jittery.

"She put her son into a coma," I say.

"She hit him with an iron."

"Could have killed him," I say.

"I wish she had."

I nod. I wish she had too.

"You know she only did a few months in jail, right?" he asks.

"I know," I tell him.

"Not much of a punishment," he says.

"Not much at all."

"More should have happened to her."

"She should never have been let out," I say.

"All of this, it all began with her. Doesn't seem right she should get away with it."

"Not right at all," I agree.

"The world needs balancing, Theo." A cell phone rings. I look down at it. It's the doctor's. "This job," he says, "we see the shittiest things."

"I know."

"Jesus," he says, and he tilts his head up and stares at the ceiling for a few seconds, and when he looks back at me I think he's trying hard not to cry. "I don't . . ." he says, then shakes his head, "I can't. I can't deal with any more children dying. Last Christmas I promised myself no more kids were going to die on my watch," he says, and I can tell he's back in that moment where he last had to deal with the horror of a child being killed. "That day in the bathtub, drowning like that, I should have left the force then. I should have left."

"Carl . . ."

"No more dead children," he says. "No more."

The phone is still ringing. I look at my watch. It's been thirty minutes. I'm shaking my head and Schroder is nodding his. He smiles. A sad, sad smile, and now the tears are there, just a few of them. "No more on my watch," he says, and his smile grows. "Give me the phone," he says.

"Why?"

"Because the world is about balance, Theo. That's why. Give me the phone."

I hand it over. He looks at it for a few seconds as if he's forgotten how to use one. The display is lit up with the number the call is coming from. "Four minutes I was dead," he says. "Four minutes and nothing, just nothing. These kids, when they die they're not moving on to a better place. We want to think so, but they're not. The only thing waiting for us is a whole lot of nothing." He presses the answer button. "This is Detective Inspector Carl Schroder," he says, talking into the phone, straightening himself up and wiping at his eyes. He changes his grip on the gun so he can spare a few fingers to tug at his pajama top and get it sitting right, as if he were about to go into a meeting.

I can hear Cole's voice coming through the speaker. "Where's Theodore Tate?"

"He's right next to me."

"Put him on," Cole says.

"No. You're dealing with me now."

"If you don't put him on I'm going to—"

"Shut up, Caleb. Just shut up and watch," Schroder says, and he fiddles with the functions on the phone and puts it on mute, and a moment later the display shows what the phone is pointing at. It shows my feet, then Schroder's, then the door frame. It shows Schroder's hand reaching out to the handle. It's blurry and dizzying. People must throw up watching his home movies.

"Carl," I say.

He shakes his head, the smile still there, and then he shrugs. "Sometimes good men have to do bad things."

"Carl—"

"Theo, shut up. This isn't your decision. This isn't for you to live with," he says, and I don't try to stop him, I just stand back and watch as he opens the bedroom door and steps through. The light is on inside. I can see Mrs. Whitby sitting up in bed, an empty vodka bottle on the nightstand next to her, her mouth hanging open and her eyes shut. The room smells of alcohol and cigarettes and cat piss. She's wearing a robe, the front of it patchy with old stains.

He turns back toward me. "It was me," he says.

"What?"

"The prison records. I was the one who skipped past Cole's. I mean, I looked at it, but . . . but fuck, I was still balancing a line between being drunk and being hungover, and of course the baby comes with a whole lot of sleep deprivation. You were right—I should never have been part of this case. I looked at that case file and I was too fucked to even notice it meant anything, and now . . . well, now I have to do what it takes to save that little girl."

"Carl . . ."

"It's true, and you know it. If I'd made that connection, most of this could have been avoided. We could have caught him when he was going for Victoria Brown, or when he took the doctor."

"You don't know that."

He sighs. "Yeah, yeah I do. We both do," he says.

"Carl . . ."

"I'm tired, Theo. Tired and I just want this to be over," he says, and he takes the phone off mute and closes the door.

I stand in the corridor and I close my eyes and I wait for the gunshot.

It doesn't take long. Five seconds. It echoes and rolls around inside my head like a bowling ball for much longer.

CHAPTER FIFTY-FOUR

Caleb watches the display on the phone and says nothing as he looks at the dead woman on the bed, just the one gunshot, right through the heart. Her eyes opened when it happened, she looked right at the phone, her mouth seemed to cave in on itself, and she didn't even have the time to raise an arm to her chest. Instead her head dropped back down to where it was when she was sleeping, her neck slumped against her massive breasts. She's in pretty much the same position she was a minute ago. He doesn't doubt she's dead. Still—he knows they can be faked.

"There's an empty bottle on the nightstand," he says.

"What? I can't hear you."

"I said there's an empty bottle on the nightstand."

"I still can't hear you," Schroder says. "You'll have to give me a minute."

"You're kidding."

"What?"

"I said you're kidding," he says, almost shouting it at the phone.

"Missing? What's missing?"

Cole doesn't answer. He keeps watching the dead woman on the screen, and then there is fast movement as the phone is lifted higher. He watches the wall swaying up and down, and he realizes the detective has his finger in his ear, twisting it back and forth. It's the gunshot. It must be. The gunshot has deafened the detective so he can't hear him. He has to wait a minute. It's a long minute, but he's excited. He's missed out on the judge. He could try the same trick and convince somebody to kill the judge for him, but he doesn't see it working, not again, not against a man who the world thinks is good.

Finally the phone moves again, and he can see the side of Schroder's face before his ear fills the screen. Obviously he's forgotten he's on speakerphone as well as video.

"What were you saying?"

"There's a bottle on the nightstand."

"So?"

"So I want you to pick it up and smash her over the head with it."

"What?"

"You heard me."

"I'm not going to do that."

"You have to."

"No. I don't have to. She's dead."

"Then she's not going to feel it, and she's not going to mind."

"No."

"I need to know she's dead."

"Yeah? Then why don't you come down here yourself and take a Goddamn look at her. I'm not hitting her with the bottle."

Caleb thinks about it. Nods. Thinks about it a little more. Nods to himself again. He believes the detective. "Do you have a marker?"

"What?"

"A pen. Find a pen."

"I have a pen."

"I want you to write on her forehead."

"I'm not going to do that either."

"You're going to do it, Detective, and here's why—I'm going to tell you where I am."

A grunt comes down the phone line. "Yeah, sure you are."

"I am," he says, looking down at the little girl that he won't have to ever cut again. "I promise you, you write on her forehead, then you and Theodore Tate can come and take me away. I give you my word. You can save Katy Stanton."

"What about her father?" Schroder asks.

"I'm still undecided about that."

"Don't hurt him, and you have a deal."

"You write what I want you to write, and I won't harm either of them. Deal?"

"What do you want me to write?"

"I want you to write *I'm an evil bitch*."

"Why?"

"Because that's what she was. You know it. We all know it."

"Then why bother writing it?" the detective asks.

"You going to write it or not? Or does our deal not stand?"

"Hang on." The footage changes again. He sees Schroder's shirt and then the bed, and the screen stays on the bed for thirty seconds. Then the phone is on the move again. It's pointed at Mrs. Whitby's face. It's all blurry and out of focus for a few seconds, but then it becomes sharp. The words are on her forehead. The handwriting is neater than his own, nice blocky lettering, but he hasn't gotten the spacing right and the last few letters have to curve up over her left eye where they get smaller.

"Good," he says.

"Now where are you?"

"Will you come alone if I tell you? Just you and Tate?" he

asks, because that's what Schroder will be expecting him to ask. He doesn't care whether Schroder and Tate come alone, or whether they bring a hundred cops with them.

"Yes."

"How do I know if I can believe you?"

"Enough games, Caleb. Just tell me where you are."

"Fair enough," he says. He gives Schroder the address of the house that's for sale, hangs up, then calls the journalist he was going to call before. He tells him who he is, and he knows the man doubts him, so he takes a photograph of Katy on the phone and sends it to him. Then he makes a few more calls, a radio station, a TV station, and he gives them all the address too. Then he walks back through to Dr. Stanton. He has five minutes, he guesses. Five minutes and then everything will be over.

CHAPTER FIFTY-FIVE

Schroder opens the door and hands me the cell phone. I get the same view I had on his way in. Mrs. Whitby is slumped in pretty much the same way, looking drunk, only Schroder has scrawled something across her forehead.

"Don't speak to me," he says.

"Shoo did the right thing," I tell him, holding my hand lightly against the side of my head. The gunshot is still rattling around in there.

He gives me a strange look, then shakes his head. "Theo, seriously, just shut the fuck up, okay? We're going for a drive and I don't want to hear a single word from you, is that clear?"

It's clear. We head out into the street. There are lights on in the neighboring houses, the gunshot having woken people. It's the first time Schroder has ever killed anybody, and I'm guessing he never thought he'd ever have to, and I know surely he could never have envisioned such a set of circumstances. He's thinking he killed an innocent woman—but he didn't. He saved one.

"Keys," he says, putting his hand out. I hand him his keys and he hands me mine. We get into his car. I don't ask where we're going. His cell phone rings and he reaches into his pocket and hangs up without answering it. Then mine rings.

"Don't answer it," he says.

I look at the display in case it's the hospital, but it isn't. It's the police station. I kill the call and put the phone back into my pocket. Schroder's starts ringing again. He flips it over, pops out the battery, and tosses both halves into the backseat. Mine rings again. He looks at it ready to do the same thing. I put it on silent and don't answer it.

I give it a few minutes, switching between watching Schroder and watching the night slowly lose its battle to the light. The headache is creeping back slowly, the work the pills had done to fight it all falling away over the last few minutes. In the distance the sky is dark blue. In a few hours people will be getting up and heading to work, hitting their stride and being productive. Right now they're mostly still asleep, they're in their dream worlds—some are being chased by monsters, some are visiting women they've seen on TV, others are flying, others are falling.

"Where are we going?" I ask.

"We're going to arrest Caleb Cole and save Katy Stanton."

"And how are we going to do that? He didn't happen to tell you where they all are, did he?"

He nods. "As a matter of fact, he did."

"What?"

"He gave me his address."

"You believe him?" I ask, rubbing at my temple.

"I do."

"Why didn't you tell me?"

"You have no right to ask that," he says. "When was the last time you came straight to me with something?"

"It's part of his endgame," I say. "Whatever he has planned, it's going to happen when we show up."

"I know that, Theo. I'm not a fucking idiot. His endgame is to die, that's what everybody is saying, but that's not going to happen. We make sure of that. We get there and we take this bastard alive because it's the last thing he wants. You get that?"

"No sholem."

"What?"

"I said 'no problem.'"

"Look, I'm serious, Tate, this fucker isn't getting off easy. He's going back to jail."

"I said no problem, okay? But . . . shouldn't we call for backup? Have you forgotten you've been suspended?"

"He told us to come alone."

"This sounds dangerous, Carl. And stupid. You're blowing any chance you have to shave your job."

"Shave?"

"What?"

He shakes his head. "I can drop you off here if you want. I won't hold it against you."

"Carl, you're fucking things up. This isn't the way to do things. We should call for backup."

He finally looks over at me. He gives me a five-second stare, which is a long time when the person giving it is also in control of a speeding car. I'm rubbing my temple harder now.

"Jesus, Theo, are you okay?"

"Are you?"

"Look, if it were the other way around, you'd go ahead and do it your way anyway. You've always done it your way. Even when you were a cop. It's always had to be the Tate way. Tate knows best. Tate doesn't have to play by the rules. Now we're doing it the Schroder way. Okay?"

"Okay, Goddamn it, okay!"

"Are you sure you're okay?"

"I said I was okay," I snap, rubbing at my head. I'm starting to worry that I'm in the process of filling out the ER doctor's prescription.

He slows down and starts looking at the street signs, takes a right, and picks up some speed again.

"Just look for the *For Sale* sign he says. Number ninety-two."

"Okay," I say, but all the numbers look blurry. Everything does as the thing inside my head continues to wake up.

Ten seconds later he spots the sign staked into the front lawn. I see it after he's slowed down. He pulls up outside it. I rub at my eyes and my vision clears a little. I shouldn't have washed the damn pills down the sink.

"No point in trying to sneak in," he says, "he's expecting us."

"So what do we do?"

"We go up to the front door and we knock. It's that simple."

"And then?"

"And then we do it the Schroder way," he says, and before we get out of the car more cars show up behind us, and the media joins us to come and arrest Caleb Cole.

CHAPTER FIFTY-SIX

The father is awake. The police are going to be here soon. He considered not letting the police know, and only calling the media. He didn't need the cops here—but ultimately he decided they wouldn't be able to stop what was happening. They are coming into a situation they know nothing about, and they'll have to be cautious. Their inclusion won't be a problem—if anything it'll just confirm Stanton's fate.

Caleb leans over and removes Stanton's gag. "I enjoyed killing your daughters," he says.

"You're an animal," Stanton says. He's crying and his face is red.

"Get up."

"What?"

"I said get up. We're going for a walk."

"Fuck you. Fuck you, you . . . you . . ."

"Animal. You said already. You want me to kill you in front of your last remaining daughter?"

"I said 'fuck you.'"

Caleb likes it. Stanton is getting braver. He's angry. "Unless you get up I'm going to strip Katy naked and put photographs of her naked body all over the Internet."

Stanton gets to his knees. "I'll kill you," he says. "I'll fucking kill you."

Caleb nods. "If I don't kill you, Doctor, will you stand up at my trial and tell the good people of the jury that none of this was my fault? That I'm just a man who snapped?"

"You're insane," Stanton says.

"Good." He reaches down and grabs a handful of Stanton's hair and starts to pull. "Now get up."

He leads Stanton out to the living room, past the bedroom with Katy who is still asleep. He switches on the lights. He holds the knife tightly in his hand and he waits, standing behind Stanton with the knife against his neck.

"What are you waiting for?" Stanton asks.

"Shut up," Caleb says.

He only has to wait a minute until the cars start arriving.

"Move," he says, and he pushes Stanton toward the door. Stanton stumbles, but he moves, reaches it, and stops. He turns them both around so his own back is to the door and Stanton is facing the hallway.

"Now what?" Stanton asks.

"Now it's time to beg for your life," he says, and he cuts through the binds on Stanton's wrists.

The doctor immediately brings his arms in front of him and starts rubbing them. "I'm going to kill you, and then your other daughter," Caleb says. "Now turn around."

Stanton turns around. There are a few feet between them, nothing more. Cole steps toward him, and as he does, he drops the knife. It thuds onto the carpet maybe a little closer to Stanton than to him.

Both men pause as they stare at each other. Caleb waits for Stanton to react. And then he does, swooping toward the knife. Caleb reaches out and kicks it, it goes behind Stanton and further down the hallway. Stanton goes after it. Caleb smiles. He reaches behind for the door handle and opens the door. It's all perfect. Just perfect.

Stanton gets the knife and points it at him. "I'm going to kill you," he says triumphantly, shaking his head. "I'm going to fucking slice you apart."

Caleb steps through the doorway. He steps onto the porch and faces the street. There are two vans, and standing in front of them are people with cameras. He raises his arms in the air, palms facing front, hands well away from his body. On the footpath coming toward him is the detective and Tate. He keeps his back to Stanton and he waits, he waits for the fucker to stab him, he waits for the death that comes with it, and in front of the cops, in front of the media, Dr. Nicholas Stanton is going to kill an unarmed man. He's going to kill a man who he thinks killed his daughters. He's going to have to answer for that, and there's going to be a trial. He'll be found guilty, the same way Caleb was guilty fifteen years ago. And then he's going to go to jail and he's going to get beaten and raped and he's going to get his fingers broken over and over by those same assholes with the aversion to symmetry, and then Nicholas Stanton is finally going to know what it's like to walk in Caleb Cole's shoes.

CHAPTER FIFTY-SEVEN

"How the hell did they figure it out?" Schroder asks.

We step out of the car. There are media vans behind us. We don't know if Cole is in there, who's dead and who's alive, we don't know if Cole is going to come quietly. As if on cue the front door to the house opens. Cole comes forward four steps, and then he raises his arms. He stares toward us, but there are lights in his face from the vans and the cameras and I can see he can't tell us apart from the journalists. People start moving forward. Cole's shoulders are shrugged up around his neck as if he's cold or expecting to be shot.

Schroder raises his gun. I move off to the side. Cole doesn't turn toward me. He doesn't take another step forward. He keeps his eyes forward, squinting hard to see.

"Don't move," Schroder yells at him.

"I'm unarmed," he shouts back. "I am turning myself in. Don't shoot."

"Detective," one of the reporters yells, "what right do you have to be here?"

I glance back to make sure Schroder isn't about to open fire on the reporters before running onto the lawn. I reach the front of the house out to the right, out of Cole's line of vision. I stay against the side and start closing the distance to the front door. Then Dr. Nicholas Stanton comes through it. He's staggering, taking long strides. He's wearing pajamas similar to Schroder's, only his have splotches of blood and vomit down them. His eyes are large and wild and his face is in a tight grimace. He's holding a very large knife in his hand, which comes into view when he raises his arm to shield his eyes from all the light. The light is helping to spotlight him, making him look like a madman. He flinches a little at all the commotion, at all the people, and he seems unsure of himself. Then he sees Cole, focuses on him, his face gets even tighter, and he moves forward. His feet land heavily on the ground. Cole must be able to hear him, yet Cole doesn't look back, he doesn't move, just keeps his shoulders shrugged up around his neck as high as they will go.

Then it hits me. The endgame. Cole wants to be stabbed. He wants Stanton to kill him in front of all these people. He wants Stanton to go to jail for killing an unarmed man.

Schroder is still yelling at Cole not to move. From Schroder's angle, Cole is blocking his view of Stanton. I keep moving forward. All of us are in the lights of the cameras. We're all being recorded for history. Schroder has to yell to be heard over the gaggle of reporters. My head is throbbing but I know in another minute this will all be over.

"Don't do it," I yell out to Stanton.

"Keep your hands in the air," Schroder says to Cole, and Schroder is moving forward now. So are the news crews, they're providing the lights and the cameras and the rest of us are providing the action.

"Your children are alive," I tell Stanton, and there's only about ten feet between us now.

Cole throws me a look, frowns at me, then looks back at the cameras.

"I killed them," Cole says, loud enough for Stanton and me but not for the media, "and one of them I raped."

"He hisent shirt them," I say, hearing the wrong words coming out. *Fuck*.

"You killed my children," Stanton says, not hearing me, only looking at Cole.

"And I enjoyed it."

Stanton takes the final step. I try to cover the distance, but I can't, not in the time it takes for Stanton to bring the knife down. If it's the middle of Cole's back he's aiming for, then it's almost a bull's-eye. If he's trying to put enough force into the blade that it sinks right down to the hilt, then that isn't quite as good—because it snags on a bone somewhere and only goes halfway. He pulls the knife out as Cole drops to his knees, giving Schroder a clear view of Stanton and of what's going on.

"Drop the knife," Schroder shouts, changing his aim from Cole to Stanton, back to Cole, then back to Stanton again.

I get within two steps of Stanton. I shout, really focusing on the words to tell him his children are fine, and I hold my arms out, palms up, and he turns toward me, this wild man with wild hair and eyes bugging out of his skull. "Shure susshen are thine," I tell him.

He looks at me with absolutely no comprehension of what I'm trying to say.

He raises the blade and this time his aim is the back of Cole's neck. I cover the final step, I get my left hand around Stanton's wrist, and I pull him forward and we both crash to the ground. I feel the stitches in my leg popping. I feel the pressure inside my skull building, the doctor's warning floating around in there on a sea of pain. Stanton pushes me off him and I roll to my side. He half sits up and sees the knife is still in his hand. He looks at Cole, then at me, then crawls toward Cole again. I get onto my feet and try to grab hold of him. He looks at me, then slashes the knife in my direction. I don't see it in time and there's no way to avoid it.

Schroder shoots him.

The gunshot sets off a whole lot of chain reactions in my head. The first one is that for a few seconds the nerves between my eyes and my brain stop working. I'm standing in the dark with no idea what's happening. Then a switch is thrown and my vision comes back, and with it a whole lot of pain. I stumble sideways, clutching my head as if I'm the one who's been shot. The lights from the news crews all point in different directions as everybody ducks and reacts. I lean against the side of the house.

Cole twists toward us. "No," he cries out, still on his knees. "No," he repeats, and this time a blood bubble grows and pops between his lips. He loses balance and falls forward. The back of his shirt is soaking with blood. He tilts down the porch steps and comes to a stop with his face on the path and his legs still on the porch.

Stanton, however, is trying to get to his feet, only he's not having such a great time of it. The front of his pajamas over his right shoulder have turned red. I've got one hand over my eye because somehow it eases the pain from whatever the fuck my brain is doing. He tries to lift the knife again, but his arm won't work. I can see in his face that he can't figure out the mechanics of it all. He keeps trying, and then he uses his good arm to take the knife out of the good hand attached to the bad arm. He looks around and starts swinging the knife, pointing it in the direction of the media, at Schroder, and then at me. He can't seem to spot Cole. He swings it toward me and Schroder takes a second shot. I can't see where this one hits Stanton, but it stops him in his tracks. He looks down at his body, then at me, and his eyes start to clear.

I try to talk to him, to tell him his children are okay, but the words just don't come out, they're all too heavy and the ones that do finally come out just don't make sense. The lights are getting brighter as the news crews come forward. Schroder reaches us. He kicks the knife further, then helps me out from beneath Stanton.

"You okay?" he asks me.

I nod.

He grabs his cell phone and calls for an ambulance. Two of them. He doesn't let go of the gun. There are lights on him, lights on me, lights on Cole and Stanton. There is blood everywhere, all of it making for good TV footage.

"He was never going to hurt them," Schroder says, talking to Stanton once he's hung up.

"I don't . . . don't understand," he says, and he looks like a man waking from a dream.

"They're fine," Schroder tells him.

"And Katy?"

"I'm sure Katy is fine too."

"He . . . he cut off her finger."

"I know, but that's all he did," Schroder says, saying it as though cutting her finger off is nothing.

"He . . . he didn't kill them?" Stanton asks.

"No," I say, and it's the first word to have come out clear.

"I should have . . ." he says, and then he starts to cough. He keeps coughing, and when he finally stops he starts to smile. "Should have known," he says, and then he doesn't say anything else, just stares up at us with that smile on his face, and it's still there when the ambulance arrives five minutes later.

CHAPTER FIFTY-EIGHT

"You sure you're okay?" Schroder asks.

"I'm fine," I tell him, knowing that if he'd heard me speak earlier he'd know I wasn't.

"Okay," he says, and climbs into the back of the ambulance with Caleb Cole.

I drive Schroder's car. I asked one of the paramedics for the strongest painkillers they had and he handed me two tablets but the headache isn't going. My ears are still ringing from the gunshots. Some of the media stay at the house, some follow, more media vans show up as the story gathers momentum. We get to the hospital. I pull in behind the ambulance with Cole in it and see it unloaded in the opposite order I saw it loaded. They rush him into an emergency room. The second ambulance pulls up and they do the same for Dr. Stanton. His daughter is carried out and rushed in too.

Seeing Katy I remember I have her finger at home. I pull out of the parking lot and head back to the house. All the boy-racers seem to have gone home. The only traffic now is made up from people finishing the graveyard shift, or those with an early start. I see a fluffy tail, two back legs, and not much else of the cat as it races away from the back door of my house. I grab the finger from the fridge. It's cold and feels solid and I tuck it into my pocket before deciding that's a bad idea, that the body heat may only damage it. I grab a drink of water and stand by the sink with my eyes closed willing the headache to disappear, but it's not listening to me, the thing living in there no longer willing to be ignored. My ears are still ringing. I head back to the hospital with the finger on the passenger seat, the same sights as before only in the opposite order and lighter too.

I can't find a parking space when I get back to the hospital. Cop cars and media vans are everywhere, and I have to park on the other side of the road by Hagley Park, the huge park in the middle of the city that even at this time has a few people jogging slowly around it. I get buzzed in by the same nurse I spoke to when I came here to see my wife. I hold up the finger and show the first doctor I come across and tell him who it belongs to. He takes it and rushes off. I find the waiting room I was in earlier. Schroder is sitting down in it. So are a bunch of other cops. I sit next to Schroder. We don't talk to each other. Others are chatting away. Schroder stares ahead and I can tell he's replaying the shootings over and over, first Mrs. Whitby, then Dr. Stanton, and I'm replaying them too, wondering if there was anything different we could have done. An hour goes by. Nobody comes, nobody goes. The replays don't get any prettier but the headache fades. I don't come up with any other scenarios that might have worked. Schroder just keeps looking at the wall. Eventually I check my cell phone for missed calls, and there are a few, most of them from the police station, one of them from Dr. Forster. My heart sinks seeing that one. The way the week has gone, I don't see it being good news. I don't call him back. I can't. Whatever he has to say, no matter how bad, if I don't hear him say it then it doesn't need to have happened.

After another hour a doctor comes out. By this point I'm pacing the room, every few minutes reaching for my phone and reminding myself there's no point, that there is only going to be pain in the message waiting for me. There's blood on the doctor's scrubs but not much of it. He looks at us and there is nothing in his face to suggest one thing or the other.

"Caleb Cole is in serious condition," he says, addressing all of us, though it's Detective Kent he looks at the most, and who could blame him? "But it looks like he's going to make it."

I don't know how I feel about that. Schroder says nothing. Kent nods at the doctor, and the doctor glances at her chest for a second before looking at the rest of us. When the doctor sees nothing else is going to be added, he turns and heads back through the same doors he came from.

"How long do you think he'll get?" I ask Schroder.

"What?"

"Cole. You think he'll ever come out of jail?"

Schroder shakes his head but doesn't answer. He gets himself comfortable and stares at the wall again. For the first time he finally looks tired. I think about Cole's game plan, and how angry he's going to be when he wakes up to find out he's still alive. He's going to go back to jail. He's going to go through the beatings he took all over again. He didn't kill himself last time—will he this time? And in twenty years, if he's released, what then? I can't see him making it twenty years.

Another hour goes by. I spend most of it with my eyes closed and my head tilted so far back it touches the wall. A different doctor from before comes out to see us, showing up from the corridor behind us. He shakes his head. "We couldn't save her finger," he says, "but aside from that, Katy is fine. We'll be able to discharge her tomorrow."

"Okay," Kent says, and we go through the same routine as the last doctor—he stands there waiting for us to add something else and nobody does, so he walks back the way he came. I wonder what will happen to the finger.

Some of the detectives start to disappear. Soon there are only five of us. Nobody is talking. Then Dominic Stevens comes along. He steps into the room and scans everybody's faces. Detective Kent finds a reason to take the others out into the corridor, leaving me and Schroder behind. Before Stevens can start in on us, a third doctor shows up, this one coming through the same doors as the first.

"Nicholas Stanton's shoulder wound isn't the problem," he says, "but the second bullet went under his armpit and into his right lung. He lost a lot of blood. We've patched the damage, and barring nothing unforeseen, he should pull through."

"Good," Stevens says, slowly nodding. "That's very, very good." He puts his hand on Schroder's shoulder. "Let's go for a walk," he tells him.

Schroder and Stevens step into the corridor and I'm left alone with the doctor. When I try to get up I lose my balance and fall back into my chair. I need sleep. All of a sudden I can barely keep my eyes open.

"Are you okay?" he asks.

"I'm fine. Just tired, that's all. Thanks," I tell him. "Thanks for saving him."

He nods. "He's not saved yet," he says, "but it's looking good."

"Okay," I tell him, but he stays there looking at me.

"Your right eye," he says, "is blown."

"What?"

He kneels down in front of me, then suddenly he points a flashlight into my eye and my brain does a somersault, but I stay in control.

"It's not dilating. You got a headache?"

"Yeah."

"When did it start?"

"About six weeks ago."

"What?"

"It comes and goes," I tell him. "I was hit in the head."

"How hard?"

"Very," I say, rubbing the dent. "I have a prescription," I tell him, then reach into my pocket, but I'm just too sleepy now to find it. My hand falls out. It falls down my side and hangs over the side of the chair.

"Wait here," he says, and disappears.

I do the opposite and I walk out of the waiting room, my right arm swinging by my side. Dominic Stevens is in the hallway talking to Schroder. Stevens is in a pair of jeans and a shirt and I've never seen him looking so casual. He also looks calm. They are keeping their voices low, and I lean against the wall and watch them. For the first half of the conversation Schroder is shaking his head, and for the second half he's nodding. Then Stevens acknowledges me with a nod, says something else to Schroder, and leaves.

"What's the verdict?" I ask, knowing the conversation had to be about Mrs. Whitby.

"I'm not being fired," he says.

"But?"

"But I've been told to step down."

"I'm sorry."

"Yeah, I'm sorry too even though it's what half of me wanted."

"And Mrs. Whitby?"

"Stevens says the scene is still sealed, but it might be called a suicide. He said there's a chance Mrs. Whitby was found with the gun in her hand. He says there's a chance she killed herself because she felt bad about what she had done, that all of this was her fault."

"You happy to accept that?"

He shakes his head, but then says, "Yeah, I'm happy. We saved the girl, right? The world is down one evil old lady, so yeah, I can live with it," he says, but I'm not so sure he can, and Stevens's plan also comes down to how quiet they can keep Cole.

"And Stanton?"

He shakes his head. "I don't know. It's not up to us, Theo. Stanton stabbed an unarmed man on national TV. That's for the lawyers to figure out. I'm going home," he says, "before my wife fires me too."

I watch him heading down the corridor. I figure Katy, Cole, and Stanton—all of them are going to be okay. I figure that's a good omen, but then I think about the balance that Schroder was talking about earlier, and how that balance is going to be my wife. I stare at my cell phone for a few moments, then finally make the call, already knowing what I'm going to hear—when was the last time anybody called me with good news? I call Dr. Forster back and he answers after the second ring and I say nothing as he talks to me, I just listen, absorbing the information.

Bridget isn't dead. She isn't in a coma. She's alert and conscious but there is another problem. He tries to explain it to me, but I can't make sense of it. I turn in the corridor trying to orientate myself, trying to figure out the floor my wife is on and how to get there from here, and after I turn a full circle I drop down to my knees and throw up. The doctor who looked into my eyes a few minutes earlier sees me and rushes toward me, but I get back up and step into the elevator. The doors close in front of him and I make my way up a few floors.

By the time I make it to my wife's room, I can barely walk straight. At first I think half of the lights have been turned off, but then I realize it's me, that I'm struggling to see. I open the door and Bridget looks at me. A smile bursts onto my face, but then the floor comes rushing up toward me, my head crashes into the side of her bed on the way down, and the thing inside my head lights up the rest of its distress flares. I lie on the floor realizing that for something good to have happened, the city has to give something bad. That's the balance Schroder was talking about. Cole, Stanton, my wife—I'm the balance for them surviving.

I can hear the door opening behind me, somebody rushing in, somebody saying "there he is," and crouching over me. I hear "Christ, this is going to be close," and then it all fades away—the lights, the pain, my wife, and I can feel the tears on my cheek and then I can't feel a thing.

ACKNOWLEDGMENTS

I would like to say thank-you to the very cool crew at Hodder & Stoughton in the UK To Ruth Tross, Kerry Hood, Cicely Aspinall, and the others – thanks so much for doing a wonderful job on these UK editions! I'd also like to thank Simon & Schuster in the US To Lisa Keim, Janice Fryer, Mellony Torres, Alexandra Arnold, Emily Bestler, and Judith Curr, and, of course, a huge thank-you to Sarah Branham – my wonderfully talented editor who once again has done a fantastic job steering me in the right direction. I'm grateful to Jane Gregory and Stephanie Glencross, for doing such a great job on this book – especially Stephanie, who's an incredible editor and who has changed my life in many ways. And thanks to Kevin Chapman, my NZ editor, a really cool guy who's always looking out for me.

And I'd like to thank you, the reader, for coming along on this journey with Tate and Schroder and the others. Thanks for your kind messages, and for coming along to festivals and signings to come and say hi. I wouldn't be able to make bad things happen in the books if it weren't for you . . .

Paul Cleave
August 2017
Christchurch

Discover more edge-of-your-seat thrillers from Paul Cleave

The Cleaner

Joe is a janitor for the police department, and then there's his "night work". He isn't bothered by the daily news reports of the Christchurch Carver, who, they say, has murdered seven women. Joe knows, though, that the Carver killed only six. He knows that for a fact . . .

The Killing Hour

Imagine waking up covered in blood – but it's not your blood, and you can't remember a thing about last night. Welcome to Charlie's world.

Blood Men

Edward Hunter has it all – a beautiful wife and daughter, a great job, a bright future . . . and a very dark past.

Collecting Cooper

A former mental patient is holding people prisoner as part of his growing collection of serial killer souvenirs. Now he has acquired the ultimate collector's item – an actual killer.

The Laughterhouse

Theodore Tate never forgot his first crime scene – ten-year-old Jessica found dead in "the Laughterhouse", an old abandoned slaughterhouse with the S painted over. The killer was found and arrested. Justice was served. Or was it?

Joe Victim

Joe Middleton's story is this: He doesn't remember killing anyone, so there's no way a jury can convict him.
But others know Joe as the infamous Christchurch Carver and they want him dead.

Five Minutes Alone

The body of a convicted rapist is found, but no one knows if it's murder or suicide. Then two more rapists go missing . . .